The Screenwriter Looks at the Screenwriter

The Screenwriter Looks at the Screenwriter

by William Froug

Silman-James Press
Los Angeles

for
Susan, Nancy, Lisa & Jon
and for Rita

First Silman-James Press Edition 1991

Library of Congress Cataloging-in-Publication Data

Froug, William.
The screenwriter looks at the screenwriter/by William Froug.
— Silman-James Press ed.
p. cm.
1. Screenwriters—United States—Interviews.
2. Motion picture authorship.
I. Title.
PN1998.2.F76 808.2'3—dc20 91-21894

ISBN: 1-879505-01-0

Cover design by Heidi Frieder

Printed and bound in the United States of America

SILMAN-JAMES PRESS
distributed by
Samuel French Trade
7623 Sunset Blvd., Hollywood, CA 90046

Acknowledgment

I would like to express my special thanks to Pat Hawkings, aide-de-camp; to Toni Partie; to the Motion Picture Academy of Arts and Sciences Library; to David Licht, friend and advisor; to Betty Anne Clarke, extraordinary Ms.; to Fay Kanin, willing listener; and most particularly to the screenwriters who gave unstintingly of their time and without whom this book obviously would not be possible.

W.F.

Contents

Preface to the Silman-James Edition

When I began work on the first edition of this book twenty years ago, I was fueled by my deep-rooted sense of moral outrage over the way filmwriters were treated by critics, educators, and all too many of their fellow workers; the auteur theory was then in full bloom—that asinine notion that the director is the true author of films.

Now, twenty years later, I am pleased to note that only the most rigid-minded die-hards still give any credence to auteur nonsense. Today, you can actually see the writer's name listed at the top of film reviews, along with the canonized director. What is the world coming to?

The bald truth, then and now, is that every movie worth seeing (and many that aren't) was first conceived in the mind of a writer who followed the ancient tradition of story tellers by putting words on paper. The fact is *the writer first sees the movie in his or her head* and does his or her best to record that vision in words.

Once the decision is made to enlarge those words into a movie, everybody thereafter involved *interprets the writer's vision*: director, actors, set decorators, dog trainers, you name it. Thus, the writer is the sole possessor of the word *author*, whether you spell it in French, in Sanskrit, or in Hollywood.

Shortly before this book came to print, Hollywood was agog with the news that William Goldman had been paid a record-breaking $400,000 for his original screenplay *Butch Cassidy and the Sundance Kid*. This year Joe Eszterhas was reportedly paid $3 million for an original screenplay *Basic Instinct*. Several former students of mine are now in the million-dollar-plus-per-screenplay category.

It would seem the screenwriter has made real progress in the long, difficult climb toward recognition during these past twenty years. How much respect has come along with the big money is an open question. As a forty-year writer-producer veteran of the Hollywood wars, I am eager to discover how the screenwriter has progressed since 1971 and am preparing *The New Screenwriter Looks at the New Screenwriter* to fully explore the current status of the writer today in American film.

Back in 1971, the response to *The Screenwriter Looks at the Screenwriter* was encouraging. A few people even bought copies. Perhaps in a small way it contributed to the demise of the simple-minded auteur theory it attacked. What it definitely did, I am happy to report, was encourage many writers to try their hands at writing for film.

During my fifteen years teaching film and TV writing at the University of California at Los Angeles, I came across many writing students who brought this tome with them to class.

But as the years passed, I ran across more and more who complained they could not find a copy of it.

The sad truth is that the original hardcover publisher treated the book as if it was so rare a treasure they didn't want to share it with the general public. Then a paperback edition was issued. It silently slipped beneath the waves before the printer's ink was dry.

For years now it has been my weekly task to answer complaining letters about the disappearance of *The Screenwriter Looks at the Screenwriter.* I have four unanswered ones on my desk as I write this Preface. At last I will be able to say, "The new Silman-James Press edition is now available."

Those of you who may be rereading this book should note that the present edition corrects the many typographical errors that haunted the pages of the first edition. The present edition also updates through 1990 the filmographies that precede each interview.

Thank you, Silman-James. My wife thanks you, my grandchildren thank you, and just maybe there are some filmwriting students out there who will also thank you. If there are, welcome aboard, we've been waiting for a long, long time.

W.F.
Ponte Vedra Beach, Florida
December 15, 1990

Introduction

Last Fall the President of the Writers Guild of America, west, a union representing almost 3,000 writers, sent the following letter:

Gentlemen:

It has been brought to the attention of our Council that your group has expressed deep concern that the Writers Guild has not given support, or displayed any enthusiasm for the First Los Angeles International Film Exposition.

The reason should be obvious to you. In the forty or more films you intend to present, your promotional material only mentions one screenwriter as such.

The highly questionable "auteur concept," whereby films are never written, merely directed, is an approach to the art of films that genuine authors have had to endure from esoteric and dilettante sources for many years. We are not inclined, however, to support such an amateurish approach.

No professional in the art, directors among them, shares the apparent view of your group that the screenplay is an unimportant aspect of filmmaking. The ancient Chinese put it rather well: "A foolish opinion believed by thousands is still a foolish opinion."

The Writers Guild hopes you have a pleasant and successful social occasion. Not being represented, however, we cannot consider it a meaningful examination of film art.

Yours sincerely,
Ranald MacDougall
President

Copies of the letter were sent to the board of trustees of the First Los Angeles Film Exposition, four of whose members were also members of the Writers Guild.

The unpublished response of the executives of Filmex, as it was called, was that the writers' credits had been simply overlooked!

The Motion Picture Academy Awards ceremony, annually the most important single event in Hollywood, an affair which is broadcast to an estimated audience of 400 million people via satellite, is considered by the corporations which finance American films their most vital single commercial effort. What happens on that one night can make or break a film, can add millions to the studio coffers, can make the difference between profit and loss for an entire year.

Hundreds of craftsmen and technicians are employed. The superstars, the men and women who parade down those gilded runways and ask, "May I have the envelope, please?!" are paid a nominal sum ($1,000) for their turn, if only to help defray the cost of their hairdressers.

Everybody pitches in and everybody does it as a labor of love with little thought of the fees involved. (What can $5,000 for one night's work mean to multi-millionaire Bob Hope?)

The screenwriters spend weeks preparing the introductions, the jokes, those "ad libs" the stars toss off so effortlessly.

The Academy Awards are the one unifying moment for all of Hollywood—that critical two or three hours during which the American film industry gathers to pay homage to itself and, just incidentally, to reassure the world that movies are better than ever.

Everybody—musicians, ushers, cameramen, engineers, stars—is paid something for his time. But not the screenwriters.

Of course, it's an oversight. Of course, there is no sinister plot afoot to avoid paying the writer $1,000 or whatever token fee is deemed fitting.

And the fact that at the dinner-dance which follows the ceremonies it is the writers who wrote the show and find themselves seated in the back of the hall, well, that's just another one of those oversights the screenwriter learns to live with.

"I've written my own lines in every picture I've ever made," an Oscar-winning actor once confided to me. "You just can't read that stuff they hand you."

"It's okay, but it needs work," are invariably the first words uttered by the director after reading the script.

"Did you read that piece of crap they're shooting next week?" or variations thereof, is what most often passes from set decorator to key grip to assistant director to cameraman to editor to propmaster to the wardrobe mistress.

In fifteen years of working the sound stages of Hollywood, of being employed by almost every major studio, I have never heard anyone connected with any film say, "We've got a great screenplay and we're going to shoot it like it is."

Everybody connected with every film knows how to make the screenplay better. Everybody is a screenwriter.

The screenwriter is beaten, battered, and belittled by film esthetes, critics, scholars, and historians whose unshakable adherence to the auteur theory goes against all logic and verifiable fact, particularly when applied to the American motion picture. He is, indeed, as Walter Newman describes him, the "nigger" of the industry.

What the French haven't done to him the eastern critics have, and what they in their romantic and pedantic ignorance haven't accomplished, his co-workers have. He has been kept, securely, in the back of the hall.

And, finally, the screenwriter himself all too often has willingly or unwittingly conspired to play the role of Uncle Tom.

Why?

Has he been sold the inferior-race myth so effectively he can no longer believe that to write is beautiful? If the screenwriter brings to his work a sense of inferiority, he had developed it out of a long history of denigration which predates the auteur theory.

Since the beginning of motion pictures, the writer has always been "boy." He began by writing placards for the silents and he moved slowly up to developing gags and suggesting story ideas. It was a painful evolution.

When sound came in he was suddenly in demand and producers and studio executives searched the eastern seaboard and the metropolises for men who might have a knack for writing "scenarios." Newspapermen like Ben Hecht and Charles MacArthur were brought out from Chicago. Reporters like Nunnally Johnson and Dudley Nichols were recruited from New York. Big Names were lured to Hollywood: Faulkner, Fitzgerald, Parker, Benchley, Nathan, et al.

Screenwriter salaries zoomed to astronomical figures. (See the Nunnally Johnson interview.)

It was not unusual for the studios to have a score of writers making $5,000 a week. And many more made $1,000 and $2,000 a week. And there were "stables" of junior writers.

But most American films in the early sound days weren't written so much as they were rewritten, and rewritten, and rewritten. The studio heads wanted to get their money's worth.

Yet even with the outrageously high salaries he received the Hollywood screenwriter gained no real stature. Behind his back he was called a hack and considered a necessary nuisance. "If we could only figure out a way to make movies without writers," one mogul was quoted as saying.

The screenwriters were the life of Hollywood's party. They were much in demand as reigning wits and raconteurs. What Nunnally Johnson said to Louella Parsons was quoted in the gossip columns the following day. Benchley's witticisms and Dorothy Parker's acerbic wit were legends even in their own time. ("Let me get out of these wet clothes and into a dry martini.")

And Faulkner's famous telegram to MGM asking whether they minded if he worked at home instead of at his studio office became the talk of the town when the writer turned up weeks later at his home in Oxford, Mississippi.

The stories were endless and charming. The screenwriter had money and notoriety, but not recognition.

And so it has continued until the present.

Why?

What has he done or not done to deserve this?

The answer is not difficult to find. It is that even in films, auteurism notwithstanding, in the beginning is the word. There is no film without a film script.

Ingmar Bergman is first a screenwriter before he can function as a screen director. Federico Fellini is first a screenwriter before he can function as a screen director. Louis Malle is first a screenwriter before he can function as a screen director. And Antonioni and Kurosawa and Truffaut and Bresson and Forman and on and on.

In films everybody's livelihood is dependent on the screenwriter. That includes the cinematographer, the editor, the key grip, the script girl, and actors, and the director. And it also includes the film critic, the film teacher, the student, et al.

As has been observed again and again and apparently cannot be observed too often: you can't shoot 120 blank pages, and you can't successfully improvise a full-length motion picture. It's been tried. (Contrary to popular opinion, writer-director John Cassavetes, certainly as close to an authentic American auteur as we are likely to see, works closely from his own screenplay. "There aren't ten lines improvised in all of *Minnie and Moskowitz*," Johnny told me "I believe in sticking to the script.")

In the film world of Hollywood or Rome, Paris or Tokyo, London or Prague, without the screenwriter, nobody works.

Is it any wonder then that, consciously or unconsciously, resentment against the writer is almost universal? Is it surprising that every ego connected with the making of a film—and the size of those particular egos are gargantuan—is offended by the quintessential truth that all of them are utterly helpless and—ultimately—unemployable until the screenwriter writes a screenplay?

Is it therefore any surprise that the French gave the word auteur to the man who conceived the film? He was the man who developed not only the style, but the characters, the story, and either wrote or co-wrote the screenplay. It was then, and only then, that he went on to direct *his* conception.

But the history of American films is diametrically opposed to the auteur concept. The director was often brought to the production long after the conceptual work had been done. His job was to interpret the work of the writer, just as the actor's job was to interpret the role, the character, that the writer had conceived.

As often as not, it was the producer working with the writer, casting the film, selecting all the key personnel, choosing the director according to his concept of the total film, who was as much "auteur" as anybody.

And who can deny the existence of those ultimate American "auteurs"—the major studio heads of Hollywood? Surely all MGM movies bore the indelible stamp of Louis B. Mayer. Directors and writers came and went but Mayer made certain there was an "MGM look" on every frame of every film his incredible factory turned out. And couldn't the same be said of Jack Warner? And Harry Cohn at Columbia who ruled his kingdom and his movies with an iron fist.

And so distorting that word, auteur, forcing it to fit the nonwriting, nonconceiving director becomes a travesty of reason and common sense. To state, as the auteur-critic is fond of telling us, that film is ultimately the "personal statement" of the director when, in fact, the director had little or nothing to do with that statement, is truly a cruel injustice. The auteurist's credo is style *über alles.*

A stunning example is the current film, *The Last Picture Show. Life* magazine recommends it weekly with the following lead: "Peter Bogdanovich's story . . . " Larry McMurtry wrote the story, created the characters, set the mood, yes, and the style, when he wrote the novel, *The Last Picture Show.* He also co-wrote the screenplay with Bogdanovich.

By what divine magic does McMurtry's creation become solely Bogdanovich's? Yet the former is rarely mentioned while the latter is declared an authentic genius in the tradition of Welles. (Shades of *Citizen Kane*! The ghost of Herman J. Mankiewicz walks again!)

But, the auteurist will reply, the true style came from the director (after all, it was Bogdanovich's idea to use black and white film instead of color) and he, therefore, is the ultimate artist in the film making art.

Nonsense. Read McMurtry's book. It's all there.

One French auteurist who wrote as well as directed his masterpieces, Jean Renoir, put it neatly: "What you have to say is much more important than the way you say it." The story, says Renoir, is what counts, technical facility is secondary. "Filmmaking should be a team, a family. It is never one man."

But go fight Dogma, Pedantry, and Cant, perhaps the oldest law firm in the history of man.

Style *is* vital, certainly, but it is meaningless without content. And style follows content, not the other way around.

I am not talking about film as words or film as literature. We are all too sophisticated to cling to the ancient notion that the screenwriter contributes only the dialogue, or that film is just another form of theater.

Today film is its own form and its own "literature" and the screenwriter, as much as anybody else, is helping shape it. Indeed, the writers I have known and worked with are preoccupied with how to tell their story with a minimum of words. (See the Lewis John Carlino interview.)

The auteurist finds it hard to believe but the fact remains that *The French Connection*'s visual excitement was in the screenplay and that is what 20th Century-Fox bought first—before the director or the actors.

"It was all there, in the script," says Mrs. Dorothy Wilde, Fox story editor. "You could see what the film would look like—you could get the feel of the entire picture."

But in review after review auteur-minded critics reported that Ernest Tidyman's "routine" screenplay was "brought to life" by the brilliant direction of William Friedkin.

It is surely not to take anything away from Friedkin's superb direction to note that the action as well as the characters were first conceived and written by the writer.

But, argue the auteurists, the screenwriter is often "merely" an adapter, translating somebody else's work to the screen. In the past that has been largely true. But who in film making is not an adapter? Isn't the director's function to adapt to film the work provided him by the writer? Yet nobody puts down the director for being supplied a script, and actors, and a cameraman, and a small army of helpers. The adaptation argument can work both ways. If, until recently, the screenwriter's efforts could not be considered "original," surely no one, by that narrow standard, was less "original" than the director.

The argument is as needless as it is endless. Film is a complex and highly collaborative form of art (or form of commerce, if you choose). "One man, one film," as some directorial egos insist, is a self-serving myth. One might just as well say one man, one spaceship.

The director has it in his power to lift what is on the paper to greater heights—or to reduce it to something less than is already there. His talent is indispensable to film. His contribution need not be minimized.

But neither should the writer's. To herald one should not denigrate the other. Coexistence is not only possible but essential.

And what of the actor? Aren't there scores of examples where the work of the *actor* brought the film to heights it might never have attained otherwise, particularly during the era of the great personality stars: Gable, Tracy, Hepburn, Grant, Cooper, David, Bogart, et al.? Is it unreasonable to suggest that Hollywood's history is replete with films in which the actor was as much auteur as either the writer or director? Stars often created an ambience that is, in retrospect, sadly missing in many films today. (See the Walter Newman interview.)

Writer, director, and actor are interlocked in the

filmmaking process. They are interdependent.

But far too little attention has been paid to the man or woman who put it all in motion, that individual without whom there simply would be no film.

If there is one thing the screenwriters in this book have in common, it is their love of film and their abiding interest in telling their story through the full use of the medium.

Screenwriters today are involved in film as they have never been before. (Perhaps in a perverse way, they have the auteur theory to thank for that.) They are determined to become what they have never been—masters of their fates and captains of their souls.

The word "hyphenate" is now an integral part of the American film language. Writer-producers, writer-directors, writer-executives, are a fact of life in Hollywood.

Young filmmakers have learned their lesson well. If they are to truly create a personal-statement film, they must participate in as many phases of the creative process as is humanly possibly. Many of them, offered the chance to sell their first screenplay, refuse to do so—unless they are employed as director as well.

There is plenty of evidence that the screenwriter has had his fill of being the industry scapegoat. For example: it is now commonplace for the writer to demand and get producer status on his film. The screenwriters I talk to have little or no interest in producing films—but it is often their only guarantee that they can exercise any meaningful control over their work.

The hyphenate issue has caused serious problems within the Writers Guild itself. As more and more members branch off into additional activities that bring them attendant responsibility and power, they become a source of irritation to the writer who remains behind—who now calls himself, with pride and with some bitterness, a "writer-writer."

As a member of the Writers Guild for over twenty years, and five years a director of the Producers Guild, as well as its current Secretary, I often find myself squarely in the middle of the controversy. I am a firm believer in Nunnally Johnson's statement that the producer makes one decision that is more important than all the other filmmaking decisions combined, and that is to make the film.

Yet nothing is going to stem the tide toward hyphenation. More and more screenwriters are going to exercise more and more control over their work by whatever methods are available to them.

Since our interview, Lew Carlino has sold his original screenplay *The Mechanic* to United Artists. It will star Charles Bronson and be directed by Michael Winner. But it will be a Chartoff-Winkler-*Carlino* Production, with Lew as a full partner in both authority and in profits.

Since our interview, Stirling Silliphant has sold a sequel to *Shaft*, a film which he helped put together not as screenwriter, but as executive producer. Silliphant will be executive producer and co-owner of the sequel as well. "That's where it's at," says Silliphant, "where the power is."

Bill Bowers, who produced his last film, *Support Your Local Sheriff*, says he is determined to direct his next. So are Buck Henry and David Giler. Giler is now at MGM writing a new screenplay based on *The Postman Always Rings Twice.* He is negotiating to serve as co-producer of the film.

The screenwriter does owe a debt of gratitude to the auteurists. Those misguided souls have given him the final humiliation he needed to force himself out of his lonely and insulated life and into the mainstream of filmmaking.

The movie business is at a low ebb just now. But the screenwriter is registering new ideas with his guild in greater numbers than at almost any other time in the guild's history. And most of those are original screenplays—another sign that the filmwriter is determined to control what is entirely his.

A couple of years ago 20th Century-Fox paid William Goldman $400,000 for his original screenplay *Butch Cassidy and the Sundance Kid.*

I asked a Fox executive recently if those kind of prices

were still possible in the face of the current economic state of the industry.

"The film will gross over $20 million," he told me. "The screenplay is the best bargain we ever got."

Mrs. Mimi Roth, story editor for United Artists on the West Coast, recently told me, "In the past we gave top priority to established properties, novels, plays, published material. Times have changed. Today we are actively searching for original screenplays. And we are particularly interested in the work of young screenwriters."

Warner's, MGM, Fox, Columbia, Universal, and the major independents, have all developed a new and positive attitude toward material written directly for the screen.

Peter Bart, vice president in charge of creative affairs for Paramount, recently announced to the press: "Paramount operates on the premise that the key to a successful movie is the story, and it's high time we all admitted that the traditional sources of new story material cannot even begin to meet our present needs."

The statement takes on added meaning in light of the fact that Paramount was one of the most ardent supporters of the auteur theory only a few years ago.

During its brief and disastrous affair with auteurism, the major studios demanded of a producer that he bring a "name" director along with a project before any financial commitment would be made. Today that situation is reversed.

"At United Artists we prefer to see the screenplay first," say Mrs. Roth, "without any commitment to a director. We can work with the producer to find the right director later."

Screenplays are receiving recognition in other ways. They are being published in increasing numbers and even the most ardent film buffs are surprised to discover they are not only readable but often exciting and stimulating.

We may not be far from the day when the comment will be heard, "I liked the screenplay better than the film."

The purpose of this book is to further that recognition,

to reaffirm the singular contribution made by the writer of films, and, in some small way, to help right the wrong that has been done to him.

W. F.
Santa Monica, California

Lewis John Carlino

1965 SECONDS *(Screenplay)*

1967 THE BROTHERHOOD *(Story and Screenplay)*,
Writers Guild Nomination

1968 THE FOX *(Joint Screenplay)*

1970 IN SEARCH OF AMERICA *(Story and Screenplay)*
LABYRINTH *(Joint Screenplay)*

1971 STRANGER IN A STRANGE LAND* *(Screenplay)*
SIDDHARTHA* *(Screenplay)*
A REFLECTION OF FEAR *(Joint Screenplay)*

1972 THE MECHANIC *(Story and Screenplay)*

1973 CRAZY JOE *(Screenplay)*

1976 THE SAILOR WHO FELL FROM GRACE WITH THE SEA *(Screenplay)*

1977 I NEVER PROMISED YOU A ROSE GARDEN *(Joint Screenplay)*

1978 THE GREAT SANTINI *(Screenplay)*

1979 RESURRECTION *(Story and Screenplay)*

1987 HAUNTED SUMMER *(Screenplay)*

*Unproduced

PLAYS

CAGES: "Snowangel" and "Epiphany"
TELEMACHUS CLAY
THE EXERCISE
DOUBLE TALK: "Sarah and the Sax" and "The Dirty Old Man"
THE BRICK AND THE ROSE
OBJECTIVE CASE
USED CAR FOR SALE
JUNK YARD
HIGH SIGN

Lew Carlino and I were introduced over breakfast at the Beverly Hills Hotel a couple of years ago. We were brought together because Lew had sold a story that needed a producer, and I was a producer in search of a story.

At first glance, Carlino appeared to be yet another Beverly Hills hippie. He wore the uniform of the young Hollywood film maker: bell-bottomed jeans, flower-printed body shirt, and an assortment of rings. His language was heavily flavored with the newspeak of the new generation: cool, heavy, right on, etc.

In fact, Carlino had flown in from New Jersey where he lived on a 104-acre farm with his wife and three children. They grew much of their own food, raised chickens and some livestock. While ersatz hippies were flooding the major studios, Lew was living the lifestyle they gave lip service to.

The rapport between us was immediate, and we went to work on a movie designed for television.

Working with Carlino was one of the most stimulating experiences I have ever known. Lew enjoyed the give and take of a story conference. He was completely open, willing to discuss and debate any story point, any character; he had no ego hang-ups.

My teenage son says about Lew that he "approaches Nirvana" and that is as good a description of the writer's unique personality as any. He is a man totally in touch with himself. There is an aura of calm and inner peace about him that is charismatic. He projects quiet reassurance.

The son of a Sicilian immigrant tailor, Carlino was born in New York City, January 1, 1932, the youngest of three children. He worked summers, as an operating-room surgical technician and as a day-camp counselor, to help pay his way through college.

He graduated from the University of Southern California with a B.A. in 1959—magna cum laude, Phi Beta Kappa, and Phi Kappa Phi. He received his master's degree in 1960.

Then he hit the road "to let the ideas cook." He spent three years bumming around the world—Japan, Greece, Spain, France, Italy, Central America, Mexico. He lived in Sicily, Tangier, and Yucatán before returning to New York.

Carlino's initial interest was in theater. He wrote one-act plays, often with a cast of only two actors, which are notable for their insight and compassion.

In 1963 Carlino had three productions running concurrently Off Broadway at three different theaters. He won the prestigious Obie Award, the New York drama critics annual award given to the best theatrical work done Off Broadway. Overnight (after seven years of writing unproduced work) he became what is known in the trade as a hot writer.

He won the Rockefeller Grant for Theater, the International Playwriting Competition from the British Drama League, a Huntington Hartford Fellowship, a Yaddo Fellowship, and was named a member of the *Société des Auteurs et Compositeurs Dramatiques.*

Thirteen of his plays are in publication and are regularly performed in a dozen languages all over the world.

Carlino became, and still remains, one of the most sought-after screenwriters in Hollywood. But, like Walter Newman, he is very choosy about what he involves himself in, turning down far more job offers than he accepts.

Last summer Lew decided New Jersey was becoming too crowded. He sold the farm, loaded his family into two cars, trailing two motorcycles, and headed west, toward nowhere in particular.

When the caravan reached Boulder, Colorado, it stopped. Lew began to build a mountainside retreat overlooking the Continental Divide.

One day he packed his cassettes into his stereo-equipped Land Rover and took off across country alone. Once again he had no destination. From time to time he could take long detours down seldom-traveled dirt roads, stopping at isolated farm houses miles from anywhere, visiting for hours with total strangers.

"It's beautiful," says Lew, "all those people living out there. Beautiful."

THE FOX

The Fox From the novella by D.H. Lawrence

FADE IN:

1. EXTERIOR FARM AND FIELDS DAWN

It is dawn. The sun is just peeping over the trees, tinting the snow a faint pink. Fog and mist blend the shapes of trees with the whiteness so that all seems to have an amorphic unreality. There are no outlines, only dark shapes, emerging, blending, merging again. All is silent. There is no wind. Now as the sun moves higher, the mist and fog begins to burn off and shapes begin to define themselves.

A — Thin fibril branches of trees and bushes, sheathed in ice, glistening against the sun.

B — The fantastic geometric patterns of frost.

C — Frozen ripples at the edge of a brook.

D — The of gossamer-like cocoons and webs, flashing, crystalline, like spun glass.

Everything is arrested, balanced, composed. It's as if we are looking at a series of Chinese paintings, where each stroke of the brush seeks to establish harmony and peace.

E — As we complete this series we are in a long shot of farm buildings in the distance. A rooster crows. Silence again for a long moment. Now the camera pans to a snow covered thicket. Suddenly a bush shakes violently and as the snow cascades downward, we follow its fall to frame a set of fresh fox tracks, leading toward the farm. We hear the distant barking of farm dogs; at first a single bark here and there, but then gradually joined by more until there is a faint chorus. Now the camera follows the tracks. We hear the angry chatter of a squirrel.

F — Cut to a branch. A squirrel runs back and forth in fright. Now the faint crunch of snow as the camera again returns to the tracks, following, to a freshly baited trap. The

FROUG: Lew, you were at the University of Southern California cinema school studying film, but you were writing one-act plays instead of screenplays. Why was that?

CARLINO: Well, basically my orientation was theater, from way back, even before SC, and I really didn't know anything about screenplays. I think, first, I had to learn something about dramatic structure. And the discipline and the regimens of creating dramatic structure in the stage form are greater than in any other form except the written word. You can always do a cutaway in film, or fill in, or do visuals, or build tension by putting zingers in, music and everything. You have all this technical arsenal with which to deal. But in a play when you've got people on stage, it's got to be there. I mean it's *really* got to be there. There's just no crutch that you can lean on in a play. And so I approached it that way, almost from an Aristotelian point of view, in terms of the poetics. I had a professor who used to say, "What is a play?" "Imitation of an action." "What is an action?" And he used to get us so that we would analyze every play that we read in terms of a prepositional sentence. Like he once hit me with, "What is the action of *Death of a Salesman*?" The action of *Death of a Salesman* is for Willy Loman to be liked. As simple as that. And when you begin to look into drama, you realize that each thing that we write about can be reduced to a single sentence, and the entire structure of your drama revolves around that Aristotelian principle in terms of an imitation of an action. That's true even today. You can learn by working with one-act forms, which are really the hardest because you've got to really deal with that forty minutes, and do a beginning, middle, and end in the space of forty minutes. You begin to get a sense of climax, denouement, dramatic catharsis, and all that. So I began writing plays, directing them. And from there, I went to the stage in New York, and did work, and then went into film.

FROUG: Would you encourage the filmwriting student to be a playwright first, perhaps on the grounds that his one-act plays cost so very little to produce that he might have a chance of building a reputation, as you did, and then be hired to write screenplays?

CARLINO: I don't know about advising anybody to do anything. I just know the way I went and it worked for me.

FROUG: But, in effect, by writing plays first and winning the Obie Award, you went into films starting at the top with *Seconds*.

CARLINO: That's right. There was no working up. I was just unknown, and in my first year I had three productions running simultaneously in New York. I went from that to my major film assignment with a major director.

FROUG: That couldn't have happened without the plays?

CARLINO: No, it couldn't have happened, because if you do a play in New York or a couple of plays, and you win some notoriety, my gosh, the cultural center of the country is focused upon you. You're written about, you achieve what everybody calls "overnight notoriety." Well, they don't realize I'd been at it seven or eight years before all that happened. I hadn't made any money or anything. But you have every major critic in the country and they're all centered there in New York. Every publication is talking about your work. Well, you become highly desirable as a producer of a product which is successful, which has a potential of making money. That's really what happened to me. Everybody has their struggle. All the work had been done prior to New York. And then after New York, I went from one assignment to another.

FROUG: How did you get the assignment to write *Seconds*?

CARLINO: It was the result of Ed Lewis and John Frankenheimer and, I think, Kirk Douglas seeing my work, especially

Cages, and coming to me with the assignment.

FROUG: You and I screened *Seconds* for my USC class, and we discussed the critics' response to the film, many of them saying it had a very strong first act, but it had no second act. It seemed to fall apart in the center.

CARLINO: Yes, it did.

FROUG: But you explained to the class and to me a whole different approach to that film which you had envisioned, and it was quite the opposite of the film that Frankenheimer turned out. Can you tell us about that?

CARLINO: Well, I more than envisioned it. It was in the screenplay. It seemed to me that the way to do that film was to create sort of a modern Willy Loman. It was really the tragedy of the Faustian thing of man trying to live a new life, and the tragedy was that once he had paid the price to live that new kind of life, he irrevocably cut off any connection with his own people. He had a daughter, and he kept talking about the fact that maybe this daughter had a grandchild and he could be of some influence, but he'd totally cut off any possibility of the continuity of his life as far as affecting other people. It seemed to me that, in the film, the middle section should be concerned with this man going back to visit his daughter and finding out that, in fact, he does have a grandchild. And the great tragedy is the sudden realization that what he's paid for this new life is his total alienation. There is no more continuity of existence for him. There was a scene in which he sees his grandson. He's left alone in the nursery. He tries to communicate with this little infant and he can't, and he tries to pick the baby up, and the daughter comes in, but she can't recognize him because he has a new face, and she chastises him because to her he's just a stranger. And he's driven out of the house. He is totally alone. That was the crux of the middle section of the film.

FROUG: That scene was eliminated?

CARLINO: I don't think it was ever shot.

FROUG: Why wasn't it?

CARLINO: I don't know. I started to have a conversation with John about it, but we really never got close on it. There was also a scene prior to that, a scene when he meets a child on the beach, and they have a magical moment in which she shares some starfish and shells with him. It was really a significant scene because she reminded him of his daughter and the continuity of his life. And he had this magic moment, and as he got close to the child, suddenly her father appears on the beach with a dog and calls her, and she runs to him, and the father puts her up on his shoulders and they go off down the beach. He watches this, and this is what makes him seek the continuity of his life again by going to see his daughter. Well, you remember in the final moments of the man's death, at the end of the picture, when they're drilling into his brain, there is a flash, in silhouette, of a man walking on the beach followed by a dog, carrying a little girl. That's the last flash in his brain—of a little girl on the beach and a man carrying this little girl, with the dog running. Well, John ended the picture that way with this flash but never used the scene of the meeting of the little girl.

FROUG: So it had no meaning?

CARLINO: So it didn't relate to anything. And I asked him about that, and he said, "Well, they'll get it. It's sort of a symbolic thing." And I said, "Wow, I don't know about symbols. Man, you know, I'm dealing in audience recollection. They see this man on the beach, this tragic figure, trying to relate to a child, and then this child goes off with her father in silhouette and this beautiful poetic moment, and that's the last flash on his brain when he's being killed." That seems to make sense. It seems to complete the circle of the man's frustrated life.

FROUG: In our discussion about *Seconds* you told the class that you had conceived of the film starting with a normal human being under normal circumstances . . .

CARLINO: That's right.

FROUG: . . . but even under the main titles the film starts in a very spooky, bizarre fashion, using out-of-focus and distorted lenses and ominous music, and the leading character is seen walking through a subway and a man is following him, and it's played very mysterioso. As a consequence, there's so much instant tension that I felt the film had nowhere to go.

CARLINO: Well, the nature of that story is so horrifying, if you just play it right—just the basic ingredients of the story—you don't have to play the horror. It is the horror of each man's alienation and his refusal to connect with life, his submission to the values of a society that he really doesn't believe in. Therein is the horror of the tale and, God, they just went the other way with it—organ music and wide-angled lenses to create a kind of Gothic, visual approach to it. And because of that, the effects were doing everything that the tale was supposed to do. It seemed to me that the horror of the story would come out of the events that were taking place, that were being accepted as commonplace, pedestrian even, rather than zinging it with organ chords and all that. The whole genre, the tapestry of the picture, was really opposite from the way that I saw it. I think that John is incredibly gifted as a director. I just don't think he relates closely enough to his writer in terms of the structure of a screenplay or how it should emerge. I don't get the feeling that John would really want to collaborate with anybody. I think the best work comes out of collaboration. One of the best things that really emerged was out of real collaboration, and was really a joyous experience. That was when I worked with Mark Rydell on *The Fox*. It was really a true collaboration in terms of the development, the evolving of that screenplay, because we worked really close.

FROUG: On a day-to-day basis?

CARLINO: Yes. And Mark was constantly giving me his viewpoint as a director and I was giving him my viewpoint as to structure. And sometimes we'd have really fierce arguments, but they resolved themselves into a picture, for the most part, which from its very origin was a collaboration, and emerged very successfully because each moment was clear. What we would do—and I've never worked like this with a director—we would reduce our day into a storytelling session, and Mark would say, "Tell me the picture." And I would say, "Okay, this is a story about two girls living on a farm, and there's a kind of latent homosexual attachment, and then one day a guy comes in . . ." and I would tell him the story, just like someone telling you a story. And he'd listen very carefully, listen to the structure emerge, and then when I would finish, I would say to him, "Tell me about this movie." And he would say, "Oh, this is a story about two girls . . ." and by listening to each other telling the story, we were able to tell if we were misinterpreting. In other words, if we had different concepts about material which we thought we agreed on by hearing somebody else tell it, those differences would emerge. And in the telling and retelling, the points where we differed would be resolved, so the directorial thrust of the story was coexistent with the structural thrust of the story. And it was really beautiful working that way. After five or six days of doing this, after we had really created the basic structure of the film, we really *knew* that film. I mean, we really saw it, moment to moment, before it ever was lensed.

FROUG: In the screenplay *I Never Promised You a Rose Garden*, which you wrote for Columbia and has not yet been filmed, you told me that you were going to write some scenes in the form of the Japanese haiku. Can you elaborate on that?

CARLINO: Well, I've really always been fascinated by the power of the haiku, by its power to illuminate a thought with all kinds of multiple meanings in such a reduced amount of words, and the final line of the haiku illuminating the whole thing, which is a rarified form of expression. And more and more I'm beginning to believe that film is essentially nonverbal, that films really are primarily behavioral rather than verbal. And I tried to evoke a style where the behavior really is what's important, and the dialogue is what releases the tension that illuminates the behavior, much as how the haiku functions. I'll give you an example: In *Rose Garden*, the first time this young girl is admitted to the mental hospital and appears in front of her psychoanalyst—it's a terrifying moment for anyone who is committed to a mental institution, and especially if the doctor happens to be a very famous doctor who specializes in classic schizophrenia.

FROUG: Is this based on a true story?

CARLINO: Yes. This is about a woman who actually went through this experience. So it seemed to me the best thing to do was to play the tension of this—because the girl is a brilliant young girl and the psychiatrist is a brilliant psychiatrist and there's an immediate challenge—like, "Well, you're the famous psychiatrist and you're going to cure me and let's see what you can do."

FROUG: These are the thoughts that are going on in the patient's head?

CARLINO: Yes. They're never expressed, but that's the situation. And the psychiatrist is wise enough just to be quiet and wait for the girl to talk, so there are several minutes which are just played in silence, and the behavior is to build the tension of this silence. Of the entire scene, which runs three or four minutes in the screenplay, the first half is just silence. Finally the psychiatrist says, "What are you thinking of?" and the girl says, "Sigmund Freud," and the psychiatrist says, "Oh?" And the girl says, "Do you know what Sigmund means?" And the psychiatrist says, "No." And the girl says, "Powerful mouth. Sigmund." The psychiatrist says, "Oh." And then there's another long silence in which you keep building the behavior. You wonder what the girl's getting to, and what is the challenge she's setting up. Finally, she says, "Do you know what Freud died of?" And the psychiatrist says, "No." And the girl says, "Cancer of the mouth." And there's a very long silence, and the psychiatrist is trying to fit this into some kind of contextual meaning, and he smiles and says to the girl, "Ah, in that case, I shall be very careful to listen more." That's the end of like a four-minute scene, and it's told in five or six lines.

FROUG: But many silences.

CARLINO: Oh, incredible silences.

FROUG: All of which are indicated in the screenplay?

CARLINO: Yeah. Oh, yeah.

FROUG: And all of which will probably be credited to the director?

CARLINO: Well, probably so. Probably so.

FROUG: In *Stranger in a Strange Land*, which you wrote for Warner Brothers and is yet to be produced, you also tried some new techniques you were telling me about, some new visual techniques, which I had never heard of before.

CARLINO: If you really get into the psychology of visual stimulation, also sound stimulation as well, you find that the human being can see and hear much more than occurs normally in our one-to-one relationship with our environment, and one of the techniques which I thought would really be good to use is when Valentine Michael Smith is on his journey to discover what makes him human. There is a computer bank in which the entire civilization of mankind is put on tapes, and he is viewing this screen which starts from the dawn of the prehistory of man and which has a series of visual images. And it's possible in a space of three or four minutes, through single- or double-frame exposures occurring at very rapid intervals, to compress the entire pictorial civilization of mankind in about three or four minutes of film at significant periods in man's civilized progressions. So Smith keeps accelerating this process and the images keep getting faster and faster as he turns them up. And in one instance, he's looking at this screen and exploring the origin of man's "civilized progressions," so-called, in quotes, and it's through the use of single-frame exposures and, at the same time, sound accompanying it that you're bombarded with rapidly changing visual stimuli or triggers into the subconscious. The subconscious can really operate that way on a connotative basis so that you understand what's happening, but not in a denotative way, not in a structured way. You're touching into the visual stimuli that lie within the subconscious, that lie within, as Jung calls collective unconscious, not subconscious, which we all possess, and you're touching those triggers. That was one of the effects that I wanted to use in the picture. The other was when he organizes his temple and he takes his initiates and they all become water brothers. To expose them to what really is the empathetic nature of being able to love another person, he takes them through a sort of historical journey of the bipolarity of male-female relationships. And he takes them right from the primitive cave figures of every civilization through time, sort of *The Golden Bough* they go through, and they each become—he and the woman he's with, Jill—each become those prototypes, prehistoric and archaic prototypes of male-female polarity. They become Eros and Venus, all through history, and their *bodies* keep changing form and finally evolving into germ cells, and the outlines of their faces are formed by the composite of thousands and thousands of lives, faces, so you have a kind of changing, almost psychedelic, tapestry of existence based on the male-female thing. I believe that true knowledge, really deep metaphysical knowledge of male-female relationships comes out of that sexual union. This is what Heinlein is talking about, you know, this is what D. H. Lawrence talked about, and I really believe that it's all tied into the creative, physically creative, process. That's another effect. I also want to do some effects in terms of Smith being able to suspend himself in midair, to do antigravitational things, and I wrote a scene of he and Jill making love at the Bonneville Salt Flats so that wherever you put the camera, in any direction, it's so flat there you go out to infinity, and just a scene of them suspended in this void, making love, a kind of Salvador Dali-esque thing of just two bodies suspended in space.

FROUG: The screenplay then embodies many advanced film techniques, solarization of the film, etc.

CARLINO: Yes. Most of the techniques as we know them today, as I've tried to find out about them, to utilize them. Of course, it's a futuristic story. It takes place in the year approximately 2000. I got into Fuller and Clark and other people who make projections about what life would be in the future. I tried to get into this business of philosophy and physics and the powers that the human being will have. Now we're developing alpha-wave control and it won't be too long, I'm pretty sure, until we'll be able to perform telekinesis, you know, the harnessing of electro-energies to move objects. That's, of course, what Heinlein was talking about. There are some experiments in parapsychology at Duke University which are being done now.

FROUG: Then you did a great deal of research beyond the book itself before writing the screenplay?

CARLINO: Yes. Heinlein has some problems when you begin to try to create a screenplay out of what he's written because, for the most part, his dialogue is really dated and it's really kind of corny, and the behavior is rather strange for the characters; it's rather a burlesque. The thing that makes the book work is the idea behind the book, the central idea of Smith being this Christ figure who comes from another planet, with his pure innocence and who is destroyed by a corrupt people, by a corrupt race, who don't understand his beauty and his innocence, and who find that his need to love them and to have them love him is terribly threatening, because it involves a huge responsibility of giving up a whole ego thing. Those are the things which made the book, I think, succeed. But when you begin to try to extrapolate those things, it all gets very ponderous and overweighted. But most of the difficulty I had was trying to find out those areas which could be made into cinematic representations—so that it became behavioral rather than philosophic. Long passages in Heinlein discussed the origins of the race and the corruptness of the legal system and cannibalism and religion and all the things that plague us as human beings. That's just talk. You know, pages and pages and pages of that. It's very interesting in a novel, but in a film you can't do it because it's not behaving. You just can't sit there and listen to all that, and the basic book is structured on those philosophical dissertations.

FROUG: Lew, you once told me *The Brotherhood*, your original story, was the least successful screenplay you have written. I felt the film had a rare sense of authenticity and reality. But it failed critically and financially. Why?

CARLINO: The screenplay went through too many changes and was pretty much eviscerated along the way.

FROUG: By you and Martin Ritt together?

CARLINO: Yes, essentially it was that, and it also had to meet certain requirements.

FROUG: Such as?

CARLINO: Well, when the screenplay was first written, it wasn't a story about two brothers. It was about a father and a son, and the crime was patricide, which is a larger crime. It has more mystical roots. Kirk Douglas' company, Marty Ritt and Kirk, had hired me to do this original. And the nature of the piece just emerged as a father and son thing and it just didn't work for Kirk. So Anthony Quinn was going to do it with a younger man as his son. The minute you start really tampering with those fundamental structural elements and begin to change them, then the whole thing started to change. And from there I really had very little control over it.

FROUG: Perhaps when the writer gets into those kind of revisions, he loses his own perspective?

CARLINO: Yes, sure, because there's incredible pressure, pressure from the star, pressure from the director. But I've run into people who say to me, "God, I read the first draft of *The Brotherhood.* What happened in the interim?" And rather than get into lengthy discussions, you just throw up your hands and shake your head because it's superfluous to answer that question, since they should know the answer themselves, being in the film industry. It's really very naive.

FROUG: Last night you and I went to see a production of *Cages* here in Hollywood and the program says, "Lewis John Carlino's *Cages*," but in film we tend to think of it as "John Frankenheimer's *Seconds*." Why is that?

CARLINO: God, I don't know. There was a ruling that the Writers Guild pushed and got through in the industry that a director can't take that possessive credit anymore unless he writes the screenplay himself.

FROUG: Still, in spite of the fact that it may not officially be advertised that way or titled on the screen that way, among film critics, film buffs, and in film journals it is generally referred to, for example, as Martin Ritt's *The Brotherhood*. Yet that was an original story and screenplay by you.

CARLINO: I guess it's just where the power structure lies in film. Essentially it's this, as compared to the play situation. Let's say I'm working with Martin Ritt on a play. If he wants to change a particular scene in the play and I say, "Gee, Marty, I don't see it that way," the Dramatists Guild contract provides the protection that allows me to say that. It says I don't have to change a word if I don't want to. Essentially it would finally reduce itself to the fact that if we really came head to head and he would say, "Well, I can't do it that way," I would say, "Well, I guess we're gonna have to get another director." In film, the opposite is true. If Marty says to me, even on my original piece of material, and says, "You know, Lew, I don't see the scene this way," and I disagree—you know, we can be very polite about it—the fact is that if I don't change it to a point where he's satisfied with it, he just hires somebody else to change it. But I worked very closely with Marty on *The Brotherhood*. He wanted me there to make changes as we went along, and he said he would never do another picture unless he had the writer right there to make the changes when there was trouble because he felt that the writer was the best qualified to do that. That's really refreshing. I really think he prefers to work that way because it takes a huge load off his back. It's the best way to work because it's a true collaboration. Some of the best scenes in *The Brotherhood* were written two days prior to them being put in the shooting schedule. On the other hand, when you write a screenplay and simply turn it over to the producer or the director, what happens is, you get to the front titles and it says "written by" and there's your name. And then halfway through the film you see this scene, and you search your mind and you just had nothing to do with the scene. You didn't write it. And it could be god-awful, and yet you have to assume the responsibility for it. You have absolutely no control. They can bring in anybody, and unless he writes 33 percent of the film, you get sole credit, also sole responsibility. So you could have a terrible, terrible scene that somebody else wrote and your name appears up there. It's the same with cutting out essential material, as happened in *Seconds*.

FROUG: Lew, you have written a screenplay which I have read, and many other people have read, and most of us think it is a tremendous accomplishment, a brilliant piece of work. Warners agreed to finance the picture after reading the screenplay, yet it remains unproduced. Can you tell us about *Siddhartha*?

CARLINO: I guess it's one of the best pieces of work I've ever done, in terms of a screenplay. And it was almost a continuous writing. It took a little under two months, including the research. Almost a month of that was research.

FROUG: A month of writing and a month of research?

CARLINO: Yeah.

FROUG: What happened to the screenplay after Warners approved it?

CARLINO: There's a foul-up in the partnership which was organized to produce the picture, between Conrad Rooks, Ed Lewis, and myself, and Ed Lewis and I are waiting to see what Conrad is going to do. He apparently hasn't decided.

FROUG: If he doesn't go forward with the project, will the rights then revert to Ed Lewis and you?

CARLINO: No, it can't work like that because Conrad is tied to the material as the director, as a condition of rights with the Hesse estate. No one else can direct it.

FROUG: Do you and Rooks have a substantial disagreement on the approach to the film?

CARLINO: Not during the writing. Then a weird thing happened. After the screenplay was written, Ed Lewis made our deal at Warners with John Calley. Locations had been scouted, and at the final meeting to resolve all of the production problems, Rooks arbitrarily announced that he couldn't shoot my script. I wasn't at the meeting, but as far as I understand, when they asked him what he was going to shoot in lieu of it, he said he didn't know just then, but would work from day to day. That wasn't acceptable to Warners. So right now the project is at a standstill until, I guess, Rooks makes up his mind what he's going to do. But because of our original agreement in which the rights were assigned to the partnership, to Ed Lewis and myself and Conrad Rooks, he can't make the picture without us, and we can't make it without him. [Since the interview Edward Lewis Productions and Carlino's agent, Dick Irving Hyland, have filed separate lawsuits against Conrad Rooks for refusing to go ahead with the Carlino screenplay approved by Warners. Lewis' suit is for $550,000. Rooks, meanwhile, has reportedly gone into production with his own version of *Siddhartha.*]

FROUG: You have another unproduced screenplay, an original, that's gotten a lot of favorable attention: *The Mechanic.* Can you tell us about that?

CARLINO: There was a partnership formed between myself and Ted Dubin, a New York entrepreneur, and a producer, Marty Poll. It was an original idea that I came up with, it grew out of the research that I did on *The Brotherhood.* And Ted Dubin put up some development money during the time that I was writing it. It's a sort of existential statement on the license to kill and what is occurring in our society, how legalized murder is occurring through our institutions. The only difference between an individual's ability to kill without paying the price for it and society's license to kill is that society institutionalizes its arms, its mechanism for committing those murders. It makes it legal. We all see what's happening around us. And I wanted to treat that with one individual's perception. This is a story of a professional killer who kills, not for hire, although he does get paid for it; but that's not the reason he kills. He functions in a symbiotic relationship with organized crime because they provide the environment in which he can do this, although he could do it himself. He kills as an existential expression of his right to the license to kill as an individual, and as an expression of his highest disdain for the hypocrisy of society by committing the cardinal sin against it. So he's truly a free individual, in an existential sense. The price he pays for that is total alienation from society. But he's willing to pay that price to be the free individual. And it becomes a sort of commentary on the nature of violence in society, in a kind of allegorical way. The individual as opposed to society, and the absolute pure and clear logic of his arguments about why to kill. You saw it with the Sharon Tate business and all that. I mean you really can root it with *Caligula*—Camus' *Caligula*—about the absolute right to eradicate individuals who are not functioning in society, who you yourself make judgment upon and say, "Okay, he doesn't deserve to live or you're not contributing as I see it, so we'll wipe you out." Well, we're doing that pretty much as a society. I mean, our institutions are doing that. I don't think that anybody quarrels with the point that somehow built into the American psyche is that an American life is more valuable because we have spirit, we are very special people. You know, yellow people are somehow quasi-human or black people are somehow quasi-human. We really can't get into the humanity of people who look different than we do. It's like shooting somebody through a telescopic lens on a rifle. You really have no sense of them at a quarter of a mile away. You can't hear them scream. There's no voice to them. They just don't exist. So, essentially, that's what the film is about.

FROUG: What will happen to *The Mechanic*?

CARLINO: Bob Chartoff of Chartoff-Winkler is behind it and, hopefully, we'll film it because I see it as more current than it was when I wrote it.

FROUG: As it relates to Vietnam?

CARLINO: Yes, as it relates to a whole kill syndrome in our society. It seems like we kill to assert our reality. [Since our interview, *The Mechanic* has been sold to United Artists and is now filming. Carlino received $100,000 for the screenplay plus one-third of 50 percent of the film's profits (an equal partnership with Chartoff-Winkler.)]

FROUG: Between assignments do you automatically continue writing originals?

CARLINO: No. Actually, the writing is really just such a small part of it. I mean the mechanics of writing. What happens is that things continue to cook, but I don't go to my desk every day and all that business. If a project is really formed in my head, I mean really formed and ready, it will write itself. But sometimes that takes four, six, eight months cooking process in which occasionally maybe I'll write a note down to myself if I have an idea. But I don't go through outlines and drafts and all that business. It's just that when it's ready, it comes.

FROUG: Lew, you and I worked together on a television film, you as the writer of the original story and screenplay and me as the producer, called *In Search of America* for ABC's "Movie-of-the-Week." Can you talk about the differences you found in writing a movie for television as opposed to a movie for theatrical release?

CARLINO: Well, that's simple. There's only one reason you create whatever you're creating on television and that's to sell a product. It's to keep the person glued to that screen so they will buy the product. The whole orientation of writing a film or writing a play or a novel or whatever, is that you write it for its own self. Whatever you write for television is a *means* to accomplish something else. So, when you buy that set of circumstances, then you also buy all the censorship and everything else that takes place, because the considerations have to be for the widest market. In other words, what's going to sell the most people. And what's going to sell the most people are the things that are not going to offend most people. It's very basic and simple and sound reasoning from the businessman's point of view. So the difference is that you have to construct the kind of drama that doesn't offend anybody, that's able to entertain in a kind of ersatz way. It's just sort of artificial all the way down the line because you can't really deal in reality. In the early days of television when you had "Playhouse 90" and other dramas where you could really deal with issues, where the whole commercial entity hadn't been that clearly formed as yet, you could do it. But now the competition is so keen, nobody wants to jeopardize the ability of their product to sell, so they all aim at the same level.

FROUG: So the television writer is, in effect, in the business of writing about nothing?

CARLINO: Yes, yes. Right. He's in the business of writing about things that are going to allow people to escape into a safe kind of a dream world, so that when the commercial comes on they won't be disturbed. It seems to me that if you are writing a really serious story dealing with sociological issues, you can only approach a certain degree of reality. The minute it gets to stink a little, the minute it gets to be a little fleshy or sweaty or people start breathing too heavily, God, when they take that break and they advertise Aunt Annie's Frozen Apple Pie, if you're seeing some black man being hung, or whatever, well, forget it. They used to talk about drama as the suspension of disbelief. Now it's a suspension of *belief* with television. That's really what it's about. In other words, as long as you can remain there safely disbelieving, then that's what they want.

FROUG: What project are you working on now?

CARLINO: I'm not working on any project now.

FROUG: What are you doing?

CARLINO: Just thinking. I realized that in the past six or seven years I've really been working feverishly from one assignment to the other, from one project to the other. And I had been working so much that I really didn't know what I was thinking. I was really concerned with writing and with that whole thing that started me out, that ability to take time and cook an idea and let it emerge in its own good time. So right now, I'm just thinking my way through to what I really want to say, and I don't really know what I want to say at this point.

FROUG: Do you feel that the collapse of the major studios, the fall-off at the box office, the economic disaster that is now facing Hollywood, is going to reduce the work available to the screenwriter so that it wouldn't be worthwhile for students to pursue it as a career?

CARLINO: I think there's more opportunity now than there was before.

FROUG: Why?

CARLINO: Well, I think there's more opportunity to operate outside of the nepotism of the studios. I think that the structure of the studios was such that they really controlled a lot of the people's lives and had them for hire, so to speak. It seems to me that even with the demise of the number of films being shot, there seems to be more opportunity for someone who's really gifted because he doesn't have to buck a very tight structure in terms of the studios. There are more people making films independently now, even though there are less films being made. In the old days, studios had stables of writers sitting in little bungalows at a certain fixed figure a week, turning in four pages a day or whatever—that kind of cubical existence. Well, you know what that was. You went through it. But I think for a person coming in today, he's only limited by his imagination. There's a tremendous amount of private financing available. Whereas, if you had a contract, the studio sort of assumed all of the financial responsibility, that kind of Big Daddy thing. But you had to pay a price for that.

FROUG: Your freedom?

CARLINO: Exactly. So now it just takes probably more drive to do it, but there's more opportunity to do it.

FROUG: Is it still possible for screenwriters to look forward to $75,000 or $100,000 for a screenplay?

CARLINO: It's still possible for established writers, or I think it's possible for a new writer who writes a script that some star—there's just a handful of them now—somebody who is immediate box office, to say, "Wow, I'm just dying to do that." A studio will buy it for him. But unless you're really established, it's difficult for a new writer, I think, to make those kinds of demands. However, that's healthy too, because it gets filmmaking on a more realistic economic scale. If a writer really has something solid, he can get more of the lion's share of his product now than he ever could.

FROUG: He'll get a percentage of the film's profit?

CARLINO: Yes. And that's really healthy because the money should be put into raw stock and cameramen and stuff like that, and all these inflated prices that went to actors and everything shouldn't be paid. It just had nothing to do filmmaking. The money should be put into making the film, and the people should receive a fair wage for their work, but the big remuneration should come out of the success of the film.

FROUG: Everybody gambles together?

CARLINO: Yes. That's my feeling. I mean, you should make enough to live on, but when you talk about people getting a million dollars for a film or a million and a quarter and all that business, it just doesn't make any sense. It's insanity, and that's what killed it all. It really killed most of that kind of filmmaking, and I think for the good.

FROUG: Lew, to what extent does film criticism affect your work?

CARLINO: It doesn't affect me at all in terms of my approach to my work. I don't try to please a critic, if that's what you mean. It may affect you in terms of your price, let's say, if a film critic really knocks your picture or several film critics reach a consensus on your picture. Then it may affect your salability in that marketplace of assignments.

FROUG: The next time out, your price may be a little lower?

CARLINO: A little lower. But it really doesn't affect you at all in terms of the film itself, and the film public, as has often been proved. Once it's created, it exists. It has its own life. It will find its audience, despite the critics. Totally different from a play. If two or three critics don't like your play—those two or three crucial men in New York—it's dead. It will never find its audience. No matter how much time you've spent in creating it, it's simply dead.

FROUG: What kind of work do you want to do in the future?

CARLINO: I've been giving that a lot of thought, especially recently. There seem to be so many pitfalls. After seeing my play last night, realizing that even in the play form, after that first production, after that premier production, you have no control. A director can take a play and completely change the ending, as happened last night. Totally the antithesis of what you intended—even using the same lines. And in a film, you have no control because the director can change anything he wants. And I've been thinking that probably the purest form is just to write novels and deal directly with your audience without the interpretation of anybody. But I don't know if that's going to be the way. It's a simpler way of life because you really don't have to deal with all the machinations and the games and all these other careers are not so dependent on you. And your work won't be changed to further somebody else's career and make them look good. So novels seem to be the purest form. But there's something about the communal ritual of what takes place in the theater that still draws me to it in a very hypnotic way. Something about sharing a really primal thing. You know, a thousand people in an audience and suddenly that electrifying thing. But you have to pay a big price for that. I don't know, as you get older, you seek some kind of control, some kind of purity in your work. Some kind of pure expression. I lean more and more toward just putting it in a book and getting it directly to the person that you've intended it for. And that exacts a price. And the price is that you're not a part of, you're not a participant in that exchange as you are in the theater. What that person is feeling is done silently in their own room as they read your book and you don't share it. But in the theater you share it with them. And maybe it's an ego trip, but you do share it directly and emotionally.

FROUG: Do you feel you share it in film?

CARLINO: No. I mean, only in an abstract way. There's only one way to share and that's with live actors and a live audience. You really share that primal ritual of catharsis in a theater. It's a pure, true experience.

FROUG: Lew, the world of the Hollywood screenwriter seems a topsy-turvy one at best. Doesn't all the madness get you down?

CARLINO: No, it's just that you really have to be able to laugh at all these intrigues and machinations and power plays, and have a sense of humor about this game that you're in and also about yourself, and how you fit in as part of this game. It's simply that.

William Bowers

1942 MY FAVORITE SPY *(Joint Screenplay)*
SEVEN DAYS LEAVE *(Joint Original Screenplay)*

1943 ADVENTURES OF A ROOKIE *(Joint Story and Screenplay)*

1944 SING YOUR WAY HOME *(Screenplay)*

1945 NIGHT AND DAY *(Joint Screenplay)*
LADIES MAN *(Joint Story Basis)*

1946 THE FABULOUS SUZANNE *(Joint Story Basis)*

1947 THE WEB *(Joint Screenplay)*
SOMETHING IN THE WIND *(Joint Screenplay)*
BLACK BART *(Joint Screenplay)*
THE WISTFUL WIDOW OF WAGON GAP *(Joint Story Basis)*

1948 LARCENY *(Joint Screenplay)*
THE COUNTESS OF MONTE CRISTO *(Screenplay)*
JUNGLE PATROL *(Story Basis)*

1949 THE GAL WHO TOOK THE WEST *(Joint Story and Screenplay)*, Writers Guild Nomination
ABANDONED *(Additional Dialogue)*
THE GUNFIGHTER *(Joint Story and Screenplay)*, Screenplay, Academy Nomination, and Writers Guild Nomination

1950 CONVICTED *(Joint Screenplay)*
MRS. O'MALLEY AND MR. MALONE *(Screenplay)*
CRY DANGER *(Screenplay)*

1951 THE MOB *(Screenplay)*

1952 ASSIGNMENT—PARIS *(Screenplay)*

1953 SPLIT SECOND *(Joint Screenplay)*
SHE COULDN'T SAY NO *(Joint Screenplay)*

1954 FIVE AGAINST THE HOUSE *(Joint Screenplay)*

1955 TIGHT SPOT *(Screenplay)*

1956 THE BEST THINGS IN LIFE ARE FREE *(Joint Screenplay)*

1957 MY MAN GODFREY *(Joint Screenplay)*
THE SHEEPMAN *(Joint Screenplay)*, Academy Nomination

1958 THE LAW AND JAKE WADE *(Screenplay)*
IMITATION GENERAL *(Screenplay)*
ALIAS JESSE JAMES *(Joint Screenplay)*

1959 -30- *(Screenplay)*

1961 THE LAST TIME I SAW ARCHIE *(Story and Screenplay)*

1964 ADVANCE TO THE REAR *(Joint Screenplay)*

1966 WAY, WAY, OUT *(Joint Story and Screenplay)*
RIDE TO HANGMAN'S TREE *(Joint Screenplay)*

1968 SUPPORT YOUR LOCAL SHERIFF *(Story and Screenplay)*, Writers Guild Nomination

John Wayne approached me at a posh Beverly Hills dinner party last night. It was a pretty spiffy crowd. Everybody was dressed to the teeth. Wayne, on the other hand, was wearing faded jeans, a well-sweated leather vest, a kerchief around his neck, boots, and spurs. He had arrived late, coming directly from the set where he was finishing shooting his latest movie, *The Cowboys.* He was still in make-up and toupee.

"Did I hear you right?" he demanded towering over me ominously, though I am just short of six feet tall. "Did you say Bowers? *Bill Bowers?*" His voice pitch went higher.

"Yes," I replied, "he and I were just talking about you today. I was interviewing him for a book on . . ."

"Well, I hate the sonofabitch and you tell him I said so!" Wayne jabbed my shoulder with his forefinger so hard I nearly fell over backward. "He went and sold that goddamn story out from under me!" he continued, "and I offered him a lot of money! It was Christmas Eve and the sonofabitch should have been grateful. But, hell no, he went and sold it to Fox and they fucked it up royal and made a rotten goddamn movie out of it! Serves the sonofabitch right. If he'd let me play that part, he'd be a big man today and it'd been a goddamn good picture instead of a piece of crap! You tell that sonofabitch Bowers I hate his fucking guts!"

Somebody handed the irate Mr. Wayne, living legend, another drink, which was just what he didn't need, and he wandered off muttering what he would do to screenwriter William Bowers if he ever laid his hands on him.

The picture under discussion was *The Gunfighter*, which won for Bowers an Academy Award Nomination, and a Writers Guild Award Nomination, and is generally considered one of the dozen great Westerns ever filmed.

What gives the incident added zest is that the picture was released in 1949 and Wayne was offered the script in 1948. For twenty-three years, during which time John Wayne became, well, John Wayne, he has nursed a grudge over one screenplay, the one that got away.

When I reported the incident to Bowers, his reaction was, as I suspected it would be, absolute delight.

"I ran across Duke recently," he told me, "and I said, 'Duke, you're a mean, nasty, cantankerous bastard, but I still like you.' And you know what Duke said to me? He said, 'Well, you're one of those goddam liberals. You *have* to like people.'"

Bill Bowers' reputation for telling zany tales about Hollywood is well supported in the following interview. Bill would rather tell stories than write—as many a producer, including this one, has woefully discovered. A story conference with him is apt to produce two or three hours of hilarious anecdotes—and no story. I once spent three months working with Bowers on a project for CBS. The conferences got longer and funnier as the weeks passed and the network got anxious.

Neither cajoling, pleading, nor dire threats produced a single page. ("Stop worrying, you'll have something tomorrow.") Our friendship became strained. Finally, in his own good time and at his own incredible pace, Bowers completed an excellent script.

Yet it is impossible not to like and respond to the loquacious writer. He possesses an extraordinary warmth and generosity. His enthusiasm is contagious, his sense of nervous excitement pervades his work. Even when not talking he is in constant motion, his fingers tapping invisible typewriter keys, his eyes darting about in search of a new idea, as he lights and relights his miniature cigar (a substitute for chain-smoking) and rubs his palms over his thinning hair all the while whistling through his teeth. When he seizes on an idea or a story his slept-in face splits wide open with a devilish smile. He takes a fiendish delight in the ridiculous.

Bowers was born in Las Cruces, New Mexico, January 17, 1916, the son of a doctor. The family moved to Dallas, Texas, when he was five, and subsequently to Long Beach, California. His speech retains a western twang.

He graduated from Long Beach Poly High School in 1933 and attended the University of Missouri from 1933 until 1937, working his way through college at the height of the Depression. During a summer vacation he wrote *Where Do We Go From Here?*, a play which subsequently was produced on Broadway by Oscar Hammerstein II in 1938.

By the age of 22 he was a senior writer at Columbia Pictures under a seven-year contract (with six-month options) at the then-respectable if not lucrative sum of $100 a week.

During the following twenty years he turned out scores of features ranging from wild comedies to melodramas to Westerns. His best work often combines elements of all three.

Our interview took place in Bowers' comfortable two-story hillside home on the fringe of Bel Air, an upper-class subdivision of western Los Angeles. The Bowers' home is a way station for itinerant writers and show people. A smile will get you room and board indefinitely. Hospitality reaches new dimensions in this hectic household.

As Bowers and I talked, Margie, his dynamic, attractive young wife, dashed in and out of the living room, sweeping up wandering children and stray toys, and offering us her usual unlimited assortment of refreshments.

The conversation ran several hours. (It is impossible to have a shorter one with Bowers.) As the tape recorder spun off reel after reel and Margie rushed in new supplies of Cokes, we covered Bowers' long career in the movies. Most of the stories were familiar. Bill and I had both been working on the Metro lot (on different films) just a couple of years before, and one of the joys of that experience was the long and sometimes hilarious lunches Bowers more or less hosted. In an attempt to revive memories and customs of Hollywood's halcyon days, no doubt, Bill had set up a writers' table in one corner of the commissary and, since there was a shortage of writers working at the studio, he welcomed producers, and even directors. It was here that Bill regaled his co-workers with stories of the fortunes and foibles of a small-town boy who came to Hollywood and made good but never ceased to look on the entire colossus of the filmmaking industry with awe and wonder.

Seasoned veteran or not, Bowers still looks at Hollywood with the wide-eyed excitement of a college freshman.

"I'm the world's biggest movie fan," he says. "There's just nothing so much fun as pictures. And besides, in what other business can you be so overpaid?"

LUKE (roaring)
Get out of my way!

The man is propelled through the doors as if he were shot out of a cannon. Luke turns back to Tom.

LUKE (Cont'd)
Are you comin'?

Tom watches after his father a moment longer, sighs, and gives in.

TOM
Yeah.

He starts for the saloon -- pushes Luke out of the way -- and enters.

EXT. JAIL - NIGHT 77

As Pa Danby walks up and hesitates at the front door. Once again he checks his gun, loosens and rotates his shoulders, determines that the gun holster is hanging in just the right position vis a vis his hand. He is a tough, cocky, mean little man. He enters the door of the jail.

INT. SHERIFF'S OFFICE - SHOT OF JASON - NIGHT 78

Seated behind his desk going through a stack of "Wanted" posters as Pa Danby enters fast, his hand near his gun. He cases the room, then concentrates on Jason who hasn't even looked up yet. Then Danby crosses to a chair in front of Jason's desk -- seats himself facing Jason. Then in a deliberate move, he takes his gun out of its holster and leans forward over the desk, pointing his gun right at Jason's heart. Then he thumbs back the hammer.

DANBY
I believe you've got one of
my children here in your jail!

Jason looks up -- regards the gun pointing at him -- then regards Danby a moment -- then he examines the fingernails on his right hand. He discovers a loose piece of cuticle on his right forefinger -- bites it off -- examines the nail again -- then shoves his right forefinger into the barrel of Danby's gun.

FROUG: According to the Writers Guild publication *Who Wrote the Movie?*, you have written forty screenplays.

BOWERS: Yes, but it's closer to fifty-five because I used to, when I was under contract to a studio, when I needed the money on the side, I would do an extra one at night. But I never could take credit for it because the contract said I was exclusive to that studio. So I've done, I imagine, fifteen more.

FROUG: Did you use various pseudonyms?

BOWERS: Once I used Rodney Carlyle, and if you'll look in the writers' book, Rodney Carlyle has a credit there. I forgot to tell them not to count that.

FROUG: When you were under contract to the studios, were you paid on the basis of a weekly salary?

BOWERS: Well, forty weeks salary a year were guaranteed.

FROUG: And how many screenplays were you expected to turn out in a year?

BOWERS: They never had any specific thing. When you signed the contract, they never said we want you to work thus and so. But I used to—the really good guys would do this—we would dig up material we wanted to work on or material that we wanted to get them to buy, and they were always delighted when you came in with ideas of your own. One of those pictures was called *The Gal That Took the West.* Now, this started out—I read a *Life* magazine story about a bunch of old gunfighters who lived in an old peoples' home up in Prescott, Arizona, and it was talking about how they got into cane fights with each other because none of them ever remembered the thing the same way as the other did, and they were a bunch of feisty old guys. So I did a picture story on it. I was under contract at Universal at that time, and a man by the name of Leo Spitz, who was a marvelous man, was chairman of the board of directors, and I called him up and I said, "Mr. Spitz, can I send you something?" And he said, "Sure." So I sent him the story, and he read it right away and he called me and said, "Come on down." And he said, "Why did you send it to me?" And I said, "Well, I think there's a story there." And he said, "Gee, I don't see how there would be a story there. You got any ideas?" I said, "No. I just tell you that there's a good story there." And he said, "What do you want?" And I said, "I'm about to go on layoff and I'd just rather not go on layoff and why don't you keep me under salary and let's see what I can develop out of that." Well, I did an original screenplay in about four weeks off of it that they were just crazy about. It was one of the best screenplays I've ever done. Somehow Billy Wilder got a hold of it, and he offered $100,000 for it, and they were about to sell it to him, and I got mad as the devil. I said, "I got exactly $3,000 for this." I was making $750 a week and I did it in four weeks. And they said, "We'll give you a big bonus." And I said, "No. The idea was, this studio's always looking for material, and I came up with a real good thing and you're going to sell it to Billy Wilder." So Leo Spitz said, "He's absolutely right. It's insane. We go out and pay a lot of money for stuff, and we're all crazy about this." Well, they were gonna do it with Susan Hayward. Then they had a meeting and they said, "Why do we always go off the lot to get people? We got people here." Well, they ended up doing it with Yvonne DeCarlo and John Russell and Scott Brady, and it went right out the window. But the idea is that they would almost let you work any way that you wanted to.

FROUG: So that in the era of the major studio system, you had perhaps more freedom than you do now?

BOWERS: You certainly didn't have any less. I think the guys who remember the studio system now remember it all wrong. Actually, it was one of the most pleasant systems in the world. I mean, they made fifty pictures a year, each one of them. They needed all this material desperately. And if you were somebody who likes to do pictures, that was just heaven. I could do three or four a year, if I wanted to do them, if I wanted to work that hard.

FROUG: Well, according to *Who Wrote the Movie?*, you were writing sometimes four a year. In 1947, you wrote: *The Web*, *Something in the Wind*, *The Wistful Widow of Wagon Gap*, and *Black Bart*.

BOWERS: Well, *Wistful Widow of Wagon Gap* was an original story I did with Bud Beauchamp. We just sold it to them.

FROUG: And somebody else wrote the screenplay?

BOWERS: They did it with Abbott and Costello, and they had their special writers. Nobody else could do that stuff.

FROUG: Your recent credits indicate you have been working alone. But in prior days, there were a lot of joint credits. Does that mean that you worked with a collaborator or that you were rewritten generally by somebody else?

BOWERS: No. I usually rewrote somebody else. Bud Beauchamp and I did a lot of stuff together because he was an old Army buddy of mine, and Bud and I could work just effortlessly together.

FROUG: Why is it, in your infamous and well-known drinking days, you were turning out three and four screenplays every year, and ever since you've been sober, you've been averaging less than one a year?

BOWERS: Well, I wasn't making that much money then. It's very expensive to drink. You gotta work all the time because it's a messy life, drinking. You know, I was always being sued by somebody and I was suing somebody else. And Bud was a big drinker, too. Bud would come over and say, "Jesus Christ, I need money like hell." And I'd say, "Well, that's too bad 'cause at this point I don't need any." And he'd say, "You're gonna help me out. Either lend me money or sit down and do a story with me." Well, I figured it was better to do a story with him.

Bud had marvelous ideas like *The Wistful Widow of Wagon Gap*. This was another case where he needed money desperately, and he said, "I suddenly remember a thing, and it shouldn't take us over an hour and a half to get a story off of this." I said, "What is it?" He said, "There is a law on the books in Montana and it says that when one man kills another man in a gunfight, he is responsible for all that man's debts and for his wife and children." And I said, "You're kidding!" He said, "No." I said, "No problem." So we had Jimmy Stewart coming through a town in Montana on his way to the gold field, and he stopped to play a little poker and gets into a thing with the guy who was cheating and there's a gunfight and he kills the other guy and inherits Marjorie Main and thirteen kids, which was a marvelous idea. I was under contract to Universal then, and I just told it in the commissary one day and Bill Dozier was head of the thing and he said, "I love it. We'll buy it. You said Bud needs money. All right, I'll give you $2,500 for it." And I said, "I'm not going to take that kind of dough." Bud said, "Yes you are. I need the $1,200 dollars." So they bought it for $2,500. We'd worked on it for an hour and a half, tops.

FROUG: And Jimmy Stewart starred in it?

BOWERS: No. They made it with Abbott and Costello. Then one time, Bud said, "Are you doing anything now?" And I said, "No." And he said, "Well, Bob Hope's got a story, and it's a hell of a good story, and he wants to do more straight than he's done before, and I need this dough very badly, and he said if you can get Bill Bowers to work on it with you I'll give you guys a deal." So I really wasn't doing anything. I was kind of interested in working with Hope. So he had a marvelous story he'd bought. It was about this insurance salesman who hadn't sold anything in one year, hadn't sold a policy; that was Hope. And he gets fired the next day, and he's in a bar that night and gets to talking to this guy and sells him a $100,000 policy, and the guy pays the premiums all in advance. And he's just delighted, and the next morning he takes the satchel of money in to the company and announces he's sold a really big policy. And they say let's see the application, and they say, "You idiot! That's Jesse James!" And so they send him west to make sure that nothing happens to Jesse James.

FROUG: It was called *Alias Jesse James*?

BOWERS: Right. Now, I said, "I haven't got much time on this thing, Bud." So you know what we did? We assigned each other sections of the script. I said, "I'll do the first twenty pages, you do the second twenty pages, I'll do the third twenty pages." We did this in four weeks. We put them altogether, and we were astounded; they fit perfectly.

FROUG: What did they pay you for the screenplay?

BOWERS: We worked on a salary for that thing. I was getting $2,500 a week then.

FROUG: That was a big raise from the $750 a week you had been getting before the war.

BOWERS: My first contract, I got a hundred bucks a week. That was in 1938, I think, but I was making more money than everybody I knew. I'd worked on a newspaper, for United Press, I got thirty dollars a week and ten dollars a week for expenses, and I was thrilled at that. But it was different then because if you started at one hundred dollars a week, your next raise was a hundred and a quarter, and your next was a hundred and fifty, and to really get into the big money, it took years. And I had written fourteen pictures before I was making $500 a week. Then from that point, it just zoomed. I went to $750, then to $1,500, then to $2,500, and I got up to $5,000.

FROUG: $5,000 a week?

BOWERS: Yeah.

FROUG: What year was that?

BOWERS: It was about '57.

FROUG: During that year, you wrote *The Law and Jake*

Wade, *Imitation General*, and *The Sheepman*, all for MGM.

BOWERS: And I did another one called *Mrs. O'Malley and Mr. Malone.*

FROUG: Now those were all major features with major stars, weren't they?

BOWERS: Yes. But that really never concerned me. I would take any job that interested me, and a lot of them were stories that they were having trouble with, and I would go on them and fix them up. I enjoyed what I was doing. I loved the studio life. I thought eating in the commissary was about as much fun as you could have. I was still the big movie fan. I just couldn't believe that I was working in pictures, that I was really working for those people.

FROUG: When you wrote a screenplay in the days of the major studios, did you have any ongoing relationship with the production? Did you meet and discuss your screenplay with the director?

BOWERS: No, not really. The directors don't want you around. You know that. They resent you like crazy—even on the last picture I did where I was also the producer.

FROUG: You're talking now about *Support Your Local Sheriff?*

BOWERS: Yes.

FROUG: You were both the writer and the producer, and it was your original story?

BOWERS: Yes.

FROUG: The director didn't want you around?

BOWERS: I could tell. He was an old friend of mine, but he watched me like a hawk for fear I might give the actors a reading. And he got very uncomfortable every time I came down on the set. This is just a bunch of crap. You know that—that they're so jumpy about writers.

FROUG: Why do directors fear writers?

BOWERS: I think they're afraid we're going to discover that they're stealing money. I remember that Lazlo Vadnay . . . you remember Lotzy?

FROUG: Yes.

BOWERS: Lotzy was under contract at MGM at the same time Billy Wilder was, and he said Billy used to sneak off—he was writing a picture—and go down on the set and watch the directors work because he was interested in becoming a director. And he used to come back and he'd say to Lotzy, "They're stealing money. They're absolutely stealing money!" Billy said, "I write the script, I tell them every move to make, and then they go down and make every move. And they're stealing money." Well, I had been aware of that for a long time. I should have started directing twenty years ago. I was just lazy. I was busy drinking, too. But this whole thing about the director, when I read in a book about Henry King's *The Gunfighter*!

FROUG: Which you wrote.

BOWERS: Which I wrote.

FROUG: For which you were nominated for an Academy Award.

BOWERS: Well, Henry King. I've never even met him!

FROUG: You've never met him?

BOWERS: No. I wrote an original screenplay at home and sold it to Fox. Now, Nunnally Johnson was the producer on it and Nunnally, being a writer, protected my lines absolutely, and that screenplay was shot absolutely 100 percent the way it was written. And having shot it the way it was written, it now becomes Henry King's *The Gunfighter*! Now, I don't think Henry King did this. I don't think he's that kind of man, you know, that would try to hog the credit.

FROUG: Robert Warshow, in his brilliant collection of film essays, *The Immediate Experience*, devotes much of the book to *The Gunfighter*, citing it as the definitive Western. Were you aware that you were writing a classic?

BOWERS: No. I thought I had a real good idea for a Western. You know, I do this terrible thing. I used to go to parties and I would tell them parts of this thing, and this went on for a year and a half. And finally my agent said, "You know, you have told me every single scene and with all the dialogue." I said, "Oh, sure. I know." And he said, "Well, write it." So by the time I sat down to write *The Gunfighter*, I knew every line in it. It took me two weeks just to put it down, but I had thought it out completely. Now, you ask if I had an idea it was going to be a classic. I don't know. Those were my drinking days. I was very surprised as I began to read reviews, that they were saying this is a completely new thing. This is an adult Western. Well, I never knew quite what that meant, and I don't think anybody else does either. But I know that the English magazine *Punch* said that this is an astounding new conception of a man who is a gunfighter, and is the top gunfighter in the West, and really doesn't want to be a gunfighter anymore and wants to get out of it and he can't. Well, that's the first time I ever thought of it in that way, and I thought, "By God, they've never done one like that before." Most Westerns are derivative, and if you don't think *The Gunfighter* has been stolen from, just watch TV. It's been stolen in television and everywhere else, which doesn't bother me; that's a real extreme form of flattery. And also, I think the whole Western picture was built where each guy was sitting on the shoulders of the guy who had done one before. If you want to say where *The Gunfighter* came from, *The Gunfighter* came from two things: I had seen *Red River*, which I thought was a marvelous Western, and I'll tell you a story about that, too. I thought Duke Wayne was so marvelous as that big, tough, tired guy, when I did *The Gunfighter*, I thought here I've got a story about the toughest guy in the West, only you never see him do anything tough. And I'm absolutely screwed if I don't have a guy that you would just naturally believe. So Duke is that guy. You know, you don't have to see him do something tough. He's just a big, tough guy, so he was perfect. And I wrote *The Gunfighter* for Duke, and I took it to him, and he flipped over it, and he offered me $10,000. And I said, "Oh, come on!" He said, "Well, you said you wrote it for me, don't you have any artistic integrity?" I said, "No." So I sold it to Fox, and I think I got $70,000 for it. And do you know to this day, Bill, every time I run into Duke he says, "You sure sold that out from under me." I say, "Well, you didn't offer me any money." He says, "Well, you said you wrote it for me! And then you go over there and let that skinny schmuck do it!"

FROUG: He was referring to Gregory Peck?

BOWERS: Yes. And I said, "Gregory Peck is a skinny schmuck?" Duke said, "Yes. And what's more, he's a liberal." And I said, "Oh, I didn't know that or I never would have sold it to him." But actually, Duke would have been superb in *The Gunfighter.*

FROUG: Isn't that the picture about which Darryl Zanuck said, "You can't sell a Western with Gregory Peck wearing a mustache." Was that the quote?

BOWERS: Zanuck was in Europe when they were shooting, and King decided he was going to make this *the* authentic Western of all times. He didn't want any Hollywood Western kind of a thing so he had Peck grow a funny kind of mustache . . . it was a straight Western mustache . . . it was a small little thing. And he had him wear kind of a funny hat in it, too. And Zanuck came back and saw it, and went right through the ceiling. And he said, "Jesus, you don't take the best-looking man in the world and put him in a funny hat and a funny mustache. This picture will never make a cent. People aren't going to pay money to see Gregory Peck that way." Well, as everything that Zanuck ever said, it made good sense. You don't take a man as good-looking as that and make him look silly. But he sure looked authentic in it.

FROUG: Did the picture make money?

BOWERS: The picture didn't do much the first time around. It got fabulous reviews. But I don't think it cost a lot of money to make. I know that over the years, it's made a lot. We were in London and I went to a theater that was running it to talk to the manager, and he said, "You know, I run this twice a year and have for twenty years." And I said, "Who comes to see it?" He said, "Same people."

FROUG: And it's running on television still, isn't it?

BOWERS: Oh, yes.

FROUG: Do you get any money out of the television run?

BOWERS: No. It was made in 1948 before the present agreements with the Writers Guild. Today we would get a small residual payment.

FROUG: From time to time I hear talk that *The Gunfighter* will be made into a TV series.

BOWERS: Now here's another thing about the position of the writer in this business: I have read on at least five different occasions that they were going to make a television series out of *The Gunfighter*. I never thought it was a very good idea, but what surprised me so was that they would think of making a series on it, and you know, nobody ever called me. It seems like they'd say, "Do you have any idea on it?" Just never occurred to them that somebody wrote that, and if they're going to do a series that I might be of some help.

FROUG: You've never concentrated in any one area as a writer, working in comedy, drama, and even musicals. For example: you wrote *Night and Day*, which was the movie musical biography of Cole Porter. How did you get from Westerns to musicals?

BOWERS: I did a lot of pictures before I did a Western. I had done a script for Cary Grant that ran into trouble at RKO, but he always liked it very much. They had two writers, Charlie Hoffman and Leo Townsend, working on *Night and Day* for two years, and they were going to start shooting, and they decided they couldn't use any of that, and Cary Grant brought me onto the picture. That was one of those insane things when what I wrote in the morning, I mean this literally, they shot in the afternoon, and what I wrote in the afternoon, they shot the next morning. It was the first time I ever had this experience.

When we were halfway through, Charlie Hoffman called me up and said, "Leo and I have decided that you have gotten all the dirty work on this picture and you deserve a solo credit." And I said, "I've seen the rushes, too, you sonofabitch, and you're not going to crawl out of it." And he said, "Well, I think you ought to get first credit." I said, "No, I'm willing to take the rap, right along with everybody else, but in the order in which we appeared on this thing."

FROUG: But the picture was a success, wasn't it?

BOWERS: Oh, an enormous success, but I still think it's the worst thing I've ever seen. And I was so embarrassed. I got to know Cole Porter really well during that period, and I was so ashamed of the picture that about a year later, I called Cole in New York and told him how sorry I was, and I asked him to have dinner. We went to dinner, and he said, "What are you doing back here?" And I said, "I came back for no other reason than to tell you how sorry I was about that picture." He said, "What picture?" And I said, "The one about your life." He said, "*Night and Day*?" I said, "Yes." He said, "Loved it. Just loved it." I said, "You did?" He said, "Oh, I thought it was marvelous. I don't really like many pictures, but that one I liked enormously." Now, the next night, I had dinner with Oscar Hammerstein, who produced my first play on Broadway, and I said, "I'm puzzled. You've known Cole Porter for a long time, and he said he just loved that picture." Oscar said, "Bill, how many of his songs did you have in it?" I said, "Twenty-seven." He said, "Well of course he loved it! They only turned out to be twenty-seven of the greatest songs of all time. You don't think he heard that stuff that went on between his songs, do you?" And Oscar was absolutely right. The songs were done beautifully, and that's really the only thing that mattered in that silly picture.

FROUG: Bill, I want to ask you now about your work patterns as a writer.

BOWERS: I wish you hadn't asked me that.

FROUG: I have to ask you because, having worked with you, I'm still unsure what they are. When you're working on a picture, do you have a regular writing schedule?

BOWERS: I should, but I don't.

FROUG: Do you just write when the spirit moves you?

BOWERS: I don't write at all anymore. Let me see how I could put this.

FROUG: What do you mean, you don't write anymore? You're working on a new Western right now.

BOWERS: Well, I'm certainly not as prolific as I used to be, and I think that is 100 percent because I make so much more money now, and I don't have to keep going all the time. I liked it much better when I was doing more pictures.

FROUG: But the market is shrinking, prices for screenplays are lower, and there are fewer pictures being shot. How is it you're making so much money?

BOWERS: Well, I owned a percentage of the last one, and I will end up making about half a million dollars off that.

FROUG: Off of *Support Your Local Sheriff*?

BOWERS: Yes.

FROUG: Is that going to be the new pattern for screenwriters, to sell their material at a low price but own a piece of the action?

BOWERS: Well, I didn't even sell that at a low price. I got $150,000.

FROUG: To write and produce it?

BOWERS: Yes. I'm counting that as part of the half million.

FROUG: And you'll make another $350,000 off of the profits?

BOWERS: Yes. I took my money through Jim Garner's company. Jim owns 45 percent of that picture.

FROUG: And what percentage do you own?

BOWERS: Ten.

FROUG: What about the new picture just released, *Support Your Local Gunfighter*?

BOWERS: I had nothing to do with it.

FROUG: Have they the right to paraphrase your title in that way? Wouldn't it appear to the average moviegoer that it's a sequel.

BOWERS: Yes.

FROUG: And doesn't it star James Garner?

BOWERS: Yes. And everybody else that was in *Support Your Local Sheriff*. Jack Elam. And Harry Morgan.

FROUG: And wasn't it directed by the same director?

BOWERS: Burt Kennedy, yes.

FROUG: Well, obviously they wanted to capitalize on your picture.

BOWERS: Yes.

FROUG: Is there any legal recourse a writer has?

BOWERS: I was about to take legal recourse. Now this is very hush-hush at this point. And just on a hunch, I called my agent, Leonard Hanser, and I said, "Check my contract for sequels." And he called me back in about half an hour, laughing like a sonofabitch, and he said, "They have to pay you $50,000 on any sequel, whether you do anything on it or not." And I said, "Really?" He said, "It's firm!" Now, I don't think they know this because that really wasn't a sequel. Burt had dug up an old Jimmy Grant story called *Latigo*, and he wanted me to do the screenplay, and I didn't like it. I said, "I'd rather start from scratch." Well anyway, Burt sat down and he did a rewrite on it, and he got Jim Garner to do it, and they made *Latigo*. It was at the last minute they decided to change the title to *Support Your Local Gunfighter*. But it was kind of crappy of them to do that. And I was going to sue them.

FROUG: They didn't ask you at all?

BOWERS: To use the title? They never asked me.

FROUG: You began as a playwright, didn't you?

BOWERS: Yes. The first play I did when I was twenty-one years old. It was on Broadway.

FROUG: What was the name of it?

BOWERS: *Where Do We Go From Here?* Oscar Hammerstein produced it. And, instinctively, I guess, I did exactly the right thing because I did a play about my fraternity house at the University of Missouri, so I was writing about something that I knew. You know, most young writers will write about Westerns, or anything but something that applies to their own life.

FROUG: What is the most important background for a young screenwriter to have?

BOWERS: I think it's important for a writer to have any background at all. I can't imagine any job that he ever would have had that he couldn't have gotten something out of that would be of value to him as a writer. The more things you have done, the less you have to depend on your imagination. I have always been an autobiographical writer. You know, I did that play about my fraternity experiences. I later did a film that was 100 percent my war experiences.

FROUG: *The Last Time I Saw Archie?*

BOWERS: Yes.

FROUG: That was about a good friend of yours, who later sued you.

BOWERS: Yes.

FROUG: Do you want to tell the story of that?

BOWERS: Well, Archie Hall was undoubtedly one of the most unique men I have ever run into. He was six foot four, a handsome man, looked a lot like a general; like a man who had been produced by eighteen generations of selective breeding to produce a man who looked like a general. But he was a buck private with me. But he talked like a general. And we never could find out what Archie did, and I used to say—this was in the picture, too—"What did you do?" And he'd get real uptight and say, "I don't know what you mean by 'what did you do?'" And I'd say, "You know, before the war." He'd say, "Well, I don't know that that's any of your business." I said, "Well, you know, you asked me and I told you I was a Hollywood writer." He said, "Well, you don't care that everybody just knows about everything about your personal life." And then he would say, "I didn't do any one thing in particular. I was involved in a lot of things, profit-making things." So he always gave me the impression of being kind of crooked. He was a delight for me in the Army. He made the whole thing worthwhile because he's a funny, funny man. Well, when I wrote the script, I based a lot of it on him and myself and the guys. And I told him, I said, "I thought it would be kind of fun if we used our real names." I said, "I'll use mine and you use yours." He said, "That'd be fun, yeah." So I used Archie Hall, and when he found out Bob Mitchum was going to play him, he was just delighted. And he came to all the parties, and he was down on the set all the time, everybody fussed over him quite a bit, and it was about a week after the picture started shooting, I get a call from United Artists and they said, "Are you sitting down?" And I said, "Why? What is it?" And they said, "Archie Hall has just filed suit against you for $50,000 for invasion of privacy." And I said, "Why that miserable sonofabi—." They said, "Wait a minute, Bill. You said he was just like the guy in the script, and that's what the guy in the script would have done." He would, too.

FROUG: Did they pay him?

BOWERS: We paid him $6,000 to call the whole thing off. And the really tragic thing about it is, I haven't spoken to him since then and I kind of miss him. I really do.

FROUG: Years ago you once told me, I've never forgotten it, that all you needed to start a screenplay was a character who was determined to get somewhere and was just passing through.

BOWERS: Oh, that's the best character in the world. And he doesn't have to get where he's going. Now, I've said this to film classes, you know, where I take *The Sheriff* and run it for them, and later I'll say to them, and this is the truth, "The night that I was sitting down and writing and had this guy say, 'Basically, I'm on my way to Australia. I'm just passing through here so I don't want to take any kind of a job here on a permanent basis,'" the minute I wrote that, "I'm basically on my way to Australia," the whole thing fell into perspective. Because he immediately became a different kind of guy. He wasn't a bum hanging around town. This was a guy who was on his way. And it never mattered if he ever got to Australia or not. I think the reason that this was so good for me—this is kind of like everybody in life—we were on our way to do something else when something happened and we never got to do that something else. You know, the girl that you met and you really didn't feel at all that you wanted to settle at that particular time, but you met this marvelous girl . . . You see what I mean by everybody's on their way to somewhere and very few people ever get there because too many things happen. Now, that's simply good dramatics.

FROUG: You used the same formula in *The Sheepman*, didn't you?

BOWERS: Yes. He was on his way to kill somebody. He was a guy who was very much in love and was going to be married, and his girl was working in a bank and some guys came in and held up the bank and in the gunfight she was killed, and so he was looking for these guys who had killed his girl, and he passes through this little town. What happened was this: he was in a poker game in Denver and he was winning all the money, and one of the guys that he was playing with put up a herd of sheep—do they call them a herd of sheep? And he won the sheep. Now he had to find some place to put them. And so he found that there was a place, this little town, where they all pastured their cattle and everything on public lands. So he came through this little town with this herd of sheep. Actually, he was still looking for the guys who killed his girl, but everybody raised so bloody much hell about him bringing sheep in there, and he was just a real stubborn guy, there ain't nobody gonna tell him that he couldn't raise sheep, and he took on the whole territory, you remember that?

FROUG: Yes.

BOWERS: Well, at the end of the story when he had just turned the whole place upside down, Shirley MacLaine comes to town, and he's loading all his sheep aboard this train. And she says, "What are you doing?" And he says, "I'm taking them up to Denver and selling them." She says, "You're selling your sheep?" "Yes," he says, "after all that fuss, nobody's ever going to tell me that I can't raise sheep if I want to. But on the other hand, once that I've made my point, nobody's gonna tell me that I have to raise them if I don't want to. And I don't want to because they're the smelliest animals that ever lived." Well, he was a marvelous character, you know.

FROUG: A great deal of your work has been in the Western field. Is the West part of your personal background?

BOWERS: Look, I was the least likely guy to ever write a Western at all. I'd never been on a horse, and I still haven't. I don't know how to ride. In a Western, like any other kind of story, the important thing is the story, not the authenticity. You have to first get a really good story then, if you put it in 1870, you go to your research department—this is what we'd do at the studio—and you'd say, "Look for any discrepancies in this script. Maybe they didn't have this kind of gun in that day." But don't do that first. You'll waste more damn time trying to make it authentic before you ever even get a good story. The story is the important thing, the characterizations are the important thing, then you just put those characters in a Western.

FROUG: In other words, people are doing the same things, essentially, no matter what period of history we're dealing with. They're loving, they're hating, etc.

BOWERS: Of course they are. For example: when I saw *Red River*, I thought it was marvelous. And I ran into Borden Chase, who wrote it, and I said, "Jesus, Borden, that's one of the best Westerns I've ever seen." He said, "You mean you didn't get it?" I said, "Get what?" He said, "I would have thought you, of all people, would have caught it." And I said, "What?" And he said, "That was *Mutiny on the Bounty.* I had always thought what a great Western *Mutiny on the Bounty* would be." So he said, "I ran the picture and I just took it right down, and I just put it in the West. Now if you think about it, John Wayne was Captain Bligh. They were on this cattle drive and he was a mean sonofabitch and he was beating up these cowboys, and Montgomery Clift was Mr. Christian. And what did they finally do? They kicked John Wayne off of the cattle drive."

FROUG: They mutinied.

BOWERS: They mutinied and threw him off and told him he couldn't come around anymore. And Wayne is saying, "If you do this to me, I'll get you if it's the last thing . . ." It was absolutely *Mutiny on the Bounty* the whole way. Didn't you ever think about it?

FROUG: No, never.

BOWERS: Well it was, and Borden did it in exactly that way. And, of course, it was a perfect Western. But you can take nearly any story, any really good story, and you can turn it into a Western, if you want to.

FROUG: By the same token, it's been said that you can take any good drama and turn it into a comedy, and any good comedy and turn it into a drama.

BOWERS: I did that on *Imitation General. Imitation General* was a *Saturday Evening Post* story, a short story, and it was very serious. And Bill Hawks had taken an option on it and he'd gotten a deal at MGM, and I was doing another picture for Bill, which was *The Law and Jake Wade*, and he had a writer by the name of Gil Doud trying to get a script on *Imitation General.* Well, Gil handed in his treatment and the studio turned it down. So Bill came to me and said, "Jesus, I'm sunk. If they don't pick up this particular picture, I don't know what I'm gonna do. I wish you'd read it." So I did and I saw him Monday morning and I said, "Do you know what your whole trouble with this story is?" He said, "What?" I said, "It's a comedy!" He said, "A comedy?" And I said, "Well, of course. When you have a G.I. putting on a general's helmet to run the battle, I started laughing because I'm an ex-G.I. You wrote in all this serious stuff and you left out all of the comedy connotations. It's a comedy, Bill, and it'd make a marvelous comedy." So he said, "Well, do you want to do it?" And I said, "Yeh, but I'm not going to do a treatment, I'll just go right on to the screenplay because it's easy as a comedy." Well, the reason it was a good comedy is that it was a well-constructed story.

FROUG: What responsibility do you think the film director has toward the script?

BOWERS: Let me put it this way: I have never known a single director that ever got a good picture with a bad script. They may have made a script better. But I don't think there's any way of making a good picture without a good script.

FROUG: Do you think that the director is obliged to follow the script?

BOWERS: It doesn't matter whether I think they're obliged to follow it or not. They won't do it. When that picture starts, the director has control of it. And there's no way you can stop him from having control of it. That's why I want to direct.

FROUG: Will you direct your next picture?

BOWERS: You know I will. I should have done it twenty years ago.

FROUG: How far do you go in your screenplays in designing the visuals for a film? Do you write only master scenes or do you include shots and angles?

BOWERS: No. I will write master scenes, nearly always, because they're easier to read. You know, I hate reading a screenplay. To me it's the dullest thing in the world. So if you can make them any easier to read, you may have a better chance of selling it.

FROUG: Do you think film schools are helpful to screenwriters?

BOWERS: Yes. I think they're absolutely necessary unless you get the incredible kind of break that I got in the beginning.

FROUG: What was that?

BOWERS: That was, that I sat home nights . . . I was doing newspaper work when I was twenty-one, and I wrote that play and I was automatically a writer. Now, I quit the newspaper business and then I had to make a living as a screenwriter so I was writing all the time.

FROUG: Why not as a playwright?

BOWERS: Basically, I always wanted to write pictures. I used to come out and make a picture and make enough money to go back and stay in New York for a while, but it was the town that intrigued me. It wasn't the stage particularly. Now you know, in this business, everybody was so impressed that I had done a play on Broadway . . . all the other writers were . . . and that never impressed me particularly at all. It was these guys that had done all these pictures that really impressed me. Oh, god, when I met Casey Robinson, I nearly fell down. And when Julie and Phil Epstein came and saw my play when we first did it out here and said, "Jesus, kid, that's one of the funniest things we've ever seen. We're gonna steal some of that stuff; we're writing a picture called *Brother Rat.*" Well, you know, Phil and Julie Epstein were just *the* biggest.

FROUG: What kind of films do you prefer to write?

BOWERS: Well, I like to do all kinds of films. I've got several ideas now. We were sitting around talking—another writer and me down at the club—and we were talking about gangster pictures, and he is an ex-reporter on a New York paper, and he started talking about Mad Dog Cole, and as he's talking it hit me and I said, "You know, that's one of the funniest comedies that's ever come along." And he said, "How?" And I said, "Well, you've described the character Mad Dog Cole. He wasn't a gangster. He didn't belong to any gang. He was a psychopathic killer. He even killed a nun one time, see." He had told me that. He said, "Okay, so he killed a nun." I said, "And I'll tell you something else. The gangs were terrified of this guy because every time he would knock over a bank and kill a dozen people, that would get the whole town down, you know, and the cops would suddenly start cleaning up things, and it hit the gangs." So I said, "I see the opening scene in this thing." Now you've got the regular gangsters, you know, from that television series. What was the name of it?

FROUG: *The Untouchables*?

BOWERS: Yes. You've got that group of gangsters and they're saying, "You know, really, Cole has got to take it a little bit easier. He's clobbering us. He goes out and kills all these people." And one of them says, "Well, what the hell. You can reason with anybody. Let's have him in." And he comes in and he has to be the coldest-eyed sonofabitch that ever lived. They're saying, "And we've got to work together now, Vince. You're hitting us where it hurts. The minute you hold up a bank, they're closing down our breweries and I know that you're an intelligent man." And when they get all through, he just spits right in their face and walks out. He doesn't give a damn for anything. This is funny. He's got to have a girl who's just terrified of him. She's a slave, an absolute slave. She doesn't leave the room. And one time she gets mad at him, crying, and she says, "And you even killed a nun!" He says, "I killed what?" And she says, "A nun!" And he says, "What's a nun? I didn't kill any nun. I don't even know what a nun is." She says, "Those sisters! You know." He says, "Oh, they wear that white stuff with the black?" She says, "Yes." He says, "Oh, that was an accident. I didn't mean . . . That's a nun? I killed a nun?" You know, he doesn't even know what he did.

FROUG: That you can see this grotesque story of a mad dog killer as a comedy is fascinating.

BOWERS: Because of what he does to the other gangsters. You know, the gangsters are pretty reasonable people and they're businessmen. They always were businessmen. They owned breweries, they owned fleets of trucks, they did everything else. Now they are made absolutely helpless, as is any other businessman or any other sane person, by a paranoid killer. He's got to terrify them because he doesn't operate in any kind of business way at all. And the minute you have that, you've got a comedy. I'll do Mad Dog Cole one of these days because it would make $85 million. A really good gangster picture, now. I mean an old kind of gangster picture. And then you make a comedy out of it. Now, they're not gonna think they're funny—the people in the picture. And Mad Dog Cole isn't gonna be funny at all. He's just gonna be funny to the audience. I think that once you've picked this as a subject, then the more ruthless you make him, the funnier the comedy gets. Now I don't know why, but it does. And I'll call it *Mad Dog Cole,* which is a marvelous title. You know what I gotta do before I do that? I gotta go to New York and I gotta dig out all the newspapers of that period. Not because I think I'm going to find out anything funny about Mad Dog Cole, but I need kind of an outline of his life. Now I don't mind taking liberties with this at all, but I will stick to his life as much as I can. You've got this one thing: at any point in this story that you want to explain Cole, it's got to be: "You know he killed a nun?" And the other guy says, "He did?!" He now becomes the most monstrous, doesn't he?

FROUG: We were last working on the Metro lot together and you were writing, as a comedy, your experiences as an alcoholic.

BOWERS: And they hated it.

FROUG: Why did they hate it?

BOWERS: I never really got a sensible answer to that. I still think it's a very good script, and I will do something with it sometime. All I gotta do is pay them back the money that they paid me. I haven't even read it since they turned it down. I just haven't done a damn thing with it. I think because it was so personal. It was about the first thirty days of being sober after twenty years of being drunk.

FROUG: You told me at lunch one day that the studio said that alcohol was out, but that drugs were in.

BOWERS: They said, "I don't know that people are interested in alcoholism anymore." I said, "I don't know that they ever were." They said, "No, we think that alcoholism is old hat. It's drugs." Well, you remember that guy who was head of the studio then.

FROUG: The hippest of the hip.

BOWERS: And he made dreadful pictures.

FROUG: Something like eight straight losers.

BOWERS: You know why? *Easy Rider* ruined this business for a long time. He thought all you had to do was hire a young guy with long hair. Remember how many of them were walking around Metro? And he figured they would make you an "in" thing like *Easy Rider*. And he was on the wrong track from the beginning. I knew he would go on his ass because he's going to try to be contemporary all the time. And you can't be contemporary doing pictures. By the time you got that picture out, the drug and hippie scene were already gone, you know, really far gone. Anyway, he didn't do good pictures. That was the clue. It doesn't matter what you're gonna make them about. It's gotta be a good picture.

FROUG: Topicality is not a factor in movies, is it?

BOWERS: Last year, if you wanted to make two pictures that couldn't possibly make money, according to the production head of MGM, *Patton* and *M*A*S*H* were those two pictures. They couldn't possibly do it because one is about the Korean War, which is out. You know, nobody's interested in that old thing anymore, and certainly not World War II. And particularly a sonofabitch like George Patton. According to his way of thinking about pictures, nobody would have gone to see those pictures. Well, there was a very good reason why everybody went and saw those pictures: they were two marvelous pictures, and it didn't matter what they were about.

FROUG: What do you think of the current phrase directors are using: "The screenplay is merely a blueprint"?

BOWERS: Well, they're full of shit. You know that. And anyway, that's not something new. Directors have always said that for as long as I can remember. Look, the directors would love it if they could arrive at a point where it is "a film by . . ." And they never have really because they still have to have a script. And they really resent the fact that they have to have a script so they do everything to put the script down. Oh, Jesus, Burt Kennedy said something to me that was so funny. He came in and he said, "I was driving by Otto Preminger's house last night, or is it a house by Otto Preminger?"

FROUG: You wrote the Academy Awards show last year, along with Iz Diamond and Leonard Spigelgass. Could you tell us about that?

BOWERS: I love the Academy and I will do almost anything for the Academy because I think it's a marvelous organization. You mean you want me to tell this whole thing?

FROUG: Yes.

BOWERS: To our horror, we found out—the three writers—we found out that we were the only ones that weren't being paid. Bob Hope got $5,000 for doing each of the shows. Well, actors all have to be paid if they appear on television, but they should get minimum, which is $300, and the Academy decided that they could afford to pay them each $1,000. So each one of those presenters and, of course, all the musicians, are paid, and *everybody's* paid except the writers.

FROUG: Why is that?

BOWERS: Well, because we don't have anything in our Guild that says we have to be paid. I really felt it was kind of crummy. Particularly since Danny Taradash is president of the Guild.

FROUG: A former vice president of the Writers Guild.

BOWERS: Yes. That's right. And I don't think it's ever occurred to them—I'm sure it didn't because Danny's a terribly nice man—that we actually didn't get anything. But what really browned us off . . . really the only thing we got out of this thing were two tickets apiece to the Academy Award ceremonies, and two tickets to the Governor's Ball. Well, when we got to the Academy Awards, we found that they had given us *the worst seats* in the whole damn place, and when we got to the Governor's Ball, the tables are in circles that get further and further away, and we're on the next-to-the-last circle. Now why they did this to us, I don't know.

FROUG: Automatically, Hollywood and, indeed, most so-called "filmmakers," tend to belittle the screenwriter. Why is that? Will the situation for writers ever change?

BOWERS: I doubt it, and I'll tell you why: The director is the absolute last guy that's on that picture. And he cuts it and then hands it to them. Now, the contribution of the writer may have been done six months before or a year before, and the contribution of the writer has no immediacy to it. It's the director that's just at the end of the line. And I don't want to take away from the director either because from the day that picture's shot, the whole thing is on his shoulders. But a director has to be a fool not to acknowledge the contribution of the writer. I think that most good directors do acknowledge it.

FROUG: In the future, will you not sell a screenplay unless you can direct it?

BOWERS: Direct or at least produce. I intended to direct *Support Your Local Sheriff* and now I know that if I had stuck to my guns that I would have done it because Jim Garner loved it that much. He talked me out of it by saying, "Look, I've made five bad pictures in a row, and I really need a good picture, and I'd be scared to death to go with a new director. So why don't you produce this one?" But I also know that if I had stuck by my guns, they wanted that script badly enough. And I should have directed it. Not that Burt didn't do a perfectly good job. But it was my script and there were things in it that I would have gotten that he didn't get. You bet your sweet ass I'm going to direct the next one.

Walter Brown Newman

1950 ACE IN THE HOLE (a.k.a. THE BIG CARNIVAL) *(Joint Screenplay)*, Academy Nomination

1954 UNDERWATER *(Screenplay)*

1955 THE MAN WITH THE GOLDEN ARM *(Joint Screenplay)*

1956 THE TRUE STORY OF JESSE JAMES *(Screenplay)*

1960 THE MAGNIFICENT SEVEN *(Uncredited)*
CRIME AND PUNISHMENT U.S.A. *(Screenplay)*

1961 THE INTERNS *(Joint Screenplay)*

1963 THE GREAT ESCAPE *(Uncredited)*

1964 CAT BALLOU *(Joint Screenplay* with Frank Pierson), Academy Nomination, Writers Guild Nomination

1966 BAGGY PANTS* *(Story and Screenplay)*

1967 CABBAGES AND KINGS* *(Story and Screenplay)*

1970 TRIAL* *(Screenplay)*
HARROW ALLEY* *(Story and Screenplay)*

1977 BLOODBROTHERS *(Screenplay)*

1978 THE CHAMP *(Joint Screenplay)*

*Unproduced

If you were to ask the cognoscenti of Hollywood to name the half-dozen best screenwriters working in American films today, the chances are Walter Newman's name would appear on every list. What makes this unusual is that Newman's body of work is so slender, and his name has actually appeared on so few films.

Yet top-flight story editors such as Mimi Roth at United Artists and Dorothy Wilde at 20th Century-Fox, whose job it is to read and evaluate material for their studios, will tell you that there is no finer writer than Newman. Mrs. Wilde states: "*Harrow Alley* is one of the best screenplays I've ever read. It's an amazing piece of work."

From time to time students of mine at UCLA will come across a bootleg copy of *Harrow Alley* and rush into my office with the excitement of wild-eyed young prospectors who've struck a rich vein. "But," they ask, "who is Walter Newman?"

Producers such as Walter Mirisch (*In the Heat of the Night*) and Ingo Preminger (*M*A*S*H*) know and admire Newman's work. Many of the new breed of promoter-producers in Hollywood do not.

Two of Newman's screenplays have been nominated for Academy Awards (*Ace in the Hole* and *Cat Ballou*), yet almost none of the attendant publicity connected Walter with the films.

Walter Newman is perhaps the most respected, least-known writer in Hollywood.

One reason for Newman's anonymity is his former penchant for removing his name from films he'd written, as well as his refusal to accept offers to adapt novels and plays for the screen. It is safe to say that for every job Newman agrees to do, he turns down twenty.

Otto Preminger asked him to write a film about Gandhi, but Walter turned it down because he said it would be impossible for him to honestly depict the life of an East Indian. Yet his finest screenplay concerns the life and times of seventeenth-century England.

Anthony Quinn, another Walter Newman fan, recently asked me to ask him if he would be interested in adapting *Across 110th Street*—a novel about Harlem. Walter's reply was typical: "What can I possibly know about the plight of the black man? You really must get a black writer."

Actually, much of Newman's anonymity has more personal roots. Until recently he has been an exceedingly shy man (years of psychoanalysis helped him overcome much of the problem) and he is inordinately modest. He is genuinely unaware of the regard people hold for his work. (When I told him Dorothy Wilde's comment about *Harrow Alley*, his response was uproarious laughter. "You're kidding," he said, "you must be kidding!")

Walter Newman's life is a Hollywood anachronism. He is still married to the same woman after thirty years. (Connie Newman is as outgoing, bubbling, and effervescent as Walter is quiet and reticent.) He maintains the same friendships he has had most of his life. He is intensely loyal. Until recently he lived in an old house in a most unfashionable neighborhood and left only because he was on the fringe of a high-crime-rate area and was concerned for his children. He drives a Plymouth of ancient vintage, battered but serviceable. Long before it was fashionable, Walter wore jeans and denim jackets to work (purchased not at Carroll's of Beverly Hills, but at his neighborhood war surplus store). His serviceable, no-nonsense steel-rimmed eyeglasses came years before youth discovered them.

Walter is quick to admit he takes a certain "glee" in defying the materialistic hang-ups of Hollywood. But aside from his enjoyment of his idiosyncratic lifestyle, he is also keenly aware that keeping his overhead to a minimum gains him the freedom that every writer the world over longs for. In

Hollywood it's officially known as "Fuck-You Money."

Our interview took place in Walter's office, which itself might be a perfect set for a Dashiell Hammett movie. It's located alongside the railroad tracks in the commercial zone of West Hollywood, above a tailor shop and a massage parlor. He has worked there since 1955.

The decor could be described as Early Maltese Falcon. The furniture is a collage of Salvation Army castoffs, and Walter's desk looks like a refugee from a warehouse sale. Until recently his office chair dripped wads of stuffing on the scarred wood floor. When the stuffing ran out he was compelled to buy a "new" used one.

His bookshelves are filled with paperbacks, worn and well-thumbed. Walter is a dedicated reader. Nature study posters are Scotch-taped to the chipped, painted walls along with a poster presenting prehistoric mammals and animals.

There is even a pin-up girl circa World War II and a filing cabinet that looks like it might contain peanut butter, yogurt, and carrot juice. Walter is a health faddist. "We've been eating yogurt since only the Bulgarians could spell it."

Walter himself is medium tall (five-foot-eleven), slim, and graying, with sparkling eyes and a quick, ready laugh. In his continuing battle to conquer shyness, he has gained a warmth and friendliness, at least among friends and fellow professionals, that takes a heavy toll on his time. Younger writers constantly phone or drop by to seek his advice on their work. He gives it unstintingly. ("Writers are my country.") Looking entirely professional, his feet comfortably propped up on the desk, he holds forth on his favorite subject: life.

Like his work, Newman is essentially a man of affirmation. It is quite easy to reduce him to helpless laughter with a good joke. He loves to recount funny stories he has recently heard. He tells them with great gusto, badly.

His hobbies are bird-watching and magic. When the work is going slowly, he will toss his binoculars into the car and drive into the hills, where he may spend an entire day scanning the skies. His magic tricks, which he performs with all the finesse of a Sunday golfer, give him great satisfaction ("Actually, Bill, it's conjuring") and were learned, no doubt, to entertain his son, Josh, and his daughter, Liz.

In the Jewish tradition, Newman is first and foremost a family man and a scholar.

In a business that thrives on chaos and chicanery, Walter Newman remains calm, serene, and apart—his own man. Perhaps that's why his most successful work almost always contains a singular theme: man's need to be true to himself and to hold on to his dignity.

HARROW ALLEY

Stet — ~~Ketch prepares to put the noose around Ratsey's neck.~~

KETCH
Any last words?

RATSEY
Let British pluck match British
generosity - Ah, to hell with it.

stet

As Ketch raises the noose, Mortimer ~~creates a disturbance~~ by slipping down the last few rungs of the ladder.

KETCH
You wants to be more careful, young
Mortimer.

MORTIMER
(approaching)
Mr. Ketch, I suddenly feels queer and
that's the truth.

He sits down heavily near the cart-wheel, holding his head.

FIELDING
Almighty God, the soul -

Then a thought occurs to him, the one that has just occurred to Ketch and Dan.

FIELDING (cont.)
It's not the plague? Boy, you don't
have the plague?

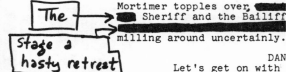

Mortimer topples over, moaning. The Sheriff and the Bailiffs stage a hasty retreat before bunching again and milling around uncertainly.

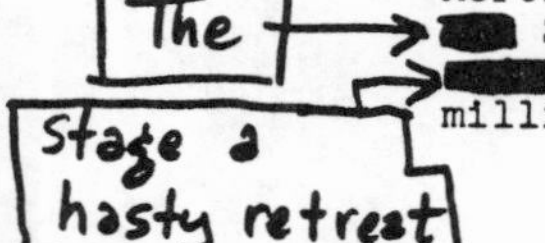

DAN
Let's get on with it, quick.

Ketch raises the noose but Ratsey jerks his head away.

RATSEY
I've changed my mind. I wants to
repent heartily of my sins.

KETCH
Oh, no, not now you don't.

FROUG: Walter, how do you feel the work of a screenwriter differs from that of a playwright?

NEWMAN: I can only speak for my own attitudes. I feel that the playwright is doing a weightier job than I am. I'm still in the grip of the status levels that are assigned in the past to theater. I would probably freeze up at the thought of writing a play. It's a carry-over from childhood. Aside from that, I don't think that there is actually any difference once I'm past the psychological barriers between writing for screen or writing for theater. At least in my kind of writing, I try to tell a story, I try to make the people as vivid as I possibly can. I work for a beginning, a middle and an end. And I use dialogue, of course. I plot my moves as carefully, I think, as any writer for the theater plots his moves. But the playwright's work cannot be tampered with without his accord. The Dramatist Guild contract guarantees that. Mine can be cut up into confetti by anyone who cares to do so.

FROUG: When you're writing for the screen do you consciously avoid telling whatever you can show, that is to say, do you make an effort to reduce the amount of dialogue?

NEWMAN: Absolutely. I work under the same rules, I think, that a spy master works with his agents. They have a rule, I understand, called *Need To Know.* You tell the spy only what he needs to know—nothing more. And I feel the same way about writing for the screen. You tell the audience only what they need to know—no more. And as little of that as possible. I feel that a great deal of tension can be given to any scene, any character, by keeping the information to a minimum. As Hitchcock said some time ago, "The one who tells you everything right away is a bore."

FROUG: How much do you yourself know about your characters?

NEWMAN: Well, I'm far from doing as complete a dossier as Lillian Hellman, for example, has done in her work for the stage. I understand that for every character, she has a full notebook with all biographical details. I need only to have an image of what the character looks like in my mind; some prime personality quirk that will enable me to hear the character talk in my head, trying always for something distinctive about the character, whether it's good or bad, and some feelings as to what the character's purpose is in the scene and how it coincides with my purpose for what I want to bring out of the scene. I long ago passed through and over the phase that a writer has of wishing to know the character's motivation. After many, many years as an analysand, I realized that motivation is a very difficult thing to determine. It takes the professional analyst years to find out what the motivation is, and I don't really see why it is necessary to know. For example, we read several times a year in the newspapers of something similar to this: There is a building burning and a mother is distraught on the sidewalk, and some passerby hears her say that her child is inside and he rushes into the building and rescues the child, puts it down and walks away. What was his motivation? I have no idea. I know what his *purpose* was, but nothing more. I think motivation is conversational coinage that directors pass around and I see no value in exploring motivations for characters.

FROUG: Do you feel that the actor, in order to play the role, needs to know more about the character than you know?

NEWMAN: I think the actor should know what he knows, and as much of that as possible. I'll give you an example of what I mean: I recently took my children to see four Humphrey Bogart films at a revival at the Encore Theater. They had never seen any of the people in these films. The films were *Treasure of Sierra Madre*, *The Maltese Falcon*, *Key Largo*, and *High Sierra*. They came out absolutely starry-eyed and talked about all the people and all the actors, *not* the characters, the actors whom they had seen. They had never seen any actors like these: Peter Lorre, Sidney Greenstreet, Edward G. Robinson, Humphrey himself, of course, Walter Huston, John Huston in a bit part in *Treasure of Sierra Madre*, and I think what they were impressed by was the larger-than-life personalities of all these people. None of these people, I am quite sure, had ever worked under the Stanislavski method. I'm not putting that down. I don't mean that in any pejorative sense. These actors did not look, as far as I can determine from some slender research into it, into themselves for characterization, but like good painters, they looked around at their experience with people—other people they had encountered during their lives—and took a bit here and a shtick there and welded them into a character for themselves, buoyed up by their own rich personalities. You had a sense that each and every one of these people had a very usable past, that they had done just about everything that a human being could do in life up until the age at which they made the film. This richness I think is lacking, and I'd like to have actors who can overlay what I have written with what they feel and know from the lives that they have observed.

FROUG: So you think perhaps the so-called "Method" has been explored to a point *ad absurdum*?

NEWMAN: I have found my reading of Stanislavski to be very helpful to me as a writer. I don't know what actors get out of it. I've seen Cassavetes' work. I don't know that I'm particularly interested in watching Ben Gazzara make up things as he goes along. I find it pointless and trivial and rather dull, and I don't mean to single out Ben Gazzara. Certainly, when he has a good part in a well-written screenplay, he does very well.

FROUG: Does improvisation conflict with the writer generally?

NEWMAN: I feel that the same observation applies to improvising in acting as it does to improvising on the concert piano. I don't think it has much to do with entertainment or beauty or excitement or anything at all. I think it's just playing with yourself. I don't think that the actor should be called upon to provide this. It's an unbearable strain upon him, obviously.

FROUG: And possibly on the audience.

NEWMAN: Yes, I don't think the actor improvising is any more interesting than any member of the audience improvising.

FROUG: What do you look for to give you that impetus to start to work on either an original or to accept a piece of work from somebody else to turn into a screenplay? What are the key qualities you search for?

NEWMAN: I will look for just a few things. At a minimum, I would like to have, as a background, an interesting arena in which to operate. I would much prefer, for example, to consider a film being made in rural Japan than in Columbus, Ohio, and that's not to say that interesting things aren't happening in Columbus. I would prefer an interesting occupation for the leading character. Given this, if I can find one living character in a book or a play against this background, that's all I need really to start moving. I can see how it will work out. I have full confidence in the project.

FROUG: Then, for you, the story really is secondary when you start?

NEWMAN: Oh, I feel confident of being able to make up my own beginnings, middles, and ends. I'm not really dismayed that the book has none of these things or that they don't work. I find my own. This has generally been true.

FROUG: What general rules or guidelines do you follow for "finding" a beginning, a middle, and an end?

NEWMAN: It has to do with decisions on the part of your leading character. The beginning has to do with the first, the big, decision he makes that starts the story going. And the middle has to do with some decisions he's faced with developing from the initial decision he made. The end is the result of all of these decisions.

FROUG: Walter Mirisch, the producer of *The Magnificent Seven*, told me that you wrote the screenplay, yet your name isn't on the film. Why is that?

NEWMAN: Yes, I wrote the screenplay. Johnny Sturges, the director, asked me to make a screenplay out of Kurosawa's film, setting it in the West, and I worked very closely with John on this. We had a lot of fun doing it. We shot every scene across the room to each other. I would tell him what I had in mind and he would counter with an objection, an idea, sometimes good, sometimes bad, which would spark me into extending myself a little further. We improvised a great deal, keeping within the absolute parallel form to the original *Seven Samurai*. When I finished, he asked me to come to Mexico to be with him while he shot it. We—my wife and I—were either having our first child at the time, or we had just recently had our first child, and I had no desire to leave the country to stand by while a movie was being shot. That's a very dull occupation. I was, at that time, a real nursery bum. I didn't want to do anything except watch the child. "The child." I sound like a novelist. To watch the "kid." Anyway, I said I wouldn't go unless it was absolutely vital and he could call me if he wanted me and I would fly down there. So he said that he would bring along somebody he knew, a writer, Bill Roberts. And he said it's just to interpolate or do whatever is necessary. You know, sometimes an actor can't say a line, you give him another line or another word or change the rhythm. And I said fine. I had written FADE OUT and I was really finished with it. Several months later, he said, "Come on over to Goldwyn studio, we're going to run a rough cut for you." So I went over to Goldwyn and sat there, just John and I, and it started to run, and after about an hour he said to me, "Jesus Christ, I've been with some tough audiences before, but you've sat there for one whole hour and you haven't said a word. What do you think of it? Won't you make any comment at all?" I said, "All right, stop the film." He stopped it. I said, "John, look, I'm not saying this is better or worse than what we had in mind. I just say it's the same but different. We talked about various things and I hear the lines and I see the actors moving this way, but it all seems very different to me. It's the same screenplay, but out of focus." At that point, I had no idea what was going to come next. He said, "Well, you know, we had certain accommodations we had to make; we couldn't get this actor to play this role so we got some other actor. Then in this scene, I know you worked very hard on it, but McQueen came to me and asked, 'Gee, can't you give me a few more lines here, daddy?' So I took some of Yul's lines and gave them to him." I said, "Well, I don't know, all the lines are in there, but some places you've changed them around and the emphasis is wrong. I'm not putting you down, John, I'm just saying it's different and I'm trying to catch my breath." And he said something that set me off, and I was a very angry fellow at the time anyway. I had only been in analysis for about eighteen years at that point, and we had hardly scratched the surface, and one thing led to another very quickly. I guess I must have been at a flash point, and I said, "All right, John, dammit, take my name off it." He said, "You don't mean that!" Well, that's all I had to hear. I said, "I sure do." He said, "If that's the way you want it. You're being a damn fool." I said, "All right. I have a right to be a damn fool." So he took my name off it. I didn't see him for a couple of years, and then I was working at Columbia on something and I stepped into the elevator one morning and there was John. He glowered at me and I glowered at him. He said, "Are you still mad?" I said, "Oh, hell no, John." He said, "Do you want to make another movie?" I said, "Sure." So I think we did make another one, I've forgotten.

FROUG: Didn't you go to work then on *The Great Escape*?

NEWMAN: Yes, that's it.

FROUG: Well, the producer told me you wrote the first screenplay for *The Great Escape*, but your name isn't on that film either.

NEWMAN: Well, ah . . .

FROUG: I have the producer's word that that's largely your screenplay.

NEWMAN: It's an embarrassing position for me. Ah, I told him to take my name off it.

FROUG: Why?

NEWMAN: John got involved in other things, and I saw very little of him during the writing of it although he insisted that we work the same way as we had on *The Magnificent Seven*. I began to get cold looks from the Mirisch brothers, who are very nice fellows and are not given to giving fellas cold looks, because eight weeks went by, ten weeks went by, eleven weeks went by; they hadn't seen a page or heard a word, and the reason for that was, I had yet to write a page. I had a lot of cards up on the storyboard and I knew what I wanted to do pretty clearly, but I was waiting for John. Finally he came in one day and said, "Look the Mirisches are very unhappy and it's been almost twelve weeks and they haven't seen anything, and dammit, Walter, neither have I!" I said, "Well, dammit, John I've been waiting for you. You told me to wait for you." He said, "Well, that's neither here nor there." I said, "All right, goddammit." And I stormed out of his office and I went down to my office and started a routine of writing from eight in the morning until six at night without lunch, coming in on weekends, too, which is a very lonely experience in a studio, and in about four or five weeks, I finished the screenplay. I was totally revolted by the whole atmosphere at this time, and I said, "John, I never want to talk to you again, and what's more, you can take my name off the goddamned script." Another writer was brought in to do the rewrite.

FROUG: Was that the end of your relationship with Sturges?

NEWMAN: No. I was walking along Santa Monica Boulevard one morning some time afterwards, and a little car, a Porsche, came by and screamed to a stop, and it was Johnny. He said, "Wanna write another movie?" I said, "Sure, John. What have you got in mind?" He said, "I'll send you something. I've got a great idea." So, it was a terrible idea. It was one of those things like, "What would happen if Christ came to Chicago?" One of those. And I listened, deadpan, as I always do when directors or producers talk to me, and I said, "Well, I'll have to think it over, John. I've got a telephone book to go over, and things like that." And so, we let it drop there. I never talked to him again about it. But then, he called me again some time later and said, "You know Michener's stories, *Tales of the South Pacific*?" And I said, "Sure." He said, "Well, they didn't use them all in that movie." I said, "Yeah, I know." He said, "I'm interested in one or two and I'll send it over to you." I said, "Okay, send it over to me." And this time I didn't bother to call him back. Just nothing there as far as I could see. I don't know what's happened to our relationship since. I haven't heard from him.

FROUG: In his recently published autobiography, *Frank Capra: The Name Above the Title*, the following appears: "I moved back into Columbia Studios in May 1964. [To make *Marooned*.] Walter Newman began writing what was to become a most magnificent script." Well, your name doesn't appear on that screenplay either. Did you remove it?

NEWMAN: No, I was the original writer on *Marooned* and I wrote a real Capra screenplay for it. You know, Frank has a wonderful combination of being oriented toward technology, so he knows all that language, and he's also got this bubbling Sicilian personality. Well, you've seen Capra films, so the idea was to try to make a film which would combine these two aspects of his character. It wasn't easy.

One was fairly gung ho, as the astronauts were, and the other was *It Happened One Night.* How do you put them together? We found a way, but unfortunately, the first draft ran about 280 pages. But we boiled it down to about 200, then 180, then 160 and so on. But then Frank was caught in some sort of studio politics. He left and I went on to another film. The writer to whom they gave the final film did a very good job and it is absolutely all his own. The only thing that was a carry-over that I had invented for the film was a sequence involving a hurricane hitting at a crucial point before launch. John Sturges called me when he took over to tell me that they were keeping that part in and asked if I had any further ideas on the subject. By that time, I couldn't even remember what the screenplay was about. I said, "No." He sent me a copy of the new screenplay, and I would say it was a very good job. I didn't see the film, but it was a very good job.

FROUG: Since we're involved in a collaborative medium, working with a director and actors, are screenwriters overly sensitive?

NEWMAN: I jib at that word "collaborative." I don't quite know what it means. When Frank Lloyd Wright designed a building and then Herman Goltz, the building contractor, came in and hired a lot of very hard working structural workers, masons, carpenters, etc., was that all a collaborative effort? I suppose in a way you could call it such, but to me, "collaboration" means actual face-to-face relationship in which everything is thrashed out.

FROUG: As you did with John Sturges?

NEWMAN: As I did with John Sturges, as I did with Capra, as I've done with one or two other directors, including Otto Preminger. But when I have written a screenplay because I've been hired by the studio or written one of my own, and nobody has seen this thing until I have written *FADE OUT* at the end of it, I don't think I've collaborated with anybody at all. I feel I've given somebody a blueprint. I hope it's followed. And that's all I can say about it. I don't see this as collaboration.

FROUG: When a director refers to the screenplay as "merely a blueprint," as so many current directors do, they imply that there is no life there, just some sketchy lines from which they will construct something of real substance. Do you feel that's true?

NEWMAN: I don't think there's that much to directing. Vince Edwards has directed, Frank Sinatra has directed, hundreds of guys have directed. There's no mystery about how to go about directing. Try to do it sometime without a script. You wind up with *Husbands.*

FROUG: What about the auteur theory?

NEWMAN: Before you came over, Bill, I found a book on my shelf called *Interviews With Film Directors,* edited and with an introductory essay by Andrew Sarris. I've never read it before. I find there are forty directors interviewed, of whom eighteen, as far as I know of my own knowledge, are writers. Now why they insist on calling them directors rather than writers, I have no idea.

FROUG: How much control do you feel you have exercised, if any, over the final results of the films that you've done?

NEWMAN: I have had no control of the final results beyond the limits imposed by a screenplay which they might or might not care to observe. I do a lot of psychological jockeying while I'm talking to producers and directors in an attempt to get them to follow the screenplay as closely as possible. All writers do this. What we face is a kind of a put-down, I think, on the part of the producer and the director. We're not in a business in which the quality of the material can be gauged by scientific methods. You can tell whether steel is strong by testing it. Here we have only opinions which can be deemed valid or invalid, depending on what the box office and the critics and your friends say after the film has come out. Before that, anybody's guess as to what makes a scene is as good as anybody else's guess, as you know. All you can hope for is that the people you are working with will understand that you have spent a lot of your time thinking about this project. And you have spent a long time learning your craft, and that they will, in effect, accede to your say-so. I can try to put them down if they suggest a scene. I use various ploys, each writer has his own. I say, "Well, that's really beneath you," and that sort of thing, or "Well, go ahead if you want to. My reputation doesn't depend on this one film," and so on. Or give them an icy stare until they shut up. But there are people on big ego trips who are not particularly interested in the film or the screenplay but in looking good or having a bigger budget than the kid down the block or putting in those jazzy camera angles that they saw on a television commercial last week. And when you come up against that, there isn't very much you can do to protect what you have put down. Even though these people may have said, "I'll buy every bit of what you've done, wouldn't change a line," they change it.

FROUG: Are you usually consulted during the filming, or has it been your personal experience that you do your job and walk away?

NEWMAN: It's been my personal experience that I write FADE OUT and I walk away. And I've had to train myself to say that's where my responsibility ends and whatever happens from now on has nothing to do with me. I would say that more than half the time I have not even gone to see the films that I've written. There are many of them that I have not seen to this day. I can't afford to feel bad, even for half a day, because it slows up my work and I don't like to feel bad personally. If something is changed which I thought was pretty good or if something is changed which I thought was ordinary and is purely arbitrary, it makes me feel very blue. I get angry and irritated and again realize my own impotence in this situation, all writers' impotence in this situation. And it can send me walking, which is my release, taking long walks.

FROUG: And bird-watching?

NEWMAN: And bird-watching.

FROUG: Have you seen *Cat Ballou*?

NEWMAN: Nope.

FROUG: You haven't seen it? You wrote the screenplay.

NEWMAN: Yes.

FROUG: What happened after you wrote FADE OUT? Another writer was brought in?

NEWMAN: Well, I left that project because I was going on to *Marooned.* I was at Columbia for about four or five years.

FROUG: But when you heard that another writer was brought in on *Cat Ballou*, did you investigate?

NEWMAN: I didn't investigate. I thought, this is very odd. I'm in the same studio, just down the hall. Nobody said anything to me about it.

FROUG: You weren't consulted?

NEWMAN: Never consulted. I'll tell you what I figured out just in the past year. Like most writers, I'm constantly brooding about the situation. We are, in effect, "the niggers" of the business, the invisible people. In moviemaking it's the hustler with the power drive who has to make it seem that he is the indispensable man in the setup. Whether he calls himself producer or director or both. He has to keep the writer in the background in order to be in the foreground. The screenplay has to become *his* and many producers and directors call it *their* screenplay and *my* writer.

FROUG: I've noted that your screenplays, from the many years I've been reading them and enjoying them, are without camera angles, only indicating a shot when it is essential to the story. Not only do you write master scenes but you describe your characters to an absolute minimum. Sometimes you say, "Joe is a banker," period. And the dialogue and the action of that character really reveal who he is.

NEWMAN: That's correct.

FROUG: Aren't most screenwriters doing that now?

NEWMAN: Yes. The screenplays by other writers that have come across my desk in arbitration proceedings do tend more and more to be written in master scenes rather than be broken up into shots.

FROUG: Is that because putting in camera angles makes the script more difficult to read?

NEWMAN: That's one of the reasons for writing in master scenes. For another, it has greater flow for me when I'm writing if I don't have to stop and consider where I want my camera. I mean, what is the point of simply putting down ANOTHER ANGLE, which is what most of these shots consist of: ANOTHER ANGLE—FROM BEHIND JIM. This is simply to fill up a page, I feel. But even though I am writing in master scenes, I very clearly indicate where the camera should be, if you care to read it.

FROUG: Would you explain that?

NEWMAN: Here's something that I'm writing now. It's an original screenplay. "A cow's skull in a patch of dead grass. There is a ragged strip of cloth torn from faded red underwear . . ." Now it's obvious that's not a long shot. Not even a medium shot. It's a close shot of a cow's skull.

FROUG: Without stating it.

NEWMAN: That's right. I say here, "The background comes into focus and we see so-and-so riding slowly toward us." Okay? So that's at least a medium shot, maybe a long shot. Then in the next paragraph I describe him. "A middle-sized bull of a man with a stolid face, etc." Well, he's coming closer, you know. You can either cut in or wait till he pulls up, if you want to spend that much footage and time on it or set up the camera and just do a close shot of him as he turns past us. You see what I mean?

FROUG: Yes.

NEWMAN: It's very clearly indicated.

FROUG: Without saying, LONG SHOT, CLOSE UP, CAMERA DOLLYING IN, PAN ACROSS. That language is out of date?

NEWMAN: I think so.

FROUG: What advice would you give someone who's interested in becoming a screenwriter.

NEWMAN: He must have confidence to begin with. You've written yourself, Bill. You still write. My God, you realize what a gut-gripping thing it is to face that blank page and to put something down, I don't care if it's the "quick, brown fox." That's yours. You're committing yourself to something here. You've got to have a hell of a lot of confidence. I have it generally when I'm fairly well into a screenplay, but that first page is frightening . . . that first blank page. Somerset Maugham recommended if you can't think of anything else to write, write your name over and over again. But even that takes confidence. Confidence that something good is going to come out. Something good by your terms, something that you'd like to see down there, that you can read over to yourself and smack your lips and say, "Boy, this will knock 'em right on their ass." You've got to feel that. See a vocation counselor and find something else if you haven't got that.

FROUG: *Ace in the Hole* was your first film credit. In working with Billy Wilder as a brand-new screenwriter, what kind of an experience was it for you?

NEWMAN: It's hard to put it in words. It was enchanting, illuminating, constantly exciting, filled with laughs, filled with good talk, constant surprises. I'm simply in awe to this day of Billy Wilder. I think he's the very best of us in all departments.

FROUG: Both as a director and writer?

NEWMAN: Absolutely.

FROUG: I've recently seen *Ace in the Hole* and I think, in some ways, it's Wilder's best film. Was it, perhaps, twenty years ahead of its time?

NEWMAN: It wasn't ahead of its time so much as it came out at a peculiar time. It came out in 1950, I believe, at the height of the McCarthy period and we had some very trenchant observations to make about certain aspects of hoopla involving most tragedies in our country, all countries, I suppose. We were shafted unmercifully by most of the newspapers—the heavies were newspaper men—and suddenly every newspaperman and every reviewer became a member of the State Department and said, "How will this film look abroad?" I still have in my files some of the only reviews of my films I've ever collected. They were so damning, and I can't tell you how good that feels.

FROUG: Why?

NEWMAN: Well, you say to yourself, I've struck a nerve.

FROUG: You hit a truth?

NEWMAN: I don't know. I just struck a nerve. The film eventually did fairly well. It took a long time to play it out. It did very well in Europe, they told me. And I ran into Billy many, many years later on the Goldwyn lot and I hadn't seen him for a while and he said, "Boy, I really lost studio power on that one." And then he said, "Fuck 'em, it was the best thing I ever did." I don't agree with that. I think he's done things which are far better.

FROUG: *Some Like It Hot*, *The Apartment* . . .

NEWMAN: *Sunset Boulevard*, *Ninotchka* . . . that sort of thing.

FROUG: I want to ask you now about what I consider the best screenplay I've ever read, *Harrow Alley*. In the current issue of the *Writers Guild Newsletter* it is called "a masterpiece" and the "most famous unproduced script in the country." You let me read it about eight years ago, shortly after you'd finished writing it, and I personally tried to interest several studio executives in it. They all said the subject matter was too grim.

NEWMAN: Oh, yes, everybody thought *Harrow Alley* was a very grim piece of business, but I thought it was very funny. In many places I actually did something I've never been able to do before or since at the typewriter: actually laugh aloud as a line occurred to me or a piece of business came into my mind.

FROUG: Why did you choose to write about the Black Plague of England?

NEWMAN: I had reached a time in life called middle age. I hit the forties and almost like a classic case it suddenly occurred to me that death exists. I don't think this will mean much to anyone younger than forty, but it, by God, exists, and I started to think about it and how do I feel about it, and then I realized that death is all over. Even though we hide it under the rug. You know, Forest Lawn, God is Love, there is no death, and so on and so on. But that's artificial, synthetic, it merely shows how much we really dread looking at it. I'd been working for a few years without a break and I had some money in the bank, so I said, "This is the time for me to examine this." And the only way I can examine things is by putting them down on paper. And then, something from my university days came to mind: the Black Plague. I knew nothing more about it other than that it hit England some time in the seventeenth century. So one hot August day I went down to the main library and took out the few books on the subject and started to read, and that's how it came into being. It's a very autobiographical screenplay.

FROUG: Why do you say that?

NEWMAN: I didn't realize it myself until several years later, when I reread it for the first time. I was surprised at seeing how I had split myself up into little fragments and given each fragment a different name and put it through its paces. One of the leading roles is a good solid citizen, which I am, who is very concerned about his first-born child, and I was and still am, and all my anxieties came out in that portion of his concern. Also part of me is pure rogue and scoundrel, and that was my other leading character, and all the other characters are me, too. From the hypocrite to the honest people, from the authoritarians to the passive ones, I have consciously recognized each and every one of them as being me. It's totally autobiographical.

FROUG: It must have struck a chord with many people because not only the cinema buffs, cinema students, but in my travels around the studios of Hollywood I have heard studio executives, even those who won't buy it, refer to *Harrow Alley* as one of the best screenplays they've ever read.

NEWMAN: It's like anything else. If you try to write honestly about yourself, you're writing about every single individual in the world, including the Bushmen. I believe that, totally.

FROUG: During the story hundreds, even thousands, of people die of the Plague. Death is on camera throughout the film, yet I feel it is an extraordinarily affirmative statement. How did you manage that paradox?

NEWMAN: I was not writing about death. I was simply writing about how do we live under such conditions. As I say, it was an examination as I went along. I'd worked it out fairly carefully on my index cards, leaving lots of room for improvisation because I just didn't know where to go at certain points. It changed constantly as I went along, so I was glad to see, in the rereading, that I was saying such a great big yes to living because I had no idea that I felt that way.

FROUG: How long did it take you to write *Harrow Alley*?

NEWMAN: I wrote it in eight weeks.

FROUG: How much time did you spend researching it?

NEWMAN: I spent over seven months researching it. If I had been in England, it would have been simpler, or even in New York City, at the main library downtown. But here, it was going to second-hand book stores, going to Huntington Library, UCLA library, USC library, and so on. It was very difficult to find something that would give me a sense of what life was like in those days. I broke myself financially writing that one.

FROUG: When your agent put *Harrow Alley* out on the market, what reaction did he get?

NEWMAN: He told me the responses from time to time. "You must be out of your mind!" That was one of them. "How dare he!" That was another one. Some studio head's wife got incensed and sent me a note—I wish I had it, I've forgotten her name—saying that I was crazy. That was generally the response. One story editor said to me, "What the hell made you write this? Boy, I read it on a rainy Sunday and damn near committed suicide," and so on. Well, all I can say is most studio people do not know how to read a screenplay. That's all there is to it. They cannot see the film in their heads as they read the words on the paper. It takes some training to do that, some ability. And it's my experience that almost all of them lack it.

FROUG: Who was the first person to option *Harrow Alley*?

NEWMAN: John Huston was the first director to ask if he could have it. I'd finished writing it in May of that year, as I remember, and in June, which was about two or three weeks later, Huston said he wanted to do it.

FROUG: Huston was unable to get financing for it?

NEWMAN: Yes. He had lost studio power. He'd put out several expensive films: *Roots of Heaven*, *The Barbarian and the Geisha*, or something like that, which had not done too well at the box office, and he had just come back from Europe with *Freud*, and everybody was getting panicky about him. He tried it for six months. He tried everything. He tried independent financing. I know he got in touch with Hunt Hartford and tried to get him to put up some of the A & P money, things like that.

FROUG: Then who was the next filmmaker who got interested?

NEWMAN: Oh, I can't remember. You know, you write these things, then you go on to make some money. I would get calls all the time from agencies. I'll just give you a typical one: four, four-thirty in the afternoon, I'm in the office, the telephone rings. Can I be in such 'n' such a saloon at such 'n such a time? Rex Harrison is driving in especially from Malibu. He has just read it, he is ecstatic, wants to do it. Can we have a drink? And I say, fine—or more than fine—hell, yes, lead me to him. And we had a drink, and oh, it's marvelous and how did I write such a thing and not being British, and so on and so on, and we're going to do it. And that's the last time I hear of him. Charlton Heston got wind of it and took me to lunch. Laurence Harvey was interested. Bryan Forbes, just before *King Rat* came out, was very, very much in demand. He took it back to England with him. I think Peter Sellers was going to do it. Then, right out of nowhere came a letter from somebody who I guess was the chief reader for the Royal Shakespeare Company saying that it had come to their attention, and would I be interested in having it done by the Royal Shakespeare Company as a play? So I just passed this over to my agent. I don't quite remember what happened with that. Oh, yes, then the Ahmanson Theater wanted to do it as a play here in Los Angeles. Elliot Martin was in charge then.

FROUG: Did you feel that it would take too much work to convert it?

NEWMAN: Absolutely not. Since I wrote it in master scenes anyway, it would take a little different blocking in the early part, that's all.

FROUG: When did George C. Scott come into the picture?

NEWMAN: Actually, he got into the picture that first summer, that June when Huston called me.

FROUG: Eight years ago?

NEWMAN: Yes. Huston, in order to show that he could bring films in on time and that they needn't be expensive, was doing *The List of Adrian Messenger* at Universal. George C. Scott was cast, one of his first films. When I went to see Huston over there one day, Scott was out front chucking a baseball with Huston's son, and Huston introduced us and Scott said that he had read *Harrow Alley* and thought it was a fine piece of work. Then several years later, like five years later, he had his agent call and say, "Look, George hasn't been able to get it out of his mind and is it available?" And I said, "Yes." But this time we weren't giving any more free options because we had discovered that what you give for nothing, nobody places any value on. And I hated to do this to Scott particularly, but I insisted on a very hefty option price. Very hefty. And he met the terms, paid out his own money for two years, maintaining that option. And then on the day it was to elapse, he sent me by Western Union a check for the full purchase price.

FROUG: Would you mind telling me how much Scott paid for the screenplay?

NEWMAN: $150,000. After federal and state taxes, agent's fees, business manager's fees, guild dues, Permanent Charities, pension plan, I finally netted a little less than $40,000.

FROUG: Do you know if Scott has any plans to make the film?

NEWMAN: I haven't been in touch with him.

FROUG: Do you think if he's ever able to film *Harrow Alley* you will be consulted?

NEWMAN: Oh, yes. Absolutely. In fact, he insisted that that be put in the contract. I told him it wasn't necessary, but I was only too ready to accede to his request. [George C. Scott has since announced he will direct, but not star in *Harrow Alley*, to be filmed in England next summer.]

FROUG: Your experience with *Harrow Alley* seems to indicate that a screenplay can assume a life of its own?

NEWMAN: All writers know this. Nothing is ever dead. A good piece of work will always be alive in some way.

FROUG: Tell me about the index cards you work with when laying out your story.

NEWMAN: Well, here's a batch. Regular five-by-seven index cards. I began to work on cards because I got tired of retyping the same pages over and over again as I made corrections or thought of better ways of doing it, other ways, making cuts, adding things. Takes me ten to fifteen minutes to type a page if there's a lot of stage business on it. So I said, "There must be an easier way." And I discovered that if I put things down on cards, scene by scene, then if I wish to make a change, it's just a question of tearing up one card or scratching a word off a card and putting another word down, changing a name, changing a line of dialogue. It makes it easier for me to work. Then when it's time for me to start putting it into screenplay form, I just go from card to card.

FROUG: In other words, these cards serve you as a step outline?

NEWMAN: As a step outline, yes. The other thing that the cards do for me is this: they keep me loose and flowing rather than inhibited, tied up in editorial work. When I start to write something, I put down on a card anything that comes to mind. Almost like free association. A name might go down on one card. That's all there'll be on one card—a name. Or a line of dialogue that spun into my head, or a very good description of a certain character. I'll just put these down in any order as they come to me and I'll do this for days and days. I'll go over my cards and some of them will serve as a stimulus to other thoughts and I'll put those down on cards. I can't tell when or how, but when I have a good thick batch of cards, I'll then sit down for the first time and do editorial work. That is, I'll rearrange the cards in some sort of sequence. If I have a character and a name, I'll put the name card and the character card together, and if I've thought of a line of dialogue, I'll put that line there, maybe some line that will occur some seventy pages in, but it goes there, until I finally have some sort of rough sequence. Then I start looking for my curtains.

FROUG: Could you elaborate on the development of curtains or climaxes?

NEWMAN: We rearrange events in a totally artificial way when we're writing screenplays because, as somebody pointed out long ago, there are no second-act curtains in life—life just flows. Whereas, in screenplays, you're aiming for a point at all times in order to get as much dramatic tension as you can. This goes for comedies, too, of course. That is, your leading characters have certain purposes and goals in mind and they wish to accomplish them and they drive and thrust toward those goals. Well, you've got to know what those goals are and, supposedly, the feelings of the reader or the audience will come from seeing them approach the goal and the hazards they meet and what obstacles they overcome and what happens to them on the way. So, just in setting up the goals, we are rearranging things artificially. Once I begin to look for scenes and curtains and climaxes, it may take two or three months. By the time I'm finished with it, I have the foundation for a screenplay that I can write without many of the attendant anxieties as to what will happen next. I know damn well what will happen next, generally.

FROUG: When you start a screenplay, do you always know where the ending is going to lie?

NEWMAN: I have a very good idea of what the ending will be, yes. I don't know how I can write the beginning unless I know the ending. You just can't ramble with a screenplay, meander down this path and that path. You've got to be heading somewhere in your own head. The trick is to keep the audience from realizing that that's what you're doing.

FROUG: You wrote the original pilot script, in radio we used to call it the "audition" script, of "Gunsmoke."

NEWMAN: Oh, yes, "Gunsmoke" number one.

FROUG: Almost every character in that first half-hour radio script, which included Matt Dillon, Kitty, Doc, and Chester, are still running and still sustaining in television today. How many years has it been?

NEWMAN: Let's see. We went down to Mexico for a weekend the day I finished writing it. We were all down there. You were down there. Johnny Meston, Dave Friedkin and Mort Fine, and Jim Poe was down there with some crazy girl. I'll tell you, that was 1953.

FROUG: So that half-hour radio script containing all the assortment of characters has sustained a series through years of radio and even longer on television for a total of over eighteen years. It must have earned millions for CBS. Do you collect a royalty?

NEWMAN: No. As a matter of fact, my name was never even printed in the reviews. The only one who bothered to review it was *Weekly Variety*. It mentioned everybody. Said it was a smash radio thing, should make a hell of a series and so on and so on. I looked in vain for my name. I couldn't find it. But I have the recording at home. It says, "Script by Walter Newman."

FROUG: How much were you paid for the script?

NEWMAN: $400.

FROUG: Many writers feel in this troubled time in Hollywood, with unemployment reaching alarming levels, that the way to survive is to fill in between screenplays with television work. You don't do that. Why not?

NEWMAN: Well, it may seem odd but it seems to me that writing for television is the hardest work of all. It's not a question of limiting yourself to a half-hour or hour of time because, as you know, we go for two hours in television these days, or an hour and a half, whatever you please. I was trained by radio. As you remember in the radio days, if I had an idea, it was simply a question of calling you up or somebody else and saying, "Hey, got an idea for so-and-so." You would say, "Yeah? How does it go?" I say, "Well, it goes this and that." No more than that. You say, "Sounds pretty good. When can we have it?" And that was all it took. And when I turned something in, it was a common experience, not just mine, there might be a brief conference with the script editor saying network censorship asked you to take this out, or can you change this line here? And you say yeah. And there was no hassle. But with television, my god, it seems to me that these TV writers sweat blood trying to clear a story, trying to get a play through to completion so they can collect their money and get on to the next one. So many people are nervous about it, talk so much about it, that writers spend a morning, an afternoon, another morning, another afternoon just in conferences. There are too many fingers in the pie. I don't think the writing, the actual writing, is any harder except when they tell you this has to be about nothing at all, we're not particularly interested in anything, we just want to keep it harmless. I tried, you know. I once got as far as talking to some guys at CBS. I had an hour or two meeting at the Fairfax offices with them, but my heart sank as the talk went on, and I realized that with the best will in the world on their part, I was up against a way of doing things that was totally obnoxious to me. So finally, I begged off. The whole business was simply tasteless. I don't mean bad taste. I mean there was no taste, no gusto about it at all. And, although I don't consider myself to be anything more than a pro, I'm ready to do anything from a one-line joke to *Oedipus Rex.* You tell me what you want and I'll turn it out for you. But this way of working in TV made me very depressed and blue and I finally said it's not worth it to me, no matter how much money they pay, to go around feeling lousy all the time.

FROUG: What subjects do you most like to write about?

NEWMAN: I never was and still am not a great lover of relevance, so-called. This sort of film, frankly, bores the hell out of me and makes me restless. I'm strictly a guy who likes penny candy. I'd much rather see an old Laurel and Hardy than *Diary of a Mad Housewife.* Call me pisher. I really am not interested in the problems that you read about in the newspapers. I'm interested in the problems that have nothing to do with these things. I'm interested in how you meet life, how you meet death, how you meet love, how you meet hate, how you express these things, what you do about them, what you do about dignity, your own, what you do about integrity, how you hang on to it, when you let go, what does it mean to compromise, is it wise, ever? I have a feeling these things engaged people while they were building the pyramids. And without being stuffy about it and not by any means thinking of myself in terms of the great Greeks or anything like that, I find naturally that these are the things that interest me.

FROUG: In the final analysis, who do you think is responsible for the success or failure of a film?

NEWMAN: Oh, it's the screenwriter. Absolutely the screenwriter. As a matter of fact, before you have even written the screenplay, you have determined the success or failure of the film simply in your choice of what to write about. At that moment, the die is cast. And you can choose something which is of no interest whatsoever and write about it beautifully. Such as the fine job Lillian Hellman did on *The Chase*—a well-acted film, well put together, done with great thought. On the other hand, you take a thing like *Cat Ballou*, which wasn't particularly well done. I put some good jokes into it, I enjoyed writing a lot of it, I knew I was doing something a little bit special that hadn't been done. That part filled me with a certain amount of glee. But I wouldn't say by any shakes it was a fine screenplay. But it didn't make any difference. I had chosen the right thing. It's this way, Bill. You see a girl at a party, let's say, and there's absolutely no flaw. The hair is right. The figure's right. The clothes are right. The face is right. And you get to her and you find out there's nothing there. She's absolutely a block of ice. You lose interest right away. On the other hand, she can be sloppy, pay no attention to her grooming, overweight or underweight, you can't remember her face, but there's something about her personality that makes you want to stay. It's the same way with your choice of subject matter. If the personality of the screenplay is right, the audience is with you. If it's not, eat your heart out. It's not going to happen.

Jonathan Axelrod

1970 SOMETIME CHAMPS* *(Joint Story and Screenplay)*

1970 EL KID* *(Joint Story and Screenplay)*

1970 THE DIRTY MOVIE *(Story and Screenplay)*

1971 GO LEFT, YOUNG MAN* *(Story and Screenplay)*

1971 EVERY LITTLE CROOK AND NANNY
(Joint Screenplay)

1972 STOWAWAY* *(Story and Screenplay)*

*Unproduced

Twenty-three-year-old screenwriter Jonathan Axelrod is a rebel with a cause. He is in revolt against not only the Establishment but against his own union, the Writers Guild of America. In fact, there are very few organizations that Jonathan doesn't hold in some sort of contempt, except "The Entertainment Industry for Peace and Justice," as he tells us in this outspoken interview.

Axelrod might appear to be just another case of Hollywood nepotism (his stepfather is famed screenwriter and Broadway playwright George Axelrod—*Seven Year Itch, Will Success Spoil Rock Hunter, The Manchurian Candidate*) except that when it comes to the screenplay, studios buy what's on the paper, not the author's family tree. A script with the name Axelrod on the cover, stepfather or stepson, is no assured sale.

Only two years ago young Axelrod, who looks like a linebacker for a high school football team, was a movie "gofer" ("Hey, you, go for coffee, go for cigarettes"), which is as low on the Hollywood scale as you can get. But in the past two years he has sold six screenplays—during a period when, for most screenwriters, the sale of one script would have been considered cause for celebration.

For a young man with minimal education and a classic poor-little-rich-boy background, plus the added fillip of divorced parents and a disapproving father, his achievement seems all the more remarkable.

Jonathan was born in New York City, July 9, 1948. His father is Arthur Stanton, a self-made multimillionaire, head of a half-dozen super-corporations; his mother is an interior decorator. After his parents separated, he was brought to California and raised in a $400,000 Beverly Hills home deep in the heart of the world's richest and most egocentric ghetto, the movie colony.

Jonathan found a rapport with his stepfather, whose talent and wit placed the senior Axelrod in the upper echelon of the industry. Jonathan took his new father's name, and perhaps, through osmosis, some of his talent. They remain good friends today, though George, like many of his fellow high-salaried screenwriters, producers and directors, has fled the now arid lotus land for London. It is quite an accurate indicator of the situation in American films that established moviemaker George is in London writing books and plays and novice Jonathan is in Hollywood making movies.

Our interview took place in Axelrod's furnished one-bedroom apartment just off the Sunset Strip. It resembles a $100-a-day suite at the Beverly Hills Hotel: elegant but worn furniture, mirror-walled dining room, gold-filigreed light fixtures.

"But I don't own anything," says Jonathan. "You can't hold on to things. From here I can walk up to the Sunset Strip where I can meet the freaks, the weirdos, the everyday people. If you live in Beverly Hills, you're finished."

The night that we talked the temperature had been hovering over ninety in Los Angeles for days, setting all kinds of records. The air-conditioning unit had collapsed. It was hot and oppressive.

Axelrod sat barefoot on the couch, wearing a T-shirt and jeans, guzzling Diet Pepsi. He was well into the second six-pack before the evening was over.

Jonathan has a quick smile and an easy warmth. He withholds nothing, he has no guile, and no malice, only a determination to fix responsibility. He named many names and attacked many sacred cows—not the least of which is his guild.

"Listen," he said to me at the end of the long, hot evening, "I don't know if I've said anything that'll help any young writers. I'd like to, but I don't know anything about that stuff. I just know what I do."

JOSEPH (v.o.)
Open up, Mr. Barnes. We know you're in there.

JACK finds his pants, but stubs his toe on the foot of the bed. He lets out a piercing scream. SYLVIA awakens, startled by JACK's holler.

SYLVIA
What . . . ?

JACK ssssh's her and motions to the window.

PAULA'S VOICE
It's hard to believe such terrible things could go on in this modern day and age.

JOSEPH (v.o.)
The Big Man wants to see you. The cheque bounced.

SYLVIA opens the window leading to the fire escape. All she has on is a nightgown. JACK, still gathering his clothes up, shouts:

JACK
What do you mean <u>bounced</u>! There's been a mistake! Send the cheque through again! Send it through again!

MURRAY (v.o.)
It's better to face the music now. Come on! Open up!

JACK finally has his clothes in his arms. He runs to the window.

JACK (whispering)
Out! Get out!

SYLVIA
I gotta get dressed, Jack.

JACK
You drive! I'll dress!

JACK truns to the door once more.

JACK (shouts)
That Bank Manager's gonna get some letter from me in the morning!

FROUG: How did you start as a screenwriter?

AXELROD: Well, when I was seventeen I had already made two short films. I wanted to be a director, and I showed a film to John Frankenheimer and he hired me as his apprentice. I worked for a year with him on a film called *The Fixer* and then later on a film called *The Gypsy Moths*, for a little while. And I realized that you couldn't walk in and say you were a director. I tried acting, which I was miserable at, so the only profession I could go into in the film business where I could support myself was by writing. It didn't cost anything to write. It was totally unintentional and I just started writing original screenplays.

FROUG: Purely on speculation?

AXELROD: Oh yeah. They were very bad because I was writing about subject matter which I was interested in. And I would go in for Pirandello effects and other things like that that I thought would be so terrific and that never worked because I wasn't dealing with people, I was still dealing with the subject matter.

FROUG: In other words, they were intellectual and not very dramatic?

AXELROD: Boring is the word. They were boring.

FROUG: How many screenplays did you write before you sold one?

AXELROD: I wrote six of them, but then I subsequently sold some of those.

FROUG: Some of the bad ones?

AXELROD: Oh, dreadful ones. The worst ones I sold.

FROUG: Where did you sell them?

AXELROD: Small places like Warner Brothers and places like

that.

FROUG: Are they shooting them?

AXELROD: No. One I sold to Warner Brothers. It was called *Sometime Champs.* They hired a director named Michael Winner who is not a winner. And it was a Western where all the climaxes were sexual instead of violence so instead of building up to a violent climax, it was a rape. Or a homosexual act. And they thought that was terrific and then Michael Winner came in and for some reason he decided that we should put back violence and take out the sex, so it turned out to be a very straight script with him. And it wasn't very good to begin with.

FROUG: Did you do the rewriting?

AXELROD: Yes, I did. And then they fired me and they hired another writer who had just written *Klute* and they invested a great deal of money in the project. They paid Michael Winner some money, and it wound up to be a terribly boring script. It was my first involvement with a director and I was able to see the destructiveness and egos of directors who can destroy scripts very easily. And also of studio heads who believe in the auteur theory and believe in the director's capacity as god.

FROUG: So because of Michael Winner and his tampering with the script it ended up as a film not being made?

AXELROD: Yeah, I got the rights back and now I'm trying to sell it again.

FROUG: In its original form?

AXELROD: Yeah, I just want to sell it.

FROUG: How old were you at this time?

AXELROD: I was twenty-one.

FROUG: Were you going to college, or had you graduated?

AXELROD: I nearly didn't make high school and I never went to college.

FROUG: Where did you go to high school?

AXELROD: Various places. Wherever they would keep me. I went to University High in Westwood for about six months. I was expelled.

FROUG: For what?

AXELROD: I didn't show up for three days in a row. And they expelled me. Before that I went back to Chadwick which is a boarding school and then to Rexford High which is a private school for maladjusted rich children.

FROUG: That's what you were?

AXELROD: No, but they put me there anyway.

FROUG: After you got out of high school, what did you do to support yourself?

AXELROD: John Frankenheimer paid me fifty dollars a week.

FROUG: Were you his "gofer"?

AXELROD: I was everything. I was his "gofer," I was like a box boy in a market. I did everything that I was asked to do. I learned a terrific amount from that man. He was sensational to me and he taught me a great deal.

FROUG: How did you get the job?

AXELROD: He had done a film with my stepfather, called *The Manchurian Candidate,* and I met him there and we became interested in each other. We would speak a great deal together. We became friends. He knew I wanted to be a director and he took me with him because he said that I had the personality of a director. Which meant I was very close to him. I had a bad temper. So I went off to Budapest and learned about filmmaking. Nothing about writing. I really never knew anything about writing at that time. Dalton Trumbo, who was there and wrote the script, would write pages and it would all seem very mystical to me. I never knew where they came from. I knew we had a brilliant man walking up and down the set. I knew his name was Dalton Trumbo, but I really didn't know what he did. I learned about filmmaking.

FROUG: When you came back from working on *The Fixer*, that's when you began writing screenplays?

AXELROD: Yeah. Well, I had very little money and I had to find a way to make a living. And I was hired by a production company called Rogallan Productions which is Roger Smith and Allan Carr, and they hired me to be an associate producer of a film. But they needed a writer. They had no idea I could write. Neither did I. They asked me to find a writer who could do the film for very little money. I was getting $100 a week which was a big raise—as the associate producer. It was a title, of course, and had no meaning. The film was never going to be made. And we all knew it.

FROUG: What was the film called?

AXELROD: It was a book, called *The Town That Took a Trip*. It was during the LSD, motorcycle craze. Anyway, I wrote a two-page opening, just for fun, and they read it. And they loved it, so they said, and they asked me to write the script. Now I really thought that they loved it and they were being honest. The problem was that I was still getting $100 a week. And I was not only working as the associate producer, I was writing the script, breaking every rule of the Writers Guild. I was not a member yet so I did not know about that. I didn't know writers should be paid. I was living like in the thirties. And it was exactly like what many New York writers in the thirties experienced, I imagine, when they came out here. I was in a little room, put away at Goldwyn studios. No one knew I was writing. What happened was that I wrote what I thought was a tremendous script, which I have read since, which may be the worst script ever attempted by man. Anyway, I continued to work for them, and suddenly I see another script with the same title. And I look at it, and it says, "By John Jordan and Jonathan Axelrod." So I'm trying to figure out who John Jordan is and I ask Roger, who I know is a fledgling writer. Now, Roger honestly believes that he is Proust, so he has a major problem in anything he does. He had taken it and rewritten it and I felt terrible. It was probably no worse than what I had done at the time, with the egos involved. But I quit and the film never got made. I guess that was my first job as a screenwriter. And after that I decided I would only write original screenplays.

FROUG: So then you sat down and just began writing them?

AXELROD: Yeah.

FROUG: How did you support yourself?

AXELROD: I lived in a house that this woman owned. I rented her back room for ninety dollars a month and I had saved money when I was working for Rogallan. At $100 a week I could save. I was living on $200 a month. And that's how I lived. And I got a job for Milton Sperling, who hired me to write a treatment based on the life and times of Edgar Cayce, the spiritualist. He was the only man who could get the rights from them, the Cayce people. Now my problem in writing it was very simple. He wanted a wonderful story about Edgar Cayce and I found out that Edgar Cayce was a total fraud, and was a very destructive man. And they were making millions of dollars from the Edgar Cayce society. Cripples walking around. And I wrote a treatment which showed that and I was, of course, immediately fired.

FROUG: You still weren't a member of the Writers Guild?

AXELROD: Oh, I had to join.

FROUG: After writing the Rogallan script?

AXELROD: Right. A friend called me up and said that unless I wanted to get into serious trouble, which I presumed at the time meant death, that I should join, which has been the biggest mistake I've made in the business so far, joining the Writers Guild.

FROUG: Why?

AXELROD: I think every writer should not join the Guild. I would fight. I'm trying to get out of it now, and I don't know how. I feel trapped. It's the most destructive crazy insane guild that ever existed, maybe. When you go to a Writers Guild screening, the marvelous thing about Writers Guild screenings is that it's the single most illiterate audience in the world. That's number one. The films that they have raved about are *Cactus Flower*, etc. Those are the films that they love. Unfortunately the Writers Guild only exists for the television writers. That's the only reason it's there now. It was formed for the motion picture writers, and television writers have taken it over. It's a very, very crazy union. For instance, they finally said, either this year or at the end of last year, if you are a member of the Communist Party you could belong. I would have been interested in the Communist Party except that I found them much too right wing for me. The Writers Guild is very stupid, I think.

FROUG: Have you actually made any move toward getting out of the Writers Guild, or is it a fantasy?

AXELROD: No, it is a fantasy, because it's one of the things where if you're out of it you can't work, and as there are so few jobs anyway now, it would be totally masochistic of me to do it at the moment. It is my dream of the future to somehow maybe separate the film writers and television writers, to somehow make the Guild more responsive to its people. I think that's true of many unions all over the country, though.

FROUG: The Writers Guild has just voted to amalgamate the television and screenwriter branches.

AXELROD: I know. It's very destructive. Because it's two different professions.

FROUG: Having now written the Rogallan script and been paid for that, what was the next step?

AXELROD: Well, the next step is I wrote some original screenplays. Some alone and some with Larry Alexander. We sold *Sometime Champs*, then we were hired to write a film at 20th Century-Fox called *El Kid* for Martin Schwartz, and that was also not a very good experience. At that time I had had all bad experiences and was looking for a good experience. And it was a terrible deal. My agents at the time, CMA, accepted the deal without telling me. I was in London and that was a problem. So I was committed to do a picture that I really didn't want to do that I knew I couldn't write effectively. About an old man going back to his home and finding his values again which is a subject that I'm totally bored with and I couldn't have cared less. I was writing it for John Wayne, who is a man whom I don't find intelligent or even important enough to write for. So we wrote the film, and very, very poorly. Richard Zanuck hated it and he was absolutely right. Threw the film out and about six months later he was fired and then Elmo Williams came in and decided it was terrific and rehired us again and we did a whole other draft of it and it was terrible, and I don't know what's happening to it. I hear rumors that they're going to make it, but I don't know. I hope they don't.

FROUG: Do you still work with Larry Alexander?

AXELROD: Oh, no. I work totally alone.

FROUG: Then what was your next step?

AXELROD: I wrote an original screenplay that sold. *The Dirty Movie.*

FROUG: Who bought that?

AXELROD: Winters-Rosen Productions. And it was made and it will be released soon. *The Dirty Movie* was what it was called at the time. It was a political satire on pornographic films. I call it a movie about Maoist fucking, which it really was about, and a comedy.

FROUG: Who is in it?

AXELROD: We had a big cast. We had Tom Skerritt, who was one of the three leads in M*A*S*H and the only one who didn't make it. We had Ron Rifkin, who is an unknown Jewish actor from New York, of very wealthy parents, who got the job through his manager, Stuart Cohen, who owns the house where Sharon Tate was murdered, and they all live there and it's a wonderful group of people. Christopher Jones and others. And big stars, Kate Woodville. Major people. I don't know how the film is. It's not what I wanted. It's not what I had planned. I wrote a pornographic film to be shot with absolutely *no* nudity. I was going to have great love scenes with people spouting Maoisms while their clothing would still be on. I really wanted that "G" or "PG" rating. Naturally they took off all the clothes and cut out most of the political references.

FROUG: So they destroyed the intent of the film?

AXELROD: I don't know. It's still interesting. The director did some interesting things. I don't think it's that good or that bad. I don't think anybody is going to pay that much attention to it.

FROUG: What happened after *The Dirty Movie*?

AXELROD: Well, then I wrote a terrific script. It was the first script that I wrote that was really 100 percent terrific. It was called *Go Left, Young Man*. It was a culmination of all my scripts put into one blockbuster. And I wrote it for Warner Brothers based on my treatment. And this was the time when they were hiring a lot of young writers. Remember there was a period of three or four months there . . .

FROUG: Absolutely. There was a period when they couldn't get enough young writers or young directors.

AXELROD: The guy in charge out there closed the studio, you know.

FROUG: It almost shut down the studio.

AXELROD: Well, my theory about being a studio head is very simple. You have to first produce fifteen flop pictures, or you have to be thrown out of another major studio. You have to be at the total bottom of your existence before they let you run a studio. Anyway, I wrote this script and I was going to produce it with a man named Norman Kurland. And it was a wonderful experience, the two of us. We had a great time with it. I wrote it and Norman was the producer. We formed a company. And it was a blockbuster script. I thought it was funny, poignant, sad, touching, meaningful. And Warner Brothers thought it was a piece of shit. So we had a basic disagreement there.

FROUG: Were they paying you at the time?

AXELROD: They were paying me. So after it was done they gave me a turnaround clause of ninety days.

FROUG: That's ninety days to sell it somewhere else?

AXELROD: Well, that script started everything else that has happened to me. Almost 90 percent of the people that have read it have either wanted to do it and have thought it was a fantastic script or they've loved the script and didn't feel they could relate to it. For instance, two months ago I went to New York and Elaine May read it and is dying to do it now. I don't know whether that will work out. Whether we can get a deal or not.

FROUG: What's it about?

AXELROD: It's about a kid who is twenty-one years old and is the son of liberal parents in New York and the parents throw cocktail parties and are members of what is commonly known now as the radical-chic. They used to be known as the black-tie left. And he has to rebel. Everybody that he knows is rebelling, but he had no place to go. His parents are very free. They let him fuck, take drugs, they want him to turn on, wonderful. So he's got to go the other way. He's got to become a reactionary. It's the only thing he can do. So he becomes a reactionary. Gets a job at Con Edison. Cuts his hair. And meets a middle-class girl from the Bronx named Nancy Drewer who is like a young Anne Jackson. Same type of part that Anne Jackson plays. Wonderful girl who only wants to decorate. Walks into a room and wants to decorate it immediately. It's all she thinks about. And reads *Cosmopolitan.* And there's a love scene where she has to convince herself to fuck him. So she says, "No, no, you can't touch me, you can't touch me. Well, you can touch me. Only my breasts." She has got to talk herself into doing things. They have a wonderful relationship until the parents decide the kid is screwing up and we've got to get him with a girl that's going to get him back where we are.

FROUG: He's too reactionary?

AXELROD: Oh, he's crazy. He loves America. And they hate it, and they say, "Will you turn on, for god's sake?" "Will you take some grass, go out and get the clap, do *something*!" So they fix him up with this girl named Julie who they think is a liberal. This is where the whole meaning of the film culminates. Julie is not a liberal, Julie is a radical. Which they don't know. The only thing a liberal hates more than a conservative on earth is a radical. Liberals can deal with the conservatives because they agree that the system works, so they are already in agreement. The only place they disagree are in minor political points, very minor, considering all the political extremes you can go to. But a radical, that's a whole other area. So the parents find out she's a radical and all hell breaks loose. And the kid, at the end, is going to at least try to find his way, his own way, some way in the political world. And the idea of the film is what Spinoza said, and that's no man can be apolitical because to be apolitical is a very political stance, because everything is political. Life, sleeping, eating, fucking, it's all political. And the script got me terrific acclaim. I mean, that's why I have this apartment. It's from that script. That's gotten me a lot of offers. I don't take too many jobs.

FROUG: Why don't you take too many jobs?

AXELROD: I hate working.

FROUG: Can you make a living being selective?

AXELROD: Yes. I took a job that I'm doing now. It's called *Every Little Crook and Nanny.*

FROUG: That was not your original screenplay?

AXELROD: No, it was not. It's a book by Evan Hunter, who wrote *Blackboard Jungle* and *Last Summer* and it's the first time I've ever adapted, which is twice as hard as an original. An original is very easy, I find, compared to this. Because here you're dealing with much more structure. And with an original you can constantly change your structure. You do not have to have one structure going on. But in a book you're already tied into something. There's some reason MGM paid all this money for this book. They don't want to see me take the book and make an original screenplay, or else they don't need the book. And it's a wonderful book, a terrific book. I got the job because Jim Aubrey and Doug Netter and Russ Thatcher read *Go Left, Young Man* and they loved it, and Cy Howard, the director, was in London and he was going to do it. And I never met him. And we have the same agent. I had left my agency and gone with IFA, Malcolm Stuart. And Malcolm said I gotta get you this film. Cy had interest in Bruce Jay Friedman, Robert Klane, and other important writers, so I had enormous competition. And Malcolm Stuart, through the greatest amount of agenting I have ever seen, I mean I found out now what an agent does, got me the job. There's no way I could have gotten it without him because, just by pestering Cy so much, Cy finally agreed to see me. On a Thursday. On the next day he agreed that I should do it, which made Metro very happy, because they wanted me anyway. And Malcolm got me that job over much more experienced writers, just as good if not better than I am. So it was a very lucky thing. And it worked out. It was a wild experience.

FROUG: Cy Howard once told me there's only one way to get the best possible work out of a writer. The first thing you do is, when he hands you the first pages, you read them and you say, "This is shit, this is the worst material I have ever read in my life, you ought to be ashamed of yourself." And he said that immediately makes the writer very competitive and it makes him rise to new peaks. Did he do that with you?

AXELROD: All the time, constantly. The problem with Cy is you can't be around him too much, because he makes you laugh so hard that you can't get any work done at all. Now, thank god, this is a comedy. I can't even express what we've gone through the last ten weeks. We have lived together, we have worked sixteen, eighteen hours a day together. We work every day, on the weekends. We are constantly improving the script. It's been an enormously enlightening experience to me. It proves to me that you have to have, and you can have a collaboration, that it does still exist, and it can happen. It's been the most tremendous experience in my life. However I'm not finished yet with the film so I don't know what will happen. But at the moment it's a dream.

FROUG: You were on the phone with Cy Howard when I walked in tonight.

AXELROD: I'm working with him now on casting, because I believe a writer has to cast the film with the director. It's vital.

FROUG: Yes, but isn't it rare that a director believes that.

AXELROD: Well, Cy does. Cy is totally open to that. There are unknowns that I have thrown at him that he is very open to. That he puts down as one of the two or three people that could get the part. It's not even particular actors as much as it is the type of actor. For instance our movie is about a Mafia chief. The theory of the film is that there's no such thing as the Mafia. We agree with J. Edgar Hoover, we agree with John Mitchell. It doesn't exist. There's no such thing. However, there is a group of Italians that does have a habit of killing people. They're very nice, sociable people, wonderful, warm, gentle people, but they do have this bad habit. It's like drinking. They kill people. And that's what the film is about. This Mafia chief, a charming, wonderful man, is in Italy. Back home in America, his son, Lewis, is kidnapped. He has an English nanny called Nanny. And Nanny, who will be played by Lynn Redgrave, is a wonderful English woman, but she knows that she can't tell the father that the son has been kidnapped because the father will fly back from Italy and knock her off. So she's got to get the kid back without anybody knowing about it. Lewis, by the way, is a twelve-year-old kid and a potential killer. He's the worst-corrupted person in the whole film. So she gets a guy called Benny Napkins who is the lowest of the low. He used to run the garbage and linen in Chicago, but he threw a brick through a guy named Domizio Galsworthy's window and then found out that it was the Mafia chieftain's brother. His real name was Dominiza Ganucci, which *is* our lead's name, Carmine Ganucci. So Benny Napkins is a pisher, and he and Nanny go off and try to get the kid back. And that's the movie. It's really a strong story about corruption.

It's these two people, working with the other members of the gang, such as Cockeye, who is a counterfeiter who counterfeits bills with George Washington's eyes crossed, and Bloomingdale, who is naturally a fence, hence the original of the name.

FROUG: These sound like Damon Runyon characters.

AXELROD: Yeah. Runyonesque, but they're very real. The book is very Runyonesque.

FROUG: Will Runyon hold up for today's audiences?

AXELROD: My friends would laugh it off the screen. So what we did is we took these same characters, and instead of straightening them out totally, by changing Bloomingdale's name to Mr. Jones, we left in the style of Runyon, but yet made the characters real. So Bloomingdale is a real fence, he is still funny and is still crazy, but he really does those things.

FROUG: In other words, he's harder. Because Runyon's characters were all very sentimental.

AXELROD: These are not. These are harder but yet there's sentimentality, of course. If you take that out then you have a straight Mafia story. It has all levels. Hopefully, it will be successful.

FROUG: Who's going to play Benny Napkins?

AXELROD: We don't know, but there are three or four actors who are being considered. The marvelous thing about people today, is you can get a lot of people that you couldn't get before. The whole price scale is gone. They have a great attitude at Metro. It's the only studio I've worked for that I think is a studio of the future, because it's the exact opposite of every experience I've ever had. For instance, we had a meeting with them. And we had a star actor, who I won't mention, who we wanted to play Ganucci. And they said, why get a star? Go with an unknown. You'll get a better actor for less money. And we said, well wouldn't you like one star for the exhibitors? And they said no, no stars. Just all unknowns. And you'll get much better actors and the audience will discover people for themselves. And stars just mean that you can get a few more theaters to begin with but after that it means nothing.

FROUG: If the film is good their theory is it doesn't need a star?

AXELROD: Right. And they pointed out *Willard* and various other hits. And they have a very positive attitude. Three days ago Cy and I were having lunch in the commissary. There was a boy sitting about two tables over. Beautiful-looking kid. And I kept looking at him all through lunch and saying, "That's Lewis Ganucci, that's our kid." Because you know how those professional kids walk in and say, "Hey, how are you?" And the mothers come in. It's crazy. You can't hire a professional kid actor. Ever. Ever. You can't. All right. This kid is sitting over there and he's sitting with a woman—and I have no idea who the woman is—and with four other kids. Like they're on a schoolday holiday. So I turn to Cy, and say, "Cy, that's our kid. That's him. I promise you, you're gonna hire that kid. Go over there and talk to them." Cy talked to the kid and he found that the woman there was Mrs. Jimmy Komack and he produces "Courtship of Eddie's Father" on the lot. And the kid is her sister's ex-husband's son. But they're very close. He lives in New Jersey. The kid's a starcker. He talks with a New York accent, you know what I mean. He's a real kid. He says, "I don't give a fuck, I'll be in your movie. What do I care?" So anyway, Cy interviewed him and tested him yesterday. A personality test. First thing, he walks into the room, looks around, looks right at Cy, didn't even give a shit that there were twenty crew members there and Jimmy Komack and his wife and me. He just didn't care. He was just a great performer.

FROUG: How old is he?

AXELROD: He's fourteen, but looks twelve, which is perfect. This kid! Like Cy said, "What would you do if you were kidnapped?" He said, "I'd negotiate." That's a fantastic, great line. Right? You know I didn't write a line that good in the script. The kid's fantastic. His name is Scott Zuckerman.

FROUG: You're working on preproduction with Cy. Are you going to get an associate producer credit?

AXELROD: No, I'm not. That was discussed at one time. It's been an exhausting experience for me.

FROUG: How long have you been on it now?

AXELROD: It seems like a long time. It's only been nine weeks. We've done six drafts.

FROUG: In nine weeks?

AXELROD: Yeah. We did the first draft in two and a half weeks. Which was great. Metro gave us the go-ahead on that first draft.

FROUG: Did you and Cy write it together?

AXELROD: Yeah.

FROUG: So you'll get co-credit.

AXELROD: Yeah. Cy gave me first credit, which is nice. It was a tremendous experience. Any writer can do a script in three weeks. The only reason that they take ten weeks is because they write six hours a day. We were doing twelve hours a day, fourteen a day, of real writing. I can sit in a room and write fourteen hours a day without stopping. That's because I'm young, I'm energetic, I can do that. That's one of the attributes of hiring a young writer, I think, is because it will usually get done in a faster amount of time. I don't have a wife. I don't have kids. I can really do that, and just that.

FROUG: When you're working alone and you're not motivated by a deadline or a salary, and you're forced into becoming a self-starter, do you work those kind of hours?

FROUG: Yeah. Always. I enjoy writing. I find it very easy, so I never find it difficult to get up in the morning and write.

FROUG: How long does it take you to write a first draft?

AXELROD: Usually I'd say three weeks.

FROUG: How long do you take developing your story?

AXELROD: Two weeks, usually. I write a full outline.

FROUG: You write a full outline for yourself?

AXELROD: Well, the first thing is I decide why I'm going to write it. I can write forty movies, but that's ridiculous. Why am I going to write it? What's the purpose, what's the point of view? Once I decide that then I say, okay, now what characters can best further that point of view. Then I invent, hopefully, terrific characters. If I get two terrific characters in five or six great scenes I'm halfway there. Then what I do is I construct what I call a book report. It's in the same style as what I used to do in high school. Of where I put scene one—Jonathan walks along the street. Then I put why the scene is in, why I need that in, what it will pay off later, what he's thinking about, and basically what kind of dialogue. Whether I want a joke, whether I want something poignant, the mood, the aura, of the scene. And once I have the outline, which usually consists of sixty scenes, then what I do is put things in scene three that I know will be in scene ten. So by the time that I begin writing I have a very full outline so that I know what I'll be able to pay off and where, which is half the battle for me.

FROUG: In other words, you always know exactly where you're going?

AXELROD: Always, every second. Now, however, that can change, but never as I'm writing it. I will write it that way and then what I'll do is I'll read it and say, well that's shitty, so then I'll restructure it again and do it the new way. I'm not very flexible as I'm writing it. As I'm writing it I usually stick to the treatment. If anything, I'll only add. I'll add a montage or some sequences, but I won't change what I have at all. I find it's the only way I can work, especially in dramatic comedy. Because in dramatic comedy you really have to know where you're going because you're not doing big jokes. I mean I don't do big jokes. They're very serious, hopefully subtle humor, so I have to be able to pay it off three or four scenes later. You can't do it within the scene. Then it becomes light comedy, which I don't write. It's like if you have a scene between two people and they're being witty back and forth and they're saying jokes—that's great, and then that's over. Then each scene is going to be that way and it's going to be a series of skits and then you're out of business.

FROUG: You've lost your dramatic tension?

AXELROD: I think so.

FROUG: How do you hold your tension along with humor?

AXELROD: It's very difficult. I don't know if you really ever do with comedy. In this film it's the first time that I think I've succeeded like halfway. We have a kidnapping sequence in the film that is about the third scene in, and then we have about seven scenes after that with Nanny and Benny Napkins, the putz, trying to figure out where the kid is, because all that we know is he's missing, but the audience already knows that he's kidnapped. So we realized that we'd lost all the tension. So all that we did was we cut out the kidnapping sequence completely so when they find out that he's been kidnapped later on, the audience will find out. Simple things like that. We went through five drafts without knowing that.

FROUG: In other words you're very conscious of the need for dramatic tension?

AXELROD: Always. That's why you can't do existential Westerns. They just can't work. They never will. I've written two existential Westerns. They just can't work, because you have no dramatic tension.

FROUG: Now that you have completed *Every Little Crook and Nanny* are you ready yet to start another screenplay?

AXELROD: I've already signed to do a picture. And I didn't want to work again because I feel lousy. I'm tired and I really want to forget about movies for a while and go on living. And I want to get laid a lot and I want to do things I haven't been doing the last eight or nine weeks. And I miss my friends. I have very close friends that I just miss being around, and having fun with, and yet I'm sure that I'll probably miss this even more than I'll miss my friends. But I had an offer to do a picture. Six months ago Stanley

Donen read *Go Left, Young Man* by accident. He was in Hollywood. He lives in London but he was here for two weeks. And he called me up and asked me to have lunch with him at the Brown Derby. And I did. And he said it was one of the funniest scripts he had ever read. And he sent it to Billy Wilder with a letter which said he couldn't do it because he could not relate to it, because he was of an age where he didn't feel he could direct it. And he gave me a book to read, not saying, "Do you want to do it?" but just giving it to me to read. It was a John Barth novel, called *The Sot-Weed Factor*, which is dreadful. And I had no courage to tell him. It's a 1,200-page satire of Henry Fielding, which you cannot transcribe on the screen. How do you do a satire of a novel on the screen? I don't know. Anyway I had no courage. I didn't write him. I left it alone. I said, well, he'll hate me, but I just don't know what to say to him, because Stanley Donen is one of the three or four American filmmakers who I really think is a major talent. So I guess it was three weeks ago a lawyer named Harold Berkowitz called up my agent and said Stanley Donen would like Jonathan Axelrod to write his next picture. And my agent got very excited and they started negotiations. I felt good about it but I wasn't sure whether I was going to do it. I called up my agent and we discussed this. Well, I don't know what it is. I do agree that he's an enormous talent but I still can't take the picture without knowing what it is. I mean that's going a little far. So, anyway, I was sent the material which was a seven-page article about a little girl who stows away on a boat, and it really didn't excite me that much. It had possibilities, but other things had much more possibilities that I was looking at and offered. So anyway, Stanley Donen calls me up and we talk about it on the phone. And he says, "Well, what type of picture do you see in it?" He's in Paris. And I said, "I see a murder mystery." And he said, "That's funny, I see a romantic comedy." So he says, "Well, I'm glad we're close." And we obviously are on the same track and we know what we're doing and we're putzes. So what are we going to do? So he said, "Listen, why don't you do the film?" And I said, "I don't know. I'm tired and I want to get away." He says, "Well, you'll come to London and write it." That was the key. So I said, "I'll come to London and write it?" And he said, "Yes. We will give you expenses, a large amount, and transportation. The money will be deposited here."

FROUG: What kind of money did they offer?

AXELROD: I'd rather not say. My agent says I'm not supposed to talk about that. But it's more than I live on here. Jesus! So I felt good. I said, "My instincts are to take the picture." A week later he calls back. And we had big problems with negotiations because they started way down. They started at nothing. And we started way up. And they tripled their offer because I turned down the film. I said, "No, I won't do it." Anyway, Stanley Donen calls me a week ago, and he says, "By the way, let's do this: I'll meet you in New York and we'll go by boat." See, the trip is even getting better now so I'm feeling better and I say, "Yeah, that's great!" He calls me two days ago at six-thirty in the morning and he says, "Listen, we'll go by boat and we'll go to London, we'll live in London a week, and then I'd like to take a vacation. So why don't we go to St. Tropez for three weeks in the south of France?" Now it's getting so fucking good that it's terrific! He doesn't know that he's never going to see a script. I know you can get laid in the south of France. In London I hear there's trouble. But in the south of France, it's incredible I've heard. And it's probably all lies, but it's summertime, remember, a lot of bikinis and a lot of tits. So, anyway, I said, "That will be terrific, Stanley. I will, of course, go with you." And I leave in two weeks.

FROUG: You're set.

AXELROD: Oh, well, the deal was set before this. This just happened. I was very ambivalent about taking this picture. I'm not sure about it yet. I'm very ambivalent even now. But it gets better all the time. So I'm thinking if that part's getting better that perhaps I can come up with an idea. But at the moment I have no idea what the picture will be. I have no characters, I have no plot, no point of view. All that I know is that it's about a girl who stows away on a boat.

FROUG: But apparently Stanley Donen is confident you will come up with a point of view.

AXELROD: He is much more confident than I am. I hope to. We were discussing the auteur theory earlier. There is no such thing as the auteur theory, except in the minds of perhaps two mindless critics in New York, one of which is Andy Sarris, and about 400 mindless critics in Paris who hate their films and love Jerry Lewis. And that's where the auteur theory exists today and that's where it has always existed. It has never existed within the filmmakers' minds. George Stevens never got up in the morning and said, "I'm an auteur." It has become a part of film school language only and is very destructive in places like the American Film Institute—which is the most negative thing that happened to young filmmakers—and other places. And every director that I know thinks that it's full of shit. If Stanley Donen believed in the auteur theory why would he want me on a boat with him for five days? Every director wants writers to live with them, every director wants a collaboration, wants an equal collaboration. They want to be told they're full of shit because they're scared. Because one mistake in a film can destroy the entire picture. And the only way not to make that mistake is to bounce it off other people. Whether it's the producer or the writer, or the prop man or the cameraman or the script girl, they need that and they want that desperately, except perhaps a director like Stanley Kubrick, who is perhaps an auteur because he is also a writer.

FROUG: I understand you were one of the first fifteen Fellows selected by the American Film Institute when it opened in Beverly Hills. Would you care to tell us about that?

AXELROD: Yeah. I applied to the American Film Institute because I wanted to learn as much as I could about directing and I was accepted on the basis of my scripts. I started work and within four weeks I was terribly disenchanted. I disliked 75 percent of the people up there, 100 percent of the people on the staff. George Stevens, Jr., I felt, was constantly running for office rather than running it. It was a total bureaucracy and I woke up one morning and I realized that I was going through enormous pain. I was writing and they weren't accepting it, and I realized that I could get paid for doing what I was doing up there and get more cooperation than what I was getting there from a studio. And it's absolutely true. The hardest time in all my experiences, and some of them were very bad, none of them have been as bad as the American Film Institute. It is one of the most destructive places for anybody who is interested in film to go. It professes the auteur theory, it does not believe in writing. It does not believe in producing. It only believes in the director. I think it is a tool for George Stevens, Jr.'s, ambition and for a lot of other people's ambition. And they've failed miserably. They have not produced anything. And that's all they are meant to do is to produce something. And they have not produced anything that has been worthwhile. I made a film up there which I never cut, never worked on, and I just left, just walked out of it.

FROUG: And after you left there, where did you go then?

AXELROD: I wrote *The Dirty Movie* up there. They wouldn't do *The Dirty Movie* because they thought it was dirty. That's one of the reasons I left. And I said, "What are you talking about, there's no censorship? Do you think it's funny?" They said, "Yeah, we really think it's funny, but it's too dirty for us, not the type for our image." I said, "Well, I mean you sound like Richard Zanuck. And that's not how you are meant to be sounding. You're supposed to be open and creative and be able to express any of the philosophy of your Fellows. That's the whole idea." It is also a sexist organization, that's why *Women in the Media*, which I have been involved in, which is a women's liberation group, have picketed them and have marched up there and said, "You are sexists, you are male chauvinist pigs." It is also a racist group of people. One of the most racist groups of people that I have ever seen. Subtle, of course. We had a token black man. One out of fifteen. Who was very token. And it's a very destructive place.

FROUG: Why is everything you do so politically oriented?

AXELROD: I think it is vitally important for anybody who is involved in filmmaking today to be involved in political action at the same time. I think without that you can never keep in touch with the people you are writing about. There's no way. I mean, I work at MGM every day and I'm in contact with only five people. You can't do that for long periods of time or else I think you're finished as a writer. There's an organization in town called The Entertainment Industry for Peace and Justice which is the first radical-based group of entertainment people. It was formed in the minds of Jane Fonda and Donald Sutherland and they formed a steering committee of ten or twelve people which I was on. I was head of the entertainment committee. It's had its ups and downs. We ran out of money and there were huge problems. And the last eight weeks really I've been out of it because of this film. But it's as big a part of my life, certainly, as filmwriting. It's something when I meet with four or five blacks from the ghetto who say to us, and we're a radical-based organization, "You're not liberal at all. We don't want to get involved with you. We want to do it ourselves, in our own neighborhood, and we don't want to be used by you. And we don't want your shows." To even deal with that you have to realize that there is no such thing as black racism. There can't be. Blacks can't be racists. It's impossible in America, because blacks have had racism perpetrated upon them. And all that they are saying is that "we hate you. We hate white people." Because they have reason. There's no reason to hate black people. There never was and there never will be. We hated them only for our own exploitation values. So this group which we've gotten together consists of a lot of other people in the film industry, people in the unions, grips, prop men. It's not just actors, it's all sorts of people. This is the only way that I've ever really heard about the unions and the unfairness of the unions to the people who are in it, to the working-class man. It's very unfair, because what I think is happening now is they're trying to cut down the salaries of the union, and yet raising the salaries constantly of actors and producers and writers and directors, and those are the most grossly overpaid people in America today. Without a doubt. We all have to come down. We all have to make much less money. It's very important. It's the only way we're going to survive. As people, let alone as a film industry. And this organization, I'm hoping, will do an enormous amount of good. I think Jane is an enormously important woman in films, beyond being our greatest actress in this country. I think *Klute* has shown that to some people. She can do an enormous service for people and I can only hope that the Writers Guild and the Directors Guild will start understanding the needs of its people. When you have 83 percent to 84 percent unemployment, obviously you're doing something wrong. It's not just them, it's you. We're all doing something wrong. And I think it's vital to be constantly politically involved and to understand that there is a Chicano environment and that there is an Asian community in this city, which nobody knows, which everybody has forgotten about. Little Asia. Which can be an enormously powerful community. We're killing their people. I guess that's been an important part of my life, if not more important than films certainly, because it's the only way that I can write, which is based on that knowledge, that experience.

Ring Lardner, Jr.

1937 NOTHING SACRED *(Joint Contributor to Treatment)*

1939 MEET DR. CHRISTIAN *(Joint Screenplay)*
KID FROM KOKOMO *(Contributor to Treatment)*

1940 ARKANSAS JUDGE *(Joint Adaptation)*
THE COURAGEOUS DR. CHRISTIAN *(Joint Story and Screenplay)*

1940 WOMAN OF THE YEAR *(Joint Story and Screenplay)*, Academy Award

1943 THE CROSS OF LORRAINE *(Joint Screenplay)*

1944 TOMORROW THE WORLD *(Joint Screenplay)*

1946 CLOAK AND DAGGER *(Joint Screenplay)*

1947 FOREVER AMBER *(Joint Screenplay)*

1948 THE FORBIDDEN STREET *(Screenplay)*

1949 FOUR DAYS LEAVE *(Dialogue)*

1965 THE CINCINNATI KID *(Joint Screenplay)*

1970 M*A*S*H *(Screenplay)*, Academy Award

1977 THE GREATEST *(Screenplay)*

He is a somewhat shy, soft-spoken, thoughtful man, fifty-six years of age. He is medium tall, slim, handsome, with black wavy hair laced with gray. He wears heavy, dark tortoise-shell glasses that do not hide gentle, innocent eyes. He is a man who seems to have a gestalt of his life and the turbulent times he has known.

Equanimity is the word for Ring Lardner, Jr.

Screenwriter Fay Kanin (who appears elsewhere in this book), president of the Screen Branch of the Writers Guild and wife of Michael Kanin, Lardner's collaborator for two years (they wrote the 1941 Spencer Tracy-Katharine Hepburn classic, *Woman of the Year*, and won an Oscar), has another word for Lardner—carefully chosen and entirely feminine. He is, she assured me, "adorable."

What makes this lavish sentiment noteworthy is that Lardner has no right to be any of these things. Knowing his background and personal history, one would expect to find an angry, embittered, even cynical, man carrying a psyche raw with open wounds. Prison often does that to a man.

Not a few of Lardner's fellow screenwriters, directors, and producers, who, for fifteen years and longer, were denied the right to earn their living in their chosen field, are so crippled. Hate breeds hate, and Hollywood has not yet fully recovered from the tidal wave of hatred that once threatened to drown the American motion picture industry.

The infamous blacklist deserves a great deal more attention than this brief introduction can give it. Books have been and are being written to acquaint those not yet born or too young to have experienced it. I will attempt to deal with it only in synopsis and as it relates to the subject of this interview who was at the very epicenter of the ugliest period in the history of Hollywood. For better or worse, Lardner and the blacklist are irrevocably linked.

Ring Lardner, Sr., in his day, was one of America's foremost writers. He was a superb humorist and satirist who, in his best work, was favorably compared to Swift and Twain. His short stories and newspaper columns were read by millions and he included among his intimate friends literary luminaries such as F. Scott Fitzgerald. Like Will Rogers, Lardner, Sr., wrote about the common man in a style that was both affectionate and incisive. He created characters who entered the language ("Alibi Ike") and even today some of his stories retain their freshness and originality ("You Know Me, Al," "Haircut," "The Love Nest"). He was a master of dialect. His short story, "Champion," became the basis for Stanley Kramer's and Carl Foreman's first and possibly best film. While he wrote most often about sports, and baseball in particular, Ring Lardner was truly a chronicler of the human condition.

Ringgold Wilmer Lardner, Jr., was born in Chicago, August 19, 1915, the second youngest of four sons. It says a great deal about their father that all four boys dreamed of becoming writers and, to the extent that their life spans allowed, they succeeded.

Ring, Sr., listed himself as a Republican but was most apolitical, his son says. "He once wrote a campaign song for Teddy Roosevelt in the Bull Moose Campaign of 1912."

The Lardners moved to Great Neck, Long Island, in 1920, where the boys were raised. It must have been a stimulating household for four young men to grow in, rich with free-flowing dialogue and ideas. Though their father died in 1933, the Lardner boys set out to improve the world.

James went off to Spain to join the Loyalists. He was killed in the war against Franco's fascists.

David became a war correspondent for *The New Yorker* and was sent to Europe. He was killed in Germany when his Jeep struck a land mine.

John, whose writing style closely resembled his

father's, became sports columnist for *Newsweek.* I used to buy the magazine solely to read his humorous comments. He died of a heart attack in 1960.

Ring, Jr., was sent to one of the finest eastern prep schools, Phillips Andover, where he spent four years, and from there to Princeton, where he became active in the Socialist Club.

In 1935, at the age of twenty, Ring turned up in Hollywood. It was rumored that David O. Selznick had sent for John to try him as an actor but Ring arrived by mistake.

In any event, Selznick gave Lardner a job in his publicity department working under the flamboyant Russell Birdwell, the zaniest press agent the movies have ever known.

Soon Ring was trying his hand at screenwriting and his first official credit was as "Joint contributor to treatment" for *Nothing Sacred,* a Ben Hecht comedy that starred Carole Lombard and was one of Hollywood's first and most successful forays into the field of black comedy. (Prior to that Ring and a young reader at the studio, Budd Schulberg, were asked by Selznick to come up with a new ending for *A Star Is Born.* They did and it was used then and in the remake.)

While learning screenwriting, Lardner became involved in the Writers Guild as a member of a group of activists who, according to some members, were trying to capture the Guild in the name of left wing causes.

It was shortly after World War II, in 1947, that Congressman J. Parnell Thomas and the House Un-American Activities Committee decided to investigate alleged Communist infiltration into American movies. The "probe," as the newspapers liked to call it, failed to uncover a single case of Marxist propaganda in any film. But no matter. Thomas and his committee were hunting headlines and votes as much as Communists and in attacking Hollywood they found the perfect vehicle for both.

In 1950, Senator Joseph McCarthy of Wisconsin jumped on the anti-Communist bandwagon and promoted the entire proceedings into the biggest roadshow attraction in America with himself as Superstar. Before the House Un-American Activities Committee was finished, it managed to turn screenwriter against screenwriter, director against director, actor against actor, and an industry against itself.

Part of the absurdity of the committee's charges lay in the makeup of the major studio hierarchy who, until recently, controlled over 90 percent of America's film output. The men who ruled the studios with an iron fist in those days, authentic moguls like Louis B. Mayer at MGM and Harry Cohn at Columbia, were politically somewhere right of Julius Caesar. Their patriotism was, if anything, rabid. (Mayer was said to have knelt by the large American flag he kept in his office and wept for love of country.)

The American Legion was an organization of enemy agents compared to many of the so-called "patriotic" groups some of the emperors of Hollywood publicly supported.

One famous and highly influential director close to the seats of power died of a heart attack during the hearings, reportedly while banging his head against his office wall shouting, "The Communists are coming, the Communists are coming!" Apocryphal or not, the incident was an accurate metaphor for the state of Hollywood.

But, in the end, it was neither patriotism nor politics that counted at the studios. It was, as always, the box office. Hollywood has traditionally operated on the bedrock principle, not unlike General Motors, that what is good for Hollywood is good for the country.

So when a handful of screenwriters, directors, and producers refused to divulge their political affiliations to the Committee on the grounds that their political beliefs were safeguarded by both the First and Fifth Amendments to the Constitution, they were called "unfriendly witnesses," fired from their jobs, and barred from employment in the industry.

Ring Lardner, Jr., was among the first ten to be called. He arrived with a position paper which he proposed to read to the Congressmen. But, after first agreeing, they abruptly changed their minds. Perhaps they feared his statement might corrupt the Committee, the press, or the public. They advised him that unless he told them whether or not he was then or had ever been a member of the Communist Party, he would be in contempt of Congress. Lardner stood on his Constitutional rights, as did nine of his fellow screenwriters, directors, and producers. The newspapers dubbed them "The Hollywood Ten" and they became the focal point of the madness.

For their refusal to testify they were sent to prison, amidst a barrage of publicity that threatened to overwhelm the Committee itself.

But there were other screenwriters, directors, and producers called by the Committee who, faced with certain unemployment, banishment, and possibly prison, talked incessantly. They confessed to political sins, named names of friends and relatives, and begged absolution.

As a consequence, hundreds of people, most of them innocent of any sort of misbehavior but guilty of being left-wing activists, were blacklisted—without a trial, hearing, or being given a chance to face their accusers. It was at this point that the term "witch hunt" came into being. To many the proceedings were a frightening re-enactment of Salem, Massachusetts.

Hollywood's daily trade papers carried full page ads—some in support of The Hollywood Ten, signed and paid for by many of the most famous stars and dignitaries in the business; others demanding that the industry throw the rascals out—signed and paid for by an almost equally impressive list of big names.

Hysteria was the order of the day. The studios, now joined by the networks (McCarthy was calling CBS "the Red network"), fell all over themselves trying to prove each was more anti-Communist than the next. Loyalty oaths were demanded, furtive lists of suspected "sympathizers" were circulated.

I was a vice president of CBS in Hollywood almost ten years after the initial hearings. The blacklist was operating at its maximum efficiency. Word had come from our New York headquarters that no one was to be employed without "clearance." Names of prospective actors, writers, directors, even secretaries, were sent to the law department for "evaluation." The entire process was kept vague; no one was told who cleared whom or by what standard of measurement people became, according to the official term, "acceptable" or "unacceptable." It was all quite Kafkaesque.

One thing was certain then. A wealthy small-town grocer in upstate New York who controlled a chain of co-ops had the power to make the entertainment industry quake. His group published a newsletter called "Counter-Attack" which listed persons suspected of being Party members or, almost as bad, "fellow travelers." The publication was required reading for all network executives. To be mentioned in "Counter-Attack" or *Red Channels,* a thick book containing lists of sympathizers, fellow travelers, and other political undesirables (which quickly became the bible of a thoroughly terrorized Hollywood) was to be instantly unemployed.

The brother of the present governor of one of our fair states once approached me in the lobby of CBS and produced a worn envelope on the back of which was scribbled in pencil the latest list of actors (all "pinkos," he assured me) who were not to be hired by the network. As a representative of one of our largest advertising agencies, this man's list carried as much weight as an official notice from the FBI.

Close friends of mine remained unemployable for years on the evidence that they once attended a concert by Paul Robeson at which funds were collected for the refugees of Stalingrad, though, at the time, the Russians were our allies.

Make no mistake about it, at the broadcasting networks or in the film studios, Hollywood officialdom united and stood as a tower of Jell-O. If, the media reasoned, the American public was to believe, even for a moment, that the enemy was within the walls of Fantasyland, financial disaster could not be far behind.

It was fifteen years before any semblance of sanity

returned to Hollywood—and twenty before the blacklist could be freely spoken of without fear.

Lately local organizations, such as the Southern California Chapter of the American Civil Liberties Union, have been trying to rectify wrongs with dinners in honor of some of the more famous victims. But these worthy gestures, twenty-four years after the fact, reveal how deep-rooted Hollywood's guilt remains.

A decade ago Ring Lardner, Jr., wrote an article for the *Saturday Evening Post* in which he said that he had, in fact, once been a member of the Communist Party but dropped out and, by 1950, had ceased to take an active role in politics. But it was not until 1965, with a co-screenplay credit on *The Cincinnati Kid,* that he was able to see his name on screen again. In 1970, with the popular and critically acclaimed *M*A*S*H,* Lardner won his second Academy Award, this time as a solo screenplay credit.

Ironically, it was *M*A*S*H,* as much as any single motion picture, that helped rescue 20th Century-Fox from the brink of financial ruin, the same studio that twenty-odd years before had fired Lardner for refusing to testify.

Our interview took place in Ring's hotel room in Beverly Hills. He was in town for two days of meetings with the producer and director of his latest project. (The Lardners divide their home between an apartment in New York City, where Ring's wife, Frances Chaney, is an actress and teaches acting, and a house in New Milford, Connecticut, Ring says he inherited.)

Mrs. Lardner is the widow of David. She and Ring married in 1946. Ring added two of his brother's children to two of his own and he and Frances contributed one son together.

Because of his crowded schedule (he had just returned from a story conference and was on his way to dinner with Dalton Trumbo—a fellow blacklistee who has made a long, difficult, and highly successful comeback), we didn't have as much time together as either of us would have liked.

I had the feeling I could have talked to Lardner all afternoon and evening and not have exhausted my supply of questions. And it was clear he was prepared to answer anything I cared to ask, as honestly and openly as he knew how.

Most of all, I was struck of the fairness of the man. Because I knew Bob Altman, *M*A*S*H*'s director, and had discussed the film with him, I was prepared for the screenwriter to be armed and defensive. Bob had made some rather odd remarks in radio and television interviews and in the press.

But Lardner exhibited no hostility. Yes, he wanted to set the record straight, but, no, he didn't feel Altman meant anything malicious by his claim to almost total conception of the film. For an explanation of the excesses of the auteur-minded director, Lardner offers fresh insight and remarkable understanding.

INT. HOT LIPS' TENT - NIGHT

Frank is sitting next to Hot Lips on her cot with a soothing arm around her.

FRANK
Godless buffoons, all of them.

HOT LIPS
(her hands on his face, turning it towards her)
It's the disrespect for you, that's what I can't forgive them.

FRANK
Oh, I'm used to it. What makes me sore is how they behave towards you.
(pulling her into a tight embrace)
They ought to be grateful to have you.
(kisses her, his hand vanishing beneath her skirt)
I certainly am.

HOT LIPS
(undoing one of his buttons and sliding her hand under his blouse)
And I'm grateful for you, Frank, especially with those boors around. We've grown very close in a short time.

He kisses her around the neck and bosom, removing such of her clothing as gets in the way.

FRANK
It isn't just chance, I'm sure of that. God meant us to find each other.

Instead of lingering on a scene that threatens to become pornographic, our attention is drawn down beneath Hot Lips' cot, where a strange object is being inserted under the canvas wall of the tent. It is a microphone.

HOT LIPS
His will be done.
(then, in excited response to an inflammatory move on his part)
~~Be a darling!~~ Oh, Frank...!

FROUG: Recently, Ring, Bob Altman came to my USC class and showed *M*A*S*H*, and while he said the screenplay was excellent, he said he thought of it as a point of departure. Do you feel that that was what you were writing?

LARDNER: I certainly didn't feel when I was writing it that it was a point of departure, and I didn't realize at any time during conferences with Bob that he had that attitude toward it. Actually he didn't come onto the project until after I had done two drafts of the screenplay, and then I had some conferences with him and Ingo Preminger [the producer of *M*A*S*H*] and then we did a final draft. Bob had some ideas which were discussed in conference and incorporated into it. I went back to New York after that and came back out here just after they had started shooting, and I went out to visit on location and got some idea of what was being done. A particular scene I was watching, the actors were obviously ad-libbing and there was no new written script. And they did stick to the main thoughts and even the main words of what was in the scene, but they were doing it again in their own words. And I discussed this a little with Bob and with Ingo, and Bob said it was the only way he could work, so then I sat with Ingo and saw an accumulation of about ten days' rushes and some of the scenes were pretty much as I had written them, and some were partly different, and a couple were entirely different. And then, there was what I consider the only really clumsy piece of direction in the whole picture. I had Hawkeye and Duke, appalled at the spectacle of their new tent-mate Frank Burns praying on his knees, break into "Onward Christian Soldiers." For some strange reason, Bob added a contrived, unrealistic bit in which other members of the unit outside the tent join in the singing, practically making a musical number out of it. There were quite new things.

FROUG: What were the new things?

LARDNER: Well, the beginning of the picture, which I saw some of in those rushes, was different. The way in which those two guys met and went to this camp. That, as a matter of fact, I didn't like. And I didn't like it in the final picture because there was a kind of slapstick business with the Jeep.

FROUG: Their falling down in the mud?

LARDNER: Yeah. And it seemed to me it started off on a wrong note. But there were a couple of other things I saw that were quite good, and it happened also that in those rushes was the Sally Kellerman in the shower thing, which was almost exactly as I had written it. Which had not been in the book and which I had devised, so I wasn't too upset. I could see that he was adhering, at least in the major respects, to the script. After that I had no contact with it. Oh, I talked to Bob a little and I talked to Ingo. Ingo persuaded me that this was the only way Bob could work and we had to leave it in his hands for better or worse, and he as a producer was doing nothing except keeping the 20th Century-Fox people away from Bob and dealing with the camera department when they said the color was murky, or the sound department when they said you couldn't hear anything. So I had no further contact with it, until I saw a press showing and preview in New York, at the same time the 20th Century people saw it, and I realized it was in fairly important respects different. And some of them I liked, and some I didn't. Everybody came out to my house afterwards, Bob and Ingo did, and we talked about it. Really, I brought up only the things I thought might still be changed. One was that I thought the football sequence had simply been allowed to go on too long and, by its very place in the script—

because he had cut out a scene that followed it so the picture ended rather abruptly—had a disproportionate place in the film, and I knew he had shot the scene that had been cut out after it. But they persuaded me that it was not going to be restored. Well, there were a few other points where I thought a little editing would be helpful, a couple of things could be cut, none of them were done.

FROUG: None of your changes were made?

LARDNER: No.

FROUG: How close do you think the final picture came to the final draft screenplay?

LARDNER: Well, in construction it was almost completely the same. Except for one major change which was made not in the shooting but in the editing. There was a character played by Jo Ann Pflug, a character called Lieutenant Dish, who had this thing with the dental surgeon and she was restoring him from suicide and then going off and leaving the camp. She was going home.

FROUG: Was that in the original script?

LARDNER: That was, but it occurred before the introduction of the character played by Sally Kellerman in the script. Jo Ann Pflug (Lieutenant Dish) was leaving at the same time the Kellerman character was arriving. Bob reversed things; in cutting he decided to do the arrival of the Kellerman character, Hot Lips, first and then do the dentist's suicide routine and the departure of Lieutenant Dish. As a matter of fact, if you look at the film very closely as the helicopter lands and Major Hot Lips goes off, you can see Lieutenant Dish in it. He just left that in because it was switched around in the editing. But that and the elimination of a scene after the football game were the only real changes in construction. But there were many changes within the scenes. And quite a lot of dialogue that was not in the script at all that was mostly background kind of dialogue. Improvisation, some of which you could hear and some of which most people couldn't hear, and most of that, incidentally, I thought was good. I thought the whole effect of that was good. To me the basic thing in relation to the whole auteur theory and to various interviews that Bob has given is really summed up in the interview he gave in the *New York Times Magazine.* He said two things: one, that he didn't like the script when he first read it, which I believe is inaccurate.

FROUG: He certainly didn't tell that to my USC class. He told us it was an excellent script.

LARDNER: He certainly told the producer and his agent, who is also my agent, George Litto, that he loved the script. But in his many interviews he is quoted as saying he didn't like it, but that he had been trying to promote a script, a picture called *Death Where Is Thy Sting-a-Ling-a-Ling-a-Ling* that Roald Dahl had written about the First World War. And that he saw the possibility of putting much of the spirit of that into this Korean War story. Well, I never read that script so I don't know how much of the spirit of *M*A*S*H* is in it. It doesn't seem to me since it concerned a group of guys who were sent from London to Switzerland to try to get to where the Germans were manufacturing the zeppelins that it could have had a very close relationship to *M*A*S*H.* And then he went on to say in this *Times Magazine* interview, "My main contribution to *M*A*S*H* was the basic concept, the philosophy, the style, the casting, and then making all those things work. Plus all the jokes, of course." This statement is pure megalomania, which is the occupational disease of movie directors. He did make everything work; that's his job and he did it damn well. As for the casting, I know Ingo Preminger had a lot to do with it because he told me so and I believe him, but I wasn't there. But essentially the concept, philosophy and style were neither Bob's or mine, but came from the book by Richard Hooker. As did quite a few of the jokes. The novel was written by a surgeon who had been through the Korean War, and rewritten by a professional writer. They got a joint pen name, Richard Hooker. The book was not a very well organized book and I did change it a great deal. The character of Lieutenant Dish didn't even exist in the book. The Hot Lips character did exist in the book, and some of the same things occurred with her, but both the overhearing of her love scene with this major, over the loudspeaker system, and the business of uncovering her in the shower to see if she was a real blonde were not in the book.

FROUG: They were the two funniest scenes in the picture.

LARDNER: Both those were added by me in the screenplay. And were shot pretty much as written. He did, also, I meant to say, when I was talking about the major changes, he did keep the Hot Lips character in the picture through the football game, and so on, where she was a camp follower and a cheerleader. And he added the business of her sneaking out of a tent with Tom Skerritt.

FROUG: And the cheerleaders were yelling, "69 . . . 69 . . . 69." Was that in the script?

LARDNER: No. That was not. In the script or in the book. Sally remained in the picture for a much longer time. However, even that tends to get exaggerated. She gave out an interview with Rex Reed shortly after the picture came out, in which she said that when she first read the script the character of Hot Lips only had nine lines and after she had been cast she was heartbroken to read the script, but fortunately Bob Altman kept building the part. Well, this was only partially true. He did extend it, but since Sally spoke specifically about lines of dialogue, it happens that all the additional lines he gave her were things where the commandant, Henry, would say, "That's six points," and she would repeat, "Six points!" A couple of things like that, through the football game. As a cheerleader. So the dialogue scenes were essentially the same. Except for the football sequence and her few appearances there. However, the impact of her part was much greater than in the screenplay because of Bob's keeping her in the action and Sally's own brilliance in the performance.

FROUG: I have a quote here from an article you wrote in the *New York Times.* You said, "The auteur theory makes no sense at all applied to 90 percent of American productions. I would present the thesis that *M*A*S*H* had three authors, Richard Hooker, who wrote the novel, myself, and Bob Altman, a writer before he became a director, and, I had recently discovered, since."

LARDNER: Yes, well I would still stick to that statement and say, like all movies, this is a collaborative job and the authorship, excluding the directorial function in itself, I mean, excluding Altman's function as a director, but thinking of his function as an author, that it was equally divided.

FROUG: A lot of screenwriters, and a lot of Hollywood people in general, felt that the Academy Award you won for *M*A*S*H* was not only a tribute to your screenplay, but in a sense, a kind of a back-of-the-hand to the auteur theory. Did you feel that that might have been true?

LARDNER: I think it's possible to some extent. But more importantly, it was a question of the way the nominations get divided, and the fact that there are two screenwriting awards and I thought I had a fairly good chance to win the award simply when I saw the nominations, because of the fact that *Five Easy Pieces, Patton,* and *Love Story* were all in the original screenplay category. Whereas the competition against *M*A*S*H* in the adaptation category was not as stiff. But there's only one directorial award so Bob was up against all those that I wasn't up against.

FROUG: The story of your trip to Cannes in connection with *M*A*S*H* winning the Golden Palm fascinates me. First off, the actors, the director and the producer were scheduled for the trip but the screenwriter was not.

LARDNER: Some time after *M*A*S*H* was invited to the Cannes Film Festival, my wife and I attended a showing of a picture of Willie Wyler's, *The Liberation of L.B. Jones,* and we ended up at a supper party afterwards, sitting at a table for six, with Otto Preminger and his wife, and Ingo Preminger and his wife. And Otto, whose picture had been invited to the Cannes Film Festival also, said, "Ring, are you going to Cannes?" And I said, "Hell, no. Nobody ever invites a writer to go." Otto said, "Ingo, how come? I'm taking my writer." And Ingo was a bit embarrassed by this, but not wanting to stand the expense himself, he called up Jonas Rosenfield at Fox and sold him the idea of taking us along on the grounds that I would be better publicity in Cannes than Altman, or Sally Kellerman, or Jo Ann Pflug, because of having been one of the Hollywood Ten. So Fox, which was the studio I was working for when I was blacklisted and which I subsequently sued for breach of contract and won an out-of-court settlement, accepted this idea that I would be good publicity.

FROUG: But at Cannes, you later wrote, you were not included in the press reception for the principals involved in the picture after it won the top prize. Again, the actors, the director and the producer were there.

LARDNER: That's true. I'm quite sure it was inadvertent. And I think probably the inadvertence was on Ingo Preminger's part. I believe I told him that I was going off to see some friends in the area the following morning, knowing that there was a press showing. I knew there was a formal showing that evening. But nobody told me there were interviews following the press showing, and Ingo just forgot, because Ingo is my very good friend of many years and I know he couldn't purposely have done that.

FROUG: When you came back to New York you told of reading in the *New York Times* Vincent Canby's coverage of the event in which you have been one of the acceptees of the award and he listed the two actresses, the producer, and the director, but he didn't mention that you, the screenwriter, were also present. Was that, too, inadvertent?

LARDNER: My first reaction to that was to call Canby on the

telephone that very day it appeared, or this happened on a Sunday and I called him Monday in his office and pointed this out and he said, "Damn it, that's right. There were five of you up there. The only explanation is that I wrote that thing at two o'clock in the morning, very tired, and I'm sorry. What can I do about it? It would seem quite odd to do a whole thing saying I inadvertently left you out." And the result of my call was a suggestion from Seymour Peck, the editor of the "Arts and Leisure" section of the *Times*, that I write a piece about it, which I did.

FROUG: Why is it that in film, and not just in Hollywood, we so frequently see the inadvertent omission of the screenwriter's name? I don't for a minute imply it is a sinister plot. I know it isn't.

LARDNER: It certainly results from the fact that the writer's role has been undervalued over a long period of time. It springs in part, I think, from the era of the thirties and forties when people like Thalberg and Selznick had those successions of writers on scripts and that as a result of that, people within the industry and without said you couldn't really tell who had written what. It also results from the assertion by directors of their authority and their dominance of pictures, and I think to a large extent that directors by their very nature, in order to be good at their job, have to be egotistical men. They really have to make quick decisions. It's an enormously complicated job, as you know, and a good director's under constant pressure having to make a succession of decisions rapidly. And I think only a man with great self-confidence can do this. And this same self-confidence leads into a quite sincere exaggeration of the function. Just to get back to *M*A*S*H* and Bob Altman at the moment: I think every word he said in that *New York Times Magazine* interview, and several other interviews, he believed. And I really think it's a delusion on his part that is almost a natural function of the job. What he really doesn't stop to think is that there could have been no such picture if Richard Hooker had not written this book, setting these particular characters in this background. And that no matter how much it might have been changed from that, the basic authorship is there in the book. As I said before, the very things that Bob attributes to himself, like concept, philosophy, style, and so on, can be traced to the book, and that several of the incidents that created the greatest attention, laughs, and so on were either in the book or added in the screenplay. But I think Bob's exaggeration of his role is quite sincere, because, and this probably applies to a lot of other directors, when he or they undertake to do a piece of material, they have to think they are reconceiving it, shaping it, as they are, to their own particular tastes and imaginations. They just tend to forget how much has gone before, and that everything they're doing is based on other people's concepts. It's probably much more true of a director who likes to get this feeling of spontaneity on the set as much as Altman does. I'm sure that there were days and scenes in which they probably departed much further from the script in the course of improvising, rehearsing, and so on, and then came back to it, without even realizing in the end where these jokes and lines had come from. So I would not accuse him or any other director in the same situation of any conscious distortion. This also applies to writers. A writer who adapts a book to the screen, unless he's doing a pretty literal adaptation, is reconceiving it, and in the course of reconceiving it, he has to begin to think of it as his original creation. And it applies to writers rewriting other writers' scripts. Some of the credit disputes that have existed in the Writers Guild are phenomenal in that both, or the two or three writers involved, might believe quite fiercely and earnestly that it's almost entirely theirs and an impartial credit committee will come out and say it's roughly half and half or half and something like that after examining all the material. But I've never heard of a credit dispute in which the writers were at all objective.

FROUG: Nor have I. I've served on the arbitration committee.

LARDNER: When I wrote this article in *The Saturday Evening Post*, "My Life on the Blacklist," the *Post* sent out word that they wanted to get photographs of the people mentioned in this, and since I had mentioned the picture *The Bridge on the River Kwai* was the joint work of two blacklisted screenwriters, Carl Foreman and Michael Wilson, the *Post* communicated with some photographer who tracked Carl Foreman down in Switzerland and asked if he could take his picture. Carl Foreman immediately called his lawyer Sidney Cohn in New York, and Sidney, whom I know, called me and said, "Carl wants to know what is being said about him in this article." So I read him this sentence: "*Bridge on the River Kwai* was the joint work of two blacklisted writers, Carl Foreman and Michael Wilson." Sidney said, "If you say that, we will sue you and the *Post*. It was 80 percent Carl's work and Mike was simply put on it at Carl's suggestion because he wasn't able to follow through on some minor rewriting that David Lean wanted during the shooting of the picture." So, having been challenged that way, I telephoned Michael Wilson in Paris, where he was living then, and reported this to him, whereupon he sent me a copy of a letter written him by David Lean from Hollywood at the time the Academy Award was given to Pierre Boulle, talking about the irony of the occasion and so on, and in this Lean letter, it said, "You and I know that 80 percent of the screenplay is yours." The fact that he used the same figure that Foreman's letter had used . . . I was put into the position of having a credit dispute between two writers, both friends of mine, whose names didn't appear on the screen. But with the backing of this Lean letter, I told Sidney Cohn that the *Post* was going ahead to print it exactly as I had written it. I knew perfectly well they wouldn't sue. And I'm quite sure that each contributed about half to the final result, and that each is firmly convinced that he contributed more than three quarters.

FROUG: Are you bored with talking about the blacklist?

LARDNER: No.

FROUG: During the Academy Awards did you feel that your former status as a blacklisted writer would affect the voting? You had won an Award for *Woman of the Year* twenty years before.

LARDNER: I didn't think so. I think that there is comparatively little awareness today of the blacklist. In the first place there are so many people who have come into the picture business since that have no direct knowledge of it, and a lot more who have just kind of blocked it out of their minds, so that I don't feel that, for instance, when I got up to receive the Award in that particular audience, the large majority were aware that there was any significance. As a matter of fact, it was sort of a special significance because the year before it had also been won by a blacklisted writer, Waldo Salt, for *Midnight Cowboy.* But I didn't get any feeling that people were much aware of this, and therefore I don't think it influenced the voting.

FROUG: Do you think that there are any significant remnants to the blacklist in Hollywood today?

LARDNER: Well, I know that there are many people, particularly writers, who were blacklisted and who never were able to get back simply because at the time they were blacklisted they weren't established enough or didn't have credits, or because they've gotten into other lines of work in the meantime, so it certainly had an effect in the sense that many careers were damaged by it. There are a few people, I think, who are or have been in the last few years still sort of on an unofficial blacklist just because, for one reason or another, they were thought of by an individual studio executive as being more troublemakers than the rest or more reprehensible or something. But I'm not even sure of that. In any case, the basic consideration has always been commercial and they have gradually hired back those they thought were of commercial value to them. I don't think there's any serious blacklist going on anymore, except in perhaps a couple of cases.

FROUG: During those fourteen years that you were on the blacklist, you continued as did many other of the really outstanding writers, Dalton Trumbo, Michael Wilson, etc., to write under various names. You went to Europe and worked on a Swiss picture. Can you reveal any other pictures you wrote?

LARDNER: I did almost no film work during that time. I did do that picture in Switzerland which was the year after the blacklist started, and during the period before we went to trial and we went to jail, when it was more relaxed than it got later. But after I got out of jail in 1951, I did a little sub rosa film work, rewriting some script, well, as a matter of fact, it was for Joe Losey, and Losey, in a book about the films of Joseph Losey, has given the credits of all the blacklisted writers who worked on his various pictures, names that were not on the screen at the time, and I think he includes mine on that one. But I then left Hollywood, worked for a couple of years on a novel, worked for the next six or seven years almost exclusively on television series which were shot in England but for American television, and this was all under pseudonyms.

FROUG: Yet television was even more sensitive to political pressure than motion pictures.

LARDNER: Yes. These series used not only myself and Ian McLellan Hunter, with whom I collaborated on scores of television films, but quite a few other blacklisted writers, like Abe Polonsky, Waldo Salt, Arnold Perl, Millard Lampell, and a number of others. And it was only known to the producer of the television films who the writers were. All kinds of names were put on the scripts.

FROUG: You once said that you had to keep changing the name you used because if you used the same name too often they would begin to want to meet the writer, or the publicity would begin to accrue.

LARDNER: Yes. The publicity would begin to accrue. Or somebody would see some of these on the television screen and, liking them, start saying, "So-and-so has written several good things on that series, you might try to locate this non-existent writer."

FROUG: Did the producer in England know who the writers were, or were the scripts sent to him from New York?

LARDNER: They were sent to *her* from New York, but she knew and had constant correspondence from us about them, and a couple of writers who could get passports even traveled there. I couldn't.

FROUG: The State Department refused you a passport, even after your release from prison?

LARDNER: Yes. I was unable to get a passport until 1958, I think it was, when there was a Supreme Court decision in a case, I believe, involving Rockwell Kent, or maybe a series of cases. And that obviously applied to all people who had been denied passports. Incidentally, after that Supreme Court decision I went down the very next day to a photographer a couple of blocks from us who had advertised passport pictures, because I was planning to apply for a passport immediately the same day. It happened that I had a strong reason for going to London in connection with this television work. So I went in to this photographer and the man said, "Well, we'll have your picture tomorrow." And I said, "Oh, I thought you could do it right away, the way they do down at the passport bureau." And he said, "Oh, sure, they can make them without a negative and you can go and have one of those made right away, but you'll end up looking like a Communist." He hadn't the slightest idea who I was.

FROUG: Was Otto Preminger the first producer to bring you off the blacklist, officially and openly?

LARDNER: Yes. And he got quite a reaction after announcing it. A letter from the American Legion, which he answered I think very nicely. However, the script I wrote for him has never been produced. And I'm pretty sure it never will be.

FROUG: Was it political?

LARDNER: Oh, no. It wasn't at all. Mainly it was a casting

thing. Otto was convinced we could only do it with one of the three stars and he couldn't get any of them at that time, and then he got interested in other things and kind of lost momentum on it. Although he kept speaking about it for several years.

FROUG: Having gone to jail because you refused to testify before a Congressional Committee as to what your political affiliations were, because you believed that the Constitution protected a man's political rights, ironically one of the first convicts you ran into was J. Parnell Thomas, the former chairman of the House Un-American Activities Committee, the man who sent you to prison. Thomas had been convicted of fraud. Did you have any discussions with the congressman in prison?

LARDNER: It happened that I didn't. Lester Cole, another one of the Hollywood Ten who was in the same prison, did, because of his prison job, have some contact with Thomas. I think Thomas was taking care of the chicken yard. Lester, passing him within the prison, said something like, "Still handling the chicken shit, I see." But I was in the Office of Classification and Parole, which involved my typing parole applications and papers and recommendations relating to all the prisoners. Thomas, I was told, was very alarmed that I would do something to sabotage his parole. But the civilian parole officer, my boss, purposely did not give me that material to type, but had a civilian clerk type it, a non-prisoner. I didn't have any chance to sabotage it, and Thomas did get parole, which none of us achieved.

FROUG: You once said, which I thought was the height of compassion, that when you saw the former congressman in jail with you, you felt pity for him because you knew that when he got out he would be finished, but that when you got out you would continue to be a writer.

LARDNER: Yes, I think that's true. And he was finished. He made an attempt to get the Republican nomination again from his district in New Jersey and was defeated in the primary. He couldn't get the organization behind him. I also felt a certain amount of sympathy for him because he lost a great deal of weight in prison, and on him it didn't look good. But the truth is, it was not any great sympathy. I, of course, disliked the man intensely.

FROUG: There was a lot of speculation about the so-called infiltration of Hollywood films by Communists in those days. Yet the Committee was unable to find any films which espoused the party doctrine.

LARDNER: It's certainly true that they didn't find Communist propaganda in films. But, nevertheless, I think they were trying to assert some control over films and, by intimidation, to affect the content of films which, looking back on them now, we would consider very mildly liberal in their themes and content. But there had been some moderately progressive films written during the war. And in the immediate postwar years there were attempts to deal with subjects !ike anti-Semitism, as in *Gentleman's Agreement*, and *Cross-Fire*, which was done by two blacklisted men, Scott and Dmytryk. I think that part of the effort was certainly to try to check any liberal sentiment coming out of Hollywood. And to a certain extent it succeeded.

FROUG: Do you think that perhaps in a different way and maybe in a more subtle way, we may be getting a little of that today with the Nixon-Agnew-Mitchell axis in power?

LARDNER: Well, as far as I know they haven't devoted much attention to movies directly, at least compared to the Agnew attacks on newspapers and television news departments, but I certainly think the threat is implicit there. Whereas I don't see another blacklist in the same sense taking place, I think it could quite easily be an effort at a new form of censorship over films. They mostly speak in terms of the so-called pornographic content and the danger to children and so on, but I think we all know once any structure is set up to censor in the sex area that it can very easily be adapted to political content.

FROUG: A lot of people feel that Agnew's attacks on the

television networks, and the news media in general, is a preliminary feeler into how far he can go in the arts, including movies. Do you think that's true?

LARDNER: Yes. And I'm sure that Nixon, basically, in his heart, would like to restrict a great many things that go on in the arts. He's a very narrow-minded man. He's almost an anachronism in some of his attitudes and beliefs. The whole business of having the government report on pornography come out, proving that pornography does not harm, doesn't create any rapists or anything, and then his just rejecting it with no evidence. It's an indication of a type of thinking that is pretty dangerous. Of course Nixon was a member of that Committee, the House Un-American Activities Committee.

FROUG: He was one of their chief investigators, wasn't he?

LARDNER: Yes. His big case was the Hiss-Chambers thing. During the Hollywood hearings he was not always present and didn't take any very active part, but, still, that was my only personal sight of him there across the table.

FROUG: Do you remember him?

LARDNER: Oh, yes.

FROUG: You once said, "All that I have done or written has been in keeping with the spirit of my father and two dead brothers."

LARDNER: Yes, that was part of a statement which I tried to read before the Committee in 1947 and which Parnell Thomas at first said I could read after he looked at it, but then, after I didn't answer the questions he forbade me to read it.

FROUG: Do you feel in looking back with the perspective of twenty-four years that you would have done anything differently—in terms of your political or your moral position?

LARDNER: I don't think so. I can raise a hypothetical question to myself, which is would I have taken the stand I took before the Committee if I knew that we would lose the case and be sent to jail, and I'm not sure of the answer.

I mean if I knew 100 percent. We thought that we probably could win this case under the First Amendment and it was really a rather close thing because those hearings occurred in 1947, the pilot trial of Trumbo and Lawson was in the spring of 1948, and in the summer of 1948 two Supreme Court Justices, Wiley Rutledge and Frank Murphy, died, considerably changing the character of the Court, because Truman appointed conservatives to succeed these two quite liberal judges. It was a practical certainty before they died that, along with Black and Douglas, Murphy and Rutledge would have given us the four votes necessary for certiorari, that is, to be heard by the court. Whereas when the cases actually came up, we were denied certiorari and the court never heard the case. As Justice Frankfurter was fond of saying, and even said in relation to this particular case, to, I believe, one of our lawyers, "You must remember that denial of certiorari does not reveal the court's opinion on the merits of the case at all." They simply have to choose which cases they'll hear at a particular time and which they won't. And there was an implication there that if they decided to hear it they would have had to uphold our position. So that anyway, it seemed to us, we had a reasonable chance, and in the same circumstances, thinking that we had a reasonable chance to win the case, I would do the same thing again. As I say, if they said, "You're going to be decapitated tomorrow if you don't answer these questions," one might have a different attitude.

FROUG: You said that you don't have very many political activities anymore. Is that still true?

LARDNER: Well, I have still fairly strong political convictions. I don't see these quite the same way I used to then. But I think my sentiments are still socialistic and revolutionary in the sense that I just don't think there's a chance in hell of solving the particular problems that the world faces, this country faces, with the present political and economic system.

FROUG: Do you feel that the young people today, and I'm now speaking about the subculture of the radicals and the hippies, do you feel that they are offering more hope than we knew in our generations?

LARDNER: Yes. I feel there's a basic soundness to the young, radical sentiment today. It hasn't been channeled into any kind of organization and movement, and it doesn't seem immediately to have much chance of radical change. But I do think that on the whole they have a more sensible attitude toward the world than at least the young people between my generation and theirs had.

FROUG: You have five children. And a number of grandchildren?

LARDNER: I have five children. And, as of now, four grandchildren.

FROUG: Are any of your children carrying on in the radical tradition of their father and grandfather?

LARDNER: When I said that about the tradition of my father and my two brothers who have been killed in wars, I really wasn't talking about a radical tradition. My father was anything but a radical. He was a registered Republican, whenever he registered anyway, and had some fairly conservative views. I was talking about a general American democratic tradition. I find that my kids, whose ages go from about twenty-two to thirty-three, are all very sensible people and all share a distaste for the kind of administration we have now, for the war in Indochina, for a lot of things they find wrong with the world. But they're so different individually in their views, I can't really categorize them.

FROUG: Is there any political organization today, do you think, that offers a way to channel the energies of these young people who are dissatisfied with the hypocrisy they've seen around them?

LARDNER: No, I don't think there is any, and that's perhaps the greatest lack on the political scene today, because I do think that organization is necessary to achieve political change. And we haven't got it. I think it could spring up quite quickly. Even by 1972.

FROUG: A young screenwriter I interviewed, named Jonathan Axelrod, said he would have been interested in the Communist Party except it's too right wing for him.

LARDNER: Yes. I think that's the attitude of many young people I know, and it certainly was true of the attitude of the young people in France in 1968 toward the French Communist Party.

FROUG: Recently you made a comment in relation to *M*A*S*H* about Hollywood's infatuation with young filmmakers that I think bears repeating.

LARDNER: I merely said, as an entrenched veteran guarding his status against the latest crop of moviemakers, I wanted to stress that a popular picture among young people in this country had been written, produced, and directed by grandfathers.

I.A.L. Diamond

1944 MURDER IN THE BLUE ROOM *(Joint Screenplay)*

1945 NEVER SAY GOODBYE *(Joint Screenplay)*

1946 TWO GUYS FROM MILWAUKEE *(Joint Screenplay)*

1947 TWO GUYS FROM TEXAS *(Joint Story and Screenplay)*
ROMANCE ON THE HIGH SEAS *(Additional Dialogue)*
ALWAYS TOGETHER *(Joint Story and Screenplay)*

1948 THE GIRL FROM JONES BEACH *(Screenplay)*
IT'S A GREAT FEELING *(Story and Screenplay)*

1951 LOVE NEST *(Screenplay)*
LET'S MAKE IT LEGAL *(Joint Screenplay)*

1952 MONKEY BUSINESS *(Joint Screenplay)*
SOMETHING FOR THE BIRDS *(Joint Screenplay)*

1955 THAT CERTAIN FEELING *(Joint Screenplay)*

1956 LOVE IN THE AFTERNOON *(Joint Screenplay)*, Writers Guild Award

1957 MERRY ANDREW *(Joint Screenplay)*

1958 SOME LIKE IT HOT *(Joint Screenplay)*, Academy Nomination, Writers Guild Award

1960 THE APARTMENT *(Joint Story and Screenplay)*, Academy Award, Writers Guild Award

1961 ONE, TWO, THREE *(Joint Screenplay)*, Writers Guild Nomination

1963 IRMA LA DOUCE *(Joint Screenplay)*, Writers Guild Nomination

1964 KISS ME, STUPID *(Joint Screenplay)*

1966 THE FORTUNE COOKIE *(Joint Story and Screenplay)*, Academy Nomination, Writers Guild Nomination

1969 CACTUS FLOWER *(Screenplay)*, Writers Guild Nomination
THE PRIVATE LIFE OF SHERLOCK HOLMES *(Joint Story and Screenplay)*

1971 FORTY CARATS *(Screenplay)*

1972 AVANTI! *(Joint Screenplay)*

1974 THE FRONT PAGE *(Joint Screenplay)*

1978 FEDORA *(Joint Screenplay)*

1981 BUDDY BUDDY *(Joint Screenplay)*

I. (for Isidore) A. L. (because he thought the letters looked interesting following I.) Diamond spent fifteen years of his writing career under the old major Hollywood studio system as a contract writer, and fifteen years as the silent partner of writer-director Billy Wilder, the Hollywood filmmaker's filmmaker.

When you use the word "silent" in connection with Iz Diamond, you are speaking both literally as well as figuratively. He has refined the low profile almost to the point of invisibility. Diamond had an office at Columbia Pictures for months, where he wrote one of their most successful films (*Cactus Flower*) and, recently, was a resident of the studio writing *Forty Carats*. Yet when I telephoned the studio, I couldn't find a switchboard operator who knew or had heard of the name. And even the supervisor said, "I.A.L. *who*?"

At the Writers Guild they gave me a phone number that was long out of date.

Our paths had crossed briefly a couple of years ago when we both worked at the Goldwyn studio, but, though we ate in the tiny executive dining room almost daily, often only a few feet apart, we had never exchanged a greeting.

I was surprised, therefore, to discover Diamond is an altogether agreeable, friendly man. He is not so much withdrawn as he is both serious-minded and preoccupied with his work. He is a twenty-four-hour-a-day writer, a chain-smoker, one of the breed whose waking hours (and, I suspect, many of his sleeping ones) are consumed with the work at hand. (Even as I am writing this introduction, Diamond is on the telephone: "Last night when I was trying to get some sleep I had a new idea I'd like to get in, if it's not too late.") He had already read and revised our interview, making meticulous changes on every page of the transcript, sometimes retyping entire sections, deleting questions, adding new (and better) ones. "The only way I'll ever stop," he finally told me, "is if you physically take it away from me."

I.A.L. Diamond is, at first glance, almost as imposing as his invented name; always conservatively dressed, freshly barbered, wearing tortoise-shell glasses. He might be your neighborhood banker or C.P.A.

But once you get past the cool, crisp exterior, you find a rather shy man who would simply rather write than talk.

Diamond was born in Ungheni, Romania, June 27, 1920, and came to America when he was nine. His father opened a dairy store in Brooklyn, and Iz and his younger sister attended public schools.

He entered Columbia University as an engineering student, but switched to journalism and began to write college shows. He graduated with a B.A. in 1941 and was hired as a junior writer at Paramount for seventy-five dollars a week. ("MGM was paying fifty dollars a week.")

"Whatever picture had just finished, you were immediately assigned to write a sequel. If Bob Hope had just done an Army picture, you were assigned to write a Bob Hope Navy picture."

For a young man in his early twenties, it must have been a heady experience, grinding out the potboilers of Hollywood and mingling with the stars and the greats of what was then truly "the film capital of the world." Diamond was and still remains a movie fan.

While his credits were not particularly distinguished, they were solid. He was known as a writer who could deliver a shooting script, no matter what the assignment.

When Wilder, a genius who knows and appreciates the value of collaboration, chose Diamond, he was asking him to replace the redoubtable Charles Brackett, Wilder's former partner and a giant in his own right.

While the team of Wilder and Diamond has won

critical acclaim (and one Oscar), their sophisticated, urbane, and dark comedies are often more appreciated in Europe than in America.

Diamond's hobbies are bridge and collecting art. He lives in a modest two-story stucco house (the same one he has lived in for twenty years, which in itself is some sort of Los Angeles county record) three blocks from the business and shopping center of Beverly Hills.

Diamond's film credo is explicit: "Movies are the biggest toy ever invented. Chaplin set out to entertain and created art. The guys who set out to create art don't even entertain."

BILLY
Me? Never. I have enough trouble keeping one woman dissatisfied.

There is the sound of a KEY turning in the lock. The door opens and Trina and Eddy come in, dressed for travelling.

TRINA
Hi.

EDDY
Hi, everybody.

TRINA
(crossing to Billy)
Look what Eddy gave me.

¶ She holds out her left hand to show him an engagement ring with a huge diamond --at least twenty carats.

BILLY
It's the thought that counts.

PETER
(in his new role as host)
What would you like to drink?

TRINA
We can't stay. We've just come to collect Granny Maud.

EDDY
(to Billy)
I just heard on the car radio that it's snowing up in Connecticut. I remember the last time we had a white Christmas ---

BILLY
Is this going to be a long story?

EDDY
(to Trina)
You know what I like about Billy? He's as mean as cat-pee on cellar stairs.

Peter chuckles.

BILLY
(to Peter)
Don't laugh. He's going to be your son-in-law.

Maud appears from the direction of the bedrooms, wearing a coat and carrying a weekend bag.

MAUD
I'm ready.

FROUG: A couple of years ago, I was at the Mirisch Company writing a screenplay for Walter, and I used to lunch in that tiny dining room across from you and Billy Wilder and in all those months I never saw you exchange a word between you. Why was that?

DIAMOND: Well, after you've been working together in the same room for fifteen years, what's there left to talk about?

FROUG: Are you still working with Billy?

DIAMOND: We just finished a script called *Avanti!*, which is going to be shot in Italy this spring. It's a comedy based on a play by Sam Taylor. That's all there is to tell about it right now. [Jack Lemmon has since been signed to star in the film.]

FROUG: Have you always had a collaborator? Or did you start writing screenplays alone?

DIAMOND: Well, with the old studio contract system, under which I worked for about fifteen years, you would either follow or precede somebody on a script. It was not uncommon to have three, four, even six writers on a screenplay. You were assigned to various stages. Either an early treatment, or a last-minute doctoring job, or somewhere in between.

FROUG: Why was that? Why didn't one writer write it and continue on through?

DIAMOND: In those days, the major studios operated on the principle that the more writers on a script, the better it was going to be. And every studio used to prepare three times as many pictures as they ever made. I remember at Metro, when I first came there, there were something like 130 writers under contract, not to mention freelance writers who came in for specific assignments. Those people had to be kept working all the time, so everybody rewrote everybody.

FROUG: Do you feel that the films benefited from these group collaborations?

DIAMOND: No, because any time you get more than two minds on something, you're going to have to start compromising. Everybody has his own notions. They may be equally good, but there's no unity to them, so you have to find the lowest common denominator. No, I don't think it was a good system.

FROUG: Milos Forman said recently in reference to his film *Taking Off* that he likes working with two writers in addition to himself because, since they rarely agree, there's always a majority of two over one on any given point.

DIAMOND: Well, the way I work with Billy is that if we disagree violently about something, we throw out both approaches and try to look for a third approach. And a good part of the time, we find something better than either of us had considered originally. So I don't think you need a third man on the picture to break the tie. It's not a question of democracy.

FROUG: When you went to Columbia to write *Cactus Flower*, which was an enormous success for the company, it was your first solo job in a long, long time?

DIAMOND: Yes, in quite a while. I had worked on one or two projects, other projects, during the time Billy and I were working, but I didn't do enough on any of them to get credit.

FROUG: How do you find the difference between collaborating and a solo job? Do you find it more difficult?

DIAMOND: Well, the first thing that happens to you is you feel terribly lonely because there's nobody else in the office to try ideas on. And then you're faced with just having to sit down and write, because you can't stall, you can't keep from working by just discussing things.

FROUG: How much time did it take you to do your first draft

of *Cactus Flower*?

DIAMOND: Oh, I think three months.

FROUG: And how much time does it take you and Billy to do your screenplays when you work together?

DIAMOND: Bill, I'd say the average time has been close to a year, but there is only one draft. You see, that's the difference. On *Cactus Flower* I did a draft, then a couple of sets of revisions. But the way Billy and I work, there is only one draft really, and a good part of the time, we don't even have a finished script when we start shooting. I mean, we do every scene as well as we can, and then we go on to the next scene, and we know nobody is going to change a word unless we decide to go back and change something ourselves. So there is no reason to try to write a quick draft and then rewrite. We just take our time.

FROUG: Considering the time that you average working with Billy Wilder, a year per screenplay, do you find that it's economically more feasible to work by yourself?

DIAMOND: Yes, in that sense, I could probably get more scripts done in a year. But with Billy, I'm usually also associate producer, so at the same time we are writing, we are also involved in production problems—casting, location hunting, and all that—and that's why it takes us longer to do the screenplay. Naturally, I prefer to be on a picture the entire way through, rather than abandoning the script and going off and just letting someone else do it.

FROUG: It's very rare, isn't it, that a screenwriter has a chance to follow through with his production?

DIAMOND: Well, I think it's all for the good. In the old days, it was not considered economically feasible to keep a writer on the set. Or usually, by the time the picture was made, the writer was off at some other studio doing some other assignment. I think that it's helpful both for the writer and for the picture.

FROUG: Iz, what, in your opinion, makes a great screenplay?

DIAMOND: Oh, god, I wish I knew, because if I knew, I would put it in a sealed envelope and sell the secret. I don't know. Something you have to feel by instinct and experience, and then one time out of three, at least, you're wrong. I don't think anybody can give you a formula, or pinpoint it that well.

FROUG: Who is your favorite screenwriter?

DIAMOND: That's hard to say. There are certain writers I have always admired, going back to Dudley Nichols and Robert Riskin. And a lot of others—Preston Sturges, Brackett and Wilder, Nunnally Johnson, Ben Hecht. I like different people for different things, or at different times.

FROUG: What movies do you like to see?

DIAMOND: Well, I'm old-fashioned in this respect, I guess. Linear movies. Movies with some dramatic drive. I want to know what happens next, not what happened last year in Marienbad. If it was last year, if it was Marienbad, if it did happen. That kind of script you can knock out on a rainy afternoon. Critics have a tendency to assume that the more obscure something is, the more profound it must be. It all rather reminds me of Gilbert and Sullivan:

> If this young man expresses himself
>   in terms too deep for me,
> Why, what a very singularly deep young
>   man this deep young man must be.

FROUG: What are your normal working hours?

DIAMOND: With Billy, when we start on a script, it's ten to five, five days a week. As we get deeper into it, it gets to be nine to six, and then we start working Saturday mornings, then Sunday mornings, and by the time we're shooting, there's a lot of weekend work and occasionally night work. So it's an expandable schedule. Working alone, at a studio, my hours are ten to five. If I'm writing something of my own, at home, and I get excited, then I work all day and after dinner, too. And weekends, naturally.

FROUG: You work seven days a week?

DIAMOND: If I'm really caught up in something, yes, sure, because I hate to put it aside.

FROUG: How many pages do you try for a day? Do you set a goal for yourself?

DIAMOND: No. You know, there'll be good days when I'll do five pages and bad days when I'll do a half a page. But in the long run that doesn't matter, because those five pages you do you may throw out the next day anyway. And the day you only did half a page will produce the next day when you'll do the five pages, because something's cooking there on the back burner.

FROUG: How long do you allow yourself for the development of your story before you begin the screenplay?

DIAMOND: Again, when I'm working alone . . . oh, I may have been thinking about a thing on and off for months or even years. But when I actually get down to work, I will spend no more than two weeks beforehand, making notes. Because I'm afraid that if I get it worked out too well, then I'm going to find the writing boring. I'd rather just have a few signposts and leave a lot of wide-open spaces, so things can happen when I'm writing. I don't like to have it down too cold or too well figured out before I start, because I think some of the excitement and enthusiasm goes out of it.

FROUG: How many pages do you figure for your first draft?

DIAMOND: That depends. Sometimes I run short, like 100 pages, and on other occasions I've come in with 200 pages. But one of the purposes of the first draft is just to lay it out for myself and see where it's too long, where it needs development, where it needs compression. That's why I like to rough it out fast so I can judge the balance of the scenes.

FROUG: How many drafts do you write for yourself before you deliver the so-called first draft to the producer?

DIAMOND: One, really, plus a lot of revision time. I mean, I spend more time rewriting than writing.

FROUG: After delivery of a draft to a studio, how many sets of revisions do you anticipate?

DIAMOND: Well, usually I'm contractually obligated to two

sets of revisions. I will normally make the first one right after the producer has read it, and save the second set of revisions till they have a cast and director. Because the director is going to want certain things, and the casting may necessitate certain changes.

FROUG: Did you find on *Cactus Flower* that you had more control over your material than you had had previously when you worked alone?

DIAMOND: Yes, because Mike Frankovich trusted me to go off and do my own first draft without interference, which is the way I prefer to do it, and we consulted at all stages, including the casting, and certainly when the director came in.

FROUG: You also adapted the Broadway hit, *Forty Carats*, for Columbia, last year. Whatever happened to that project?

DIAMOND: They're casting it now. According to what I read in the trade papers, they're trying to get Elizabeth Taylor.

FROUG: Iz, to what extent do you draw upon your own life experiences for your characters, your story, your scenes?

DIAMOND: Well, maybe not consciously, but where else does your material come from if not from your own experiences? And what you've read.

FROUG: How important, in your opinion, is a literary background to the writer of films?

DIAMOND: Well, I'm not going to prescribe for anybody else. A lot of kids today are not well-read, they don't consider it relevant. I read everything, and the only thing that I regret when I'm working is that I don't have enough time to read. I think you cannot be illiterate and write, let's put it this way.

FROUG: Do you believe that the cinema courses that are now available to college students throughout the world will be helpful toward their goal to become filmmakers?

DIAMOND: Well, yes. I should think that anybody who has some idea of what to do with a camera, and knows the basic rules of cutting will come into the field with certain advantages. But "professionalism" has become a dirty word in this business. It's much easier to get financing these days if you can prove you've never made a picture before. It's like a surgeon who's never operated before. Naturally, he hasn't lost any patients.

FROUG: To what extent does film criticism affect your work?

DIAMOND: Not at all, in a sense. I bleed like everybody else when I get bad reviews, and I'm a little smug when I get good reviews. I don't think it makes me sit down and write the next script in any different way, or with an eye to pleasing a critic.

FROUG: After the successes that you and Billy had with *Some Like It Hot* and *The Apartment*, you were lambasted pretty badly on *Kiss Me, Stupid*. Did that affect your next project?

DIAMOND: It depressed us for a while, and we had trouble getting started on the next one. But you can't let things like that get you down. Occasionally you guess wrong, or you misjudge the temper of the public at the moment. We just happened to make a dirty picture five years ahead of time, that's all. I mean, today that would be considered a Disney picture, for god's sake. But there was a big hullabaloo about it at the time, and it was the sort of last gasp of the Legion of Decency. After that, they went underground.

FROUG: Do you find film criticism of any value?

DIAMOND: No, not really. I mean, I enjoy reading Pauline Kael, although I don't agree with her most of the time. I would say the same for Penelope Gilliatt and Judith Crist. And I liked Wilfrid Sheed when he was reviewing. But as a moviemaker, I have yet to find a critic who could distinguish between writing, direction, and performance. I have seen directors credited with "touches" which I know were in the script. And I've seen actors acclaimed for performances which I knew were painfully pieced together by the director, line by line, using a blackboard and clever intercuts, because the actor couldn't sustain a performance. And how can a critic possibly judge when a picture has been salvaged by the producer and the cutter, after it was botched up by the director?

FROUG: Can you separate yourself when you're reading film criticism?

DIAMOND: Yes, because having read some of the nonsense written about my own movies, and having been disappointed by so many pictures they rave about, I tend to discount all movie criticism. After all, it's purely subjective. You like something or you don't, and then you rationalize it. What I resent is when the critics try to impose their taste on everybody else, when they feel that the only pictures that should be made are the kind they like. I think there should be room for *Mary Poppins* and Russ Meyer and everything else. I may not want to go to see them, but I'm not going to stop anybody else from seeing them, or anybody from making them. I think all kinds of pictures can coexist, and not just the limited range that particular critics seem to like.

FROUG: There's sometimes a tendency among film critics or film journalists to read into a film all sorts of bizarre, hidden meanings that were never intended in the first place, and you referred a moment ago to some of the nonsense that had been written about your own films. Can you give me any particular examples where you found something read into a film that was never intended and never there?

DIAMOND: Well, I don't remember who the critic was . . . it was a lady writing in *Film Quarterly*, or maybe *Films in Review*. Anyway, there was a review of *Some Like It Hot*, and she made a list of phallic symbols in the picture—everything from the saxophone to the machine gun to references to the Graf Zeppelin and a squeezed-out tube of toothpaste. Now, of course, I just marvel at this. It reveals a lot more about the critic's mind than the writer's. Another incident—my daughter told me this. She was going to Sarah Lawrence at the time. Some English professor there, lecturing about movies, got around to *The*

Apartment and he said, "You realize, of course, that this is a parable about heaven and hell. The office is hell and the apartment is heaven. And it's significant that the girl runs an elevator, which is what connects heaven and hell. The key to the apartment, of course, is a phallic symbol . . ." You know, I listen to this stuff and it just amuses the hell out of me. To think that the ending of *The Fortune Cookie* gave aid and comfort to Leslie Fiedler. I think more crap is being written about films today than was ever written about Abstract Expressionism. I wish they weren't so solemn about it.

FROUG: How do you go about researching material for a screenplay?

DIAMOND: I've never really been on a project where I've had to do very much research.

FROUG: *The Private Life of Sherlock Holmes*, for example . . .

DIAMOND: Yes. That just consisted of reading all the material. There must be a hundred books on Sherlock Holmes . . . more than Doyle ever wrote about him.

FROUG: You read a hundred books?

DIAMOND: Well, we went through most of the important ones. But that was just to get a feeling for the characters, for the background, so that we were completely familiar with them. Then we could go off in our own direction, but in the spirit of what Doyle had written.

FROUG: To what do you account the lukewarm reception for that film?

DIAMOND: Well, I don't know. It is not the picture that we conceived or wrote or shot. The version that was shown was an hour and fifteen minutes shorter than what we had shot.

FROUG: An hour and fifteen minutes?

DIAMOND: Yes. What had happened was that at the time the project started, which was about four years before it was released, it was supposed to be a road-show picture. We wrote a 220-page script, and had a first rough-cut of three hours and twenty minutes. But by this time, the distributors had soured on road-show pictures except for a few musicals, and we were faced with cutting down a three-hour-and-twenty-minute picture to slightly over two hours. It was conceived in episodes, more or less: three comedy episodes, which were supposed to come before the intermission, and a more serious episode in the second half. We wound up cutting two of the first three sequences and, therefore, it did not have the shape that we had originally intended for it. It was an aborted version.

FROUG: Was it also designed as a major star vehicle in the beginning?

DIAMOND: No, that, never. It was always assumed that the star was Sherlock Holmes, and not the actor who played him.

FROUG: How long did you spend on that project then, from the very beginning?

DIAMOND: I think we spent altogether about three and a half years, including shooting, post-production and everything else.

FROUG: Will it ever earn back its negative cost?

DIAMOND: That I don't know. I don't know about cost figures, or how much is in or what it did foreign, or what the television sale will be, or any of that.

FROUG: Have you ever written for television?

DIAMOND: No, not at all. I've never had any other job in my life except screenwriting.

FROUG: What responsibility do you think the film director has toward your script?

DIAMOND: Well, I've worked under different systems. One where I was working with the director throughout the picture, which is one kind of moviemaking. The other, back in the old days, where you never even meet the director, and you were not welcome on the set. That was a different kind of filmmaking. I think it is the director's responsibility to work with the writer if there's going to be a meeting of minds. Under the old studio system, that rarely happened. The director would be off shooting some other picture at the time, and usually he wouldn't see a script until a few weeks before he was ready to go. They'd say you've got a Gable and Loy, and you start three weeks from Wednesday. In those days, the directors refused to get involved with the writer during the writing of the script. They wanted to keep an option open to say yes or no after the script was finished. They were afraid if they worked with the writer and the studio heads turned the script down, they would be considered responsible. They didn't want that responsibility. They wanted to come in at the end, and read the script, and say okay or I won't do it. I think that those days are gone. As Billy once said, "The trouble with most directors is not that they can't write, but that they can't read." And I've had this experience, where I've sat in conference with a director who had just read the script, and he'd say, "I don't understand this scene. I wouldn't know how to do it." And then I'd start to question him, and it would turn out that he'd misread, or neglected to read, a key paragraph in the script. Or, again, I'd find myself on the set, and I'd point out to a director that he couldn't do something because it conflicted with a previous scene, or would undercut a future scene. So he'd reluctantly abandon the idea, and half an hour later he'd come back and say, "Now tell me once again why I can't do that." One of the cornerstones of the auteur theory is that the director is the one man who keeps the overall conception of the film in his head. But as anybody who's ever spent any time on movie sets knows, the script girl usually has a better grasp of the overall conception than the director, because he's too busy organizing all the technical details, shot by shot.

FROUG: How far should the screenwriter go in designing the visuals for a film?

DIAMOND: There, again, working in close association with Billy, who is also the director, we never bother with things like that. I mean, there is no sense putting them into the script because we are writing the script for ourselves.

FROUG: In adapting a play or novel—let's say in the case of *Cactus Flower*, an already well-established and popular hit play that's familiar to an important segment of your audience—do you feel compelled to preserve the original material intact?

DIAMOND: No, not intact. I'm not going to just throw out something which I know worked on the stage, and which I know is the reason they bought it. But I will take into consideration the fact that a stage audience is usually fifteen years older, on the average, and quite a bit more prosperous than a movie audience. I will also take into consideration the fact that on Broadway, *Cactus Flower* was slanted toward Lauren Bacall, who was their star. In rewriting, I cut that role in half, because I thought that was more important from the movie audience's point of view.

FROUG: Because of Goldie Hawn?

DIAMOND: Even before we had Goldie Hawn. Of course, we got Goldie, and I was very happy about it. But simply because of the difference in age brackets between a theater and movie audience.

FROUG: When you and Billy were writing *The Apartment*, *Some Like It Hot*, and *The Fortune Cookie*, were you as concerned then about a particular audience that you were playing to?

DIAMOND: No. I don't think the audience in those days was as fragmented as it is now. I think there was still, to some extent, a mass audience, people who went to movies more or less regularly. I think now there is definitely a young audience that will line up on Third Avenue and wait for hours to see any picture they want to see. There is the audience that comes out once a year, to see *Sound of Music* or *Doctor Zhivago*. And there are in-between audiences and, of course, combinations of various audiences. A picture like *The Graduate* obviously cut across the lines and brought in both the kids and the older people, who went to see why the kids liked it.

FROUG: When you and Billy were writing *The Apartment*, were you conscious of the fact that you were working in an area rarely known at that time to American films, black comedy?

DIAMOND: No. I don't think we were conscious of that. We were conscious of something else, however, that we were trying to combine a basically serious story with jokes. It was especially critical in one scene where Lemmon has picked up a girl in a bar, and brings her home to the apartment, and MacLaine has attempted suicide in the other room. He was playing a comedy seduction with one girl while another girl was dying, and when he discovers MacLaine, he tries to get rid of this girl. There was a delicate balance there between drama and comedy, and we were afraid that if we got a laugh in the wrong place, the whole picture would go out the window. When we sat through the preview, when they accepted that, when they laughed at the right places and took the rest seriously, then I think we knew we were in, because that was the really tricky part. It's Huxley's *Point Counterpoint*—while Smith is pushing the pram, Jones is murdering his wife. I mean, this shuttling back and forth between tragedy and comedy. On that occasion it worked for us.

FROUG: Bob Altman says that on *M*A*S*H* they cut the film to audience reaction. That is, they previewed it, noted the audience response, then recut it, then previewed it again, then recut it again, until they were finally certain exactly where the laughs would come and how long they'd last. Did you and Billy preview your films and recut them according to audience reaction?

DIAMOND: No. Hardly at all. For one thing, Billy shoots very tightly. The film is designed to be cut a certain way. There's very little leftover footage, and very little coverage of scenes. So usually we'd end up taking four minutes out of a picture. We never had preview cards. We just did it to get a feel of the audience and how they were reacting to it. I remember the preview of *Some Like It Hot*. We took it to the Bay Theater in Pacific Palisades and there was a Tennessee Williams picture playing on the same bill. It was a middle-aged audience, and the picture just lay there. Nothing happened. And I remember when we came out, Joe Mankiewicz was there and he put his arm around Billy's shoulder and said, "Well, it happens to all of us." That was on a Wednesday night. Now, without cutting a frame, we took it out again on Friday night to the Village Theater in Westwood, where there was a young UCLA audience, and the house came down. And it was the same picture. Nothing was changed. Not one frame. So go tell about previews.

FROUG: Do you find, aside from your long and successful collaboration with Billy, that in other experiences the writer and the director tend to be rivals?

DIAMOND: No. I don't know any director who isn't going to want to get the best script he can. My general experience over the years has been that people who have confidence in themselves will listen to others and accept advice. It's only the people who feel insecure who don't want to hear anybody else's opinion, because they're afraid that it detracts from their authority or threatens their position somehow. But I think that any competent professional is going to look for all the help he can get.

FROUG: You spoke of several occasions in working with Billy over the years where you were writing on the set. What pictures were those?

DIAMOND: Practically every picture. I don't think we ever started with a complete script. That sounds worse than it is. The third act is always constructed, but it's not down on paper yet, because certain things happen once you get on the set, certain performances begin to come to life, certain things you see and feel help you in writing the third act.

FROUG: Did you always shoot in continuity?

DIAMOND: Insofar as it was feasible, considering set construction and locations and all that. But we'd just be feeling our way through the first weeks of the picture, before committing ourselves to paper on the last act.

FROUG: Did the actors object?

DIAMOND: No. I think it was sort of interesting for them, too, because they were curious about where we were going. For instance, on *Some Like It Hot,* very early in the shooting of the picture, we were on location in Coronado, and we knew that Lemmon and Curtis and Monroe were going to go off with Joe E. Brown at the end, we knew that much. We also knew that there were going to be a lot of costume changes in the last act, that they were going to change from girl's clothes to men's clothes and back again. We didn't know exactly where we would come out. But we felt they would probably wind up in girl's clothes, and we shot it that way. If, in the writing, it had turned out we were wrong, that they ended up in men's clothes, we would have had to go back and reshoot it.

FROUG: Then you really didn't know your ending when you began the picture?

DIAMOND: We had no last scene, no dialogue, nothing there. We just knew we needed a shot of the motor boat pulling away from shore toward the yacht.

FROUG: When did you get that marvelous tag line?

DIAMOND: That was sort of desperation time. We had not yet written the ending when Monroe took sick, and we suddenly found ourselves having to shoot around her, and there was very little in that picture that we could do without her. And so we found ourselves having to write the tag. Now, if you recall the picture, when you go to the close-up of Lemmon and Brown in the front seat of the motor boat, you don't see Tony and Marilyn behind. You don't see her because she was not on the set that day. What we did ultimately when we shot her and Tony is, he kisses her and bends her out of the shot to justify the fact that you can't see her in the next scene. We wrote it the night before we had to shoot it, and I mentioned a line I'd considered using at some earlier point. And Billy said, "Do you think it's strong enough for the tag of the picture?" And I said, "I don't know." But it was getting to be eleven o'clock at night, so we wrote it that way, and he said, "Well, maybe we'll think of something better on the set." Fortunately, we didn't think of anything better on the set.

FROUG: Jack Lemmon says, "I'm not a girl, I'm a man." And Joe E. Brown says, "Well, nobody's perfect."

DIAMOND: It was actually a rhythm joke. The lines Brown had just before that were "It doesn't matter," "I don't care," "I forgive you." They all fell into the same pattern, which lulled the audience and set them up for the topper.

FROUG: What was the origin of *Some Like It Hot*?

DIAMOND: That was based on an old German picture called *Fanfares of Love*. It was written back in the Depression days, in the early thirties, and it was just about two musicians who were unemployed and took a variety of jobs. They dressed up as gypsies to play in a gypsy orchestra, they put on blackface to play in a jazz band, they dressed up as women to play in an all-girl band. Anyway, the only compulsion for these guys to get into drag, and stay in drag, was hunger. Well, we figured we needed a stronger reason than that. It would have to be a matter of life and death. So we invented this situation where one of the musicians is in hock to a bookie, and they go to the bookie's office to plead for an extension, and while they're there the bookie gets murdered, and they're the only two witnesses. Now, that's as much as we had when we first started. We had no idea of doing it in period yet. And then we began to discuss the question of costuming and makeup. If they looked too good, like drag queens, then a lot of the fun would go out of it. On the other hand, if they looked too sloppy, then everybody in the picture becomes an idiot for not realizing that they're really men. And while kicking these problems around, I remember pointing out that, no matter how many times *Charley's Aunt* is revived, it's always done in period. Because when all the costumes look peculiar to us, a guy in drag looks no more peculiar than anybody else. And that's the way we left it at the end of the day. The next morning Billy came in and said, "Driving home last night, I was thinking about what you said, and I think I have the solution . . . Chicago, 1929, St. Valentine's Day Massacre . . ." And suddenly we were in business. Because the period thing gave us all the other elements, you know, characters and backgrounds that we hadn't even thought of at that point. And I think that's what really made the picture, the bootleggers and the millionaires in Florida and all that.

FROUG: How long had you been working before you hit on that notion?

DIAMOND: Oh, it was in the very early stages of the discussion. Probably only a few weeks.

FROUG: What's the origin of *The Apartment*?

DIAMOND: Well, that's a little more complicated. Ever since Billy had seen *Brief Encounter*, he'd been turning over a notion about the guy who owns that apartment where the two lovers meet. I mean, what's it like for him when he comes home and the bed is rumpled and the ashtrays are full and there are dirty glasses to clean up? But we never had a plot for it. And then something happened in this town—I won't mention names, you'll know who I mean—where a producer caught his wife with an agent, and shot him. And it turned out that the agent was using the apartment of a subordinate of his in the same agency, and suddenly that gave us the plot. Of course, instead of the shooting, we used the suicide, but really, that's where the two things, that's where *Brief Encounter* and this local scandal meshed together and we had our story.

FROUG: Do you feel that the best comedy is based on life and death issues?

DIAMOND: Not necessarily life and death issues, but on a substructure that's as strong as it would be in a drama. I think any comedy, with a slight change in emphasis, should be able to play as a drama. Even a farce. It's like a captive balloon. At some point, it has to be anchored to reality. If it's free-floating, then there's no frame of reference.

FROUG: The opening of *Cactus Flower* is a suicide attempt. In *The Fortune Cookie*, the leading character is possibly paralyzed for life. At least, that's the fraud.

DIAMOND: Yes, each of those could go in a completely serious direction.

FROUG: We haven't discussed *One, Two, Three*, which was an unusual film. Was it, perhaps, ahead of its time?

DIAMOND: Actually, it was an attempt to go back and do the kind of fast-paced comedy they were doing in the thirties. What we were really trying to do was *Front Page*. We wanted something with that kind of momentum. And, I don't know, maybe it was too much for an audience to absorb. That's a wearing picture, because it never stops. It just keeps moving for two hours. There are no quiet spots in it. And maybe that hurt it. Also, while we were shooting in Berlin, the border was closed, and the situation became very serious. Suddenly we had a crisis in Berlin, and maybe people were in no mood for jokes about it.

FROUG: What was the origin of *Kiss Me, Stupid*?

DIAMOND: That was an Italian play, and it was laid in eighteenth-century England. It was about a church organist who has composed an oratorio, and the sheriff of London is coming through this small town, and he'd like to get the oratorio performed in London. But the sheriff is a notorious womanizer, and the organist is afraid to trust him with his wife, so he gets rid of the wife and hires the town courtesan to impersonate her. But he becomes jealous anyway, and throws the guy out. The sheriff then goes to what he thinks is the town courtesan, who is really the wife, and to our hero's surprise, his oratorio gets performed in London. It's the same plot we used, but we were not interested in doing a picture about greed and sex in eighteenth-century England. We wanted to translate it into modern terms, which is why Las Vegas and Hollywood and popular songwriting. What we were really trying to do was a Restoration comedy in modern dress, but nobody caught on to that. I mean, when Mankiewicz did *The Honey Pot*, everybody knew he was doing *Volpone*, and whether he succeeded or failed, at least the critics realized what he was up to. But in our case, unless we'd had a foreword, we couldn't communicate that. A lot of the things we were criticized for, the names of the characters, the costuming, some of the double entendres, that was a pure attempt to update a Restoration comedy. And like all such comedies, it was a moral and cautionary tale. A jealous husband goes to such extremes to protect his wife's virtue that she winds up losing it. The Italian title was *L'Ora della Fantasia*. For one hour a prostitute gets to act out the fantasy of being a married woman, and a married woman gets to act out the fantasy of being a prostitute. We got great reviews in London and Paris. The critics there realized that we were trying to make a statement about contemporary America. But in this country, the critics were so obsessed with looking for smut that they couldn't see anything beyond that. One television writer came to me and said, "It reminded me of Congreve's *The Way of the World*," and I wanted to throw my arms around him, because he understood what we were aiming for. But while the *New York Herald-Tribune* was knocking it, the *Paris Herald-Tribune* was saying that it was a more bitter look at America than *Virginia Woolf*. And in England it has a big cult following, like another of Billy's failures, *Ace in the Hole*. I think what it is, people don't like to be told they're corrupt. If they're going to pay money for it, they want to hear that they're honest and loyal and warm and friendly and lovable.

FROUG: Was *Kiss Me, Stupid* your most disappointing film in the sense of failing to reach your audience?

DIAMOND: Yes. I don't think we ever expected such a backlash of criticism. We felt we were doing a mildly suggestive comedy. Not something that was going to corrupt the morals of the young or something.

FROUG: Many of the so-called auteur directors refer to the screenplay as a blueprint. Do you think that's an accurate description?

DIAMOND: To an extent, yes. I mean, what does an architect do except draw a blueprint? But I don't think anybody considers the head of the construction crew as the creator of the building. And nobody goes around saying that architecture is a "contractor's medium." To say that the director is the "author" of a film is semantic nonsense. Unless he writes his own script, he's an interpreter. As Frederic Raphael, the author of *Darling* and *Two for the Road* put it, "A director who can't originate a character or develop a situation is like a pastry cook who puts curlicues on somebody else's cake." You never saw an ad for a concert that said "Bernstein's Ninth, written by Beethoven." I'm not knocking directors, I'm just trying to redress the balance. It took thirty years before Herman Mankiewicz finally started to get some recognition for the script of *Citizen Kane.* Ask any writer-director which of his functions he considers more important. In fact, I don't think the auteur theory is even fair to directors. If you look at the heroes of *Cahiers du Cinéma*, you'll find that they make essentially the same picture over and over again. What the critics recognize as a "signature" is mostly self-plagiarism. But if a director is versatile enough to tackle a wide range of subjects, they can't find a convenient pigeonhole for him. Any standard of judgment that elevates Aldrich and Fuller and Boetticher and Nick Ray above Lean and Wyler and Wilder and Stevens and Zinnemann has got to be a big put-on. Just compare their credits. Another thing you'll notice about the American directors considered auteurs is that they deal mainly in violence. As if this were somehow the highest expression of screen art, rather than the most facile. Naturally the French critics overstress the visual elements, because they don't dig English dialogue. That's why they admire Jerry

Lewis, and ignore a dozen better comedy directors who deal in verbal wit rather than mugging and pratfalls. Nobody is going to deny that Fellini and Bergman and Lubitsch and Ford and Hitchcock belong on any list of top directors. And everybody is entitled to have an occasional *Zabriskie Point.* But when they treat Hawks' *Man's Favorite Sport* as if it were the relic of some saint . . . I'm not speaking as a writer now, but as a moviegoer, somebody who has slept through the entire output of Joe Losey. But I'm glad to see that not all directors take it seriously. When an interviewer said to Don Siegel, "I understand that Jean-Luc Godard is a fan of yours," he said, "Well, I'm not a fan of Jean-Luc Godard."

FROUG: How does the collapse of the major studio system of filmmaking in Hollywood affect the writers' market today?

DIAMOND: Well, I think for the creator, whether writer, director or anybody else, it can only be for the good. And yet, let's not overlook that a lot of great pictures were made in this town under the old studio system, despite the abuses. They'll tell you what Hollywood did to Orson Welles, but his two best pictures were made right here.

FROUG: Are the independent production companies taking up the slack, or do you feel that we're going to move into CATV, cassettes, and so forth, to replace movies as a popular art form?

DIAMOND: Well, I don't know how many people are going to sit down and watch a movie on a cassette, unless it's a pornographic movie. No. I think some of the slack has been taken up. It seems to me anybody who can raise a few bucks now is going into the movie business, but that's fine. There can't be too many movies made. The ones who don't have anything to contribute are going to drop out sooner or later, and the survivors will become the new majors, in effect.

FROUG: Who do you think is ultimately responsible for the success or failure of a film?

DIAMOND: Well, you know, this is a collaborative medium.

I don't think you can pin that down . . . there are just too damned many elements. Sure, the director is highly visible, but I don't know of any director who's made a great picture out of a lousy script. On the other hand, I don't know of any director who can completely ruin a good script. I just don't think you can say any one element contributes to failure or success. I'd say more often it's the script than the director. After making *Look Back in Anger* and *A Taste of Honey* and *Tom Jones*, Tony Richardson turned out *The Loved One* and *Madame* and *Sailor From Gibraltar*. Now what happened to him? Did he suddenly lose his talent, or did he just have poor scripts? And is it even possible that he can't tell a poor script from a good one?

FROUG: Have you had any instances in working with the major stars where you feel the star's performance has added a dimension that was never conceived in the screenplay?

DIAMOND: Well, I don't know about a dimension that's never been conceived, but let's put it this way: when you write a script, you hope, I mean under the ideal circumstances, that you're gong to get back 100 percent of what you wrote. Usually you're lucky if you get back 75 or 85 percent. But on rare occasions there is an actor who's going to give you 110 or 120 percent, and those are the ones to be cherished by all writers.

FROUG: What actors do you recall who have given you that?

DIAMOND: Well, I will name you two offhand. Lemmon and Matthau . . . always. And certainly Audrey Hepburn.

FROUG: How will the present trend toward low-budget films affect the screenwriter? Particularly the veterans, such as yourself, who are used to commanding rather substantial fees for screenplays?

DIAMOND: Well, I'm all for cutting costs of pictures. But there's a difference between, say, an actor or a director taking a little money up front and a large percentage of the profits, and a writer doing the same thing. Simply because when the director or the actor is hired, they're pretty damn sure the picture is going to be made. When you sit down to write a script, you have no such assurance. A lot of things can happen. Maybe they can't cast it, maybe the budget is too high, so you wind up with no money and a big percentage of nothing. The writer is gambling a lot more than the director or the actor and I think that has to be taken into consideration. If you write a play that isn't produced, you at least still own it. But you put in six or nine months on an unproduced screenplay, and you have nothing to show for it.

FROUG: In adapting *Irma La Douce*, which was originally a musical, you and Billy eliminated the music. Why?

DIAMOND: Some of the critics pounced on us for that, for throwing the music out. But the music just wasn't very good, and we were not interested in doing a musical. We just liked the one simple plot idea of the guy who's both the pimp and the best customer of his girl. That idea appealed to us. We did not use the music except for underscoring. And yet, financially, it was the most successful comedy we ever had. It made a lot more money than *Some Like It Hot* or *The Apartment*.

FROUG: Do you and Billy ever work on ideas or screenplays that simply never pan out to your satisfaction?

DIAMOND: We've started a lot of things which never got off the ground simply because we didn't know how to solve them, or we just couldn't work them out to our satisfaction, and then abandon them. At the beginning of each assignment we start with about three different ideas and work on them alternately until one of them falls into place. Sometimes it's just Project X or Project Y, without knowing what we're going to do when we start.

FROUG: You mean, Billy will just say . . .

DIAMOND: "It's time to do another picture."

Buck Henry

1964 THE TROUBLEMAKER (*Joint Story and Screenplay*)

1967 THE GRADUATE (*Joint Screenplay*), Academy Nomination, Writers Guild Award

1968 CANDY (*Screenplay*)

1969 CATCH-22 (*Screenplay*)

1970 THE OWL AND THE PUSSYCAT (*Screenplay*)

1972 WHAT'S UP, DOC? (*Joint Screenplay*)

1973 THE DAY OF THE DOLPHIN (*Screenplay*)

1980 THE FIRST FAMILY (*Story and Screenplay*)

1984 PROTOCOL (*Screenplay*)

Someone once described Buck Henry as looking like a cross between Jack Lemmon and Wally Cox and I can't improve on that. He is a slight man, with a boyish, unlined face, appearing far younger than his forty-one years. His eyes, behind studious, horn-rimmed glasses, are inquisitive and just a little sad. He has sloping shoulders, and bone-thin arms and ankles.

He was wearing a green and white playground shirt, gym shoes and khaki slacks the day we met at Warner Brothers Studios in Burbank, and when he turned to lead me to his office I expected to see a fielder's glove stuffed in his rear pocked. He is Skippy come to life.

As I have noted elsewhere (see the David Giler introduction), writers' studio offices are traditionally barren, but Henry's has reached new peaks. No secretary, no typewriter, no scripts, no books, no paper, no pencils. A telephone, worn and shabby furniture (courtesy of the studio), and a couple of framed prints on the walls that surely arrived with Al Jolson.

"I'm never here, anyway," said Buck, dismissing the emptiness. But I suspect if Henry were there nothing would be changed.

As we talked, Buck's eyes were riveted to the tape recorder—as though it was a cobra poised to strike.

He was born in New York City, he admitted somewhat reluctantly, December 9, 1930. His parents are Paul and Ruth Taylor Zuckerman. His father is a stockbroker and a general in the Air Force Reserve. His mother was an actress in the silent movie era and appeared in Mack Sennett comedies. She lives in Palm Springs, California.

Buck squirmed in his seat. The biographical questions were making him nervous. I pressed on quickly.

He graduated from Dartmouth with a B.A. in English in 1952. He served two years in Army Air Maintenance as a helicopter mechanic. ("You put that in there and nobody will believe it.")

After service he lived on unemployment insurance and wrote stories and TV plays that nobody bought. "I refused to work. I sold Bibles for two weeks."

In 1959 he joined an off-Broadway improvisational theater group called The Premise.

"Are you married?" I asked.

"Really, must we get into all of that?" He was clearly in pain.

Henry is a man of mixtures. There is Buck Henry, the comic, who is a witty, wacky, and unpredictable clown. Then there is Buck Henry, the actor, who gave a first-rate performance as the star of Milos Forman's film, *Taking Off*, and did a creditable job in a secondary role for Mike Nichols in *Catch-22*.

Finally, and according to Henry, foremost is Buck Henry, the screenwriter, whose film adaptations of *The Graduate*, *Catch-22*, and *The Owl and the Pussycat* have placed him among the most sought-after (and highest paid) writers in Hollywood.

If Buck Henry's penchant for privacy sometimes pushes him into near panic, his openness and willingness to talk about the craft and/or art of filmwriting is rich and rewarding. While he is cautious in the extreme, it is not a result of indecision but rather the reflection of a sober, thoughtful man who weighs his opinions very carefully and wishes to be precisely represented. Our conversation was frequently punctuated with long pauses, while Buck decided exactly how he wanted to phrase his response, what his true feelings were, and how he might avoid seeming dogmatic or pretentious.

"I am Mr. Inarticulate," said this extraordinarily shy, modest, and articulate man.

I was not surprised, therefore, that following his reading of the transcript of our interview, he asked to see it again after I had edited it. There followed almost a month of telephone calls back and forth between us as Henry agonized over whether he had been too harsh on a critic (Sarris), whether he should have said more positive things about other filmmakers, whether he should have amplified some answers and revised others. He asked for additional time to rewrite and add new material.

The weeks passed as he commuted back and forth to New York, appearing in town suddenly and disappearing just as abruptly a few days later, amid apologies for holding me up. We communicated through Buck's business partner's secretary; he would leave no phone number or even addresses for himself.

One day I asked the secretary (by now we had become telephone friends) if there wasn't some way I could get whatever notes or changes Buck had in mind. My deadline was getting close.

"I'll do my best," she said. "I really don't know where he is. Maybe Palm Springs."

Late one night Buck called.

"I've got to go to New York in the morning," he said. "I'm sorry to hang you up, really. But I'll be back soon."

"When?" I asked.

A long pause.

"I don't know."

"Can I get your changes?"

"I haven't had a chance to do them. I'll call you."

"When?"

"I don't know. You see, I don't know where I'll be."

"My friend," I said, "you are a very elusive man."

"Yes," said Buck, with a deep sigh, "I am, I really am. I guess I just have to escape."

McWATT'S VOICE
(filtered; yelling)
Help him. Help him.

YOSSARIAN
(into mike; yelling)
Help who?

McWATT'S VOICE
(filtered; yelling)
Help the bombardier.

YOSSARIAN
(into mike; yelling)
_I'm_ the bombardier. I'm all right.

McWATT'S VOICE
(filtered; yelling)
Then help him. Help _him_.

Yossarian starts to look behind him, back into the stomach of the plane.

INT. HOSPITAL TRUCK - DAY

The truck starts to move forward. Yossarian's eyes open.

YOSSARIAN
Snowden.

MEDIC ONE
What'd he say?

YOSSARIAN
Snowden.

MEDIC TWO
He said - Snowden.

MEDIC ONE
Snowden's dead.

Yossarian closes his eyes.

YOSSARIAN
Snowden?

MEDIC TWO
Why is he talking to a dead man?

MEDIC ONE
He's Captain Yossarian.

(CONTINUED)

FROUG: What are you this week, an actor or a writer?

HENRY: I'm in between everything this week. I'm never really an actor, I'm just a writer that sometimes somebody hires as an actor.

FROUG: But you started as an actor?

HENRY: Well, true. Yes.

FROUG: With The Premise. And were you also with Second City?

HENRY: Yes.

FROUG: Did that influence you in terms of becoming a writer—the fact that you were really inventing your own material, so to speak?

HENRY: No. Everyone in the group wrote the material as we went along. And refined it. And shaped it. I was writing before that. I just wasn't selling anything. I was writing television plays that I couldn't sell, and one-act plays that I couldn't sell, and short stories that I couldn't sell.

FROUG: But the experience was improvisational theater. Did that reshape your thoughts toward writing?

HENRY: No. It just sort of redirected them into an area of the medium that I hadn't thought of, which was variety television. I was hired from The Premise to work for Steve Allen, which is something I had wanted to do. That is, Steve Allen was the only person in television that I wanted to write for. And, fortunately, around that time he was setting up a new show. It wasn't a particularly happy experience for me but I learned a lot, really, about jokes. About comedy in its most basic sense. I worked with a guy by the name of Stan Burns who is, I think, one of the funniest men in the world. Stan had worked for Steve for a long time. And watching him and listening to him, and watching the way his alleged mind worked taught me a lot.

FROUG: Then you were learning to deal with structured material?

HENRY: Well, oddly enough, the idea of live actors constructing scenes on the spot has a lot more to do with structure than it appears. A lot of it is a game, a lot of it is strategy, but it has a great deal to do with structure, much more so in The Premise, than, say, in Second City, because some of our rules had to do with keeping things relatively short, going for punch lines, trying to make sure that the scene entertained. Second City would go for twenty- or thirty-minute improvised scenes, where they wouldn't really try to build to anything until the characters were firmly entrenched. What we tried to do was to create characters immediately, and to shape the scene so rapidly that we could get a playlet in five to ten minutes, which involves both the specific skills of improvisation, like accents, and invisible props, and also the tricks about scenes that you learn after a while, patterns that you impose on scenes that seem to come naturally out of beginnings so that the actors begin instinctively to know what kind of end they are working toward.

FROUG: Did you work toward a set punch line?

HENRY: Never purposely, no. You do learn tricks that take you in certain directions, particularly when you get stuck. For instance, if we were in deep trouble in a scene, sometimes you could find an area for the scene to go by transference. One character becoming the other character, or a character turning into something, like a tree or a dog or a prop. It's very vague, and very hard to talk about. One never knew exactly where the scene would end, because there was always an actor off-stage working the lights, and it was for that actor to determine where the scene ended.

FROUG: By dimming the lights?

HENRY: By suddenly doing a blackout or a dimout. And over a period of time, naturally, one would develop a sort of sixth sense about where a scene was going and what the actors were working toward, what kind of an end. But we always tried to go for a punch line, for a big laugh. We were, I think, more comics than Second City was. They were a little more actors than we were.

FROUG: Having worked in The Premise did you then begin to sell material?

HENRY: No. I never sold anything freelance to anybody ever at all in my life at any time.

FROUG: In other words, Steve Allen hired you directly and you contributed material.

HENRY: I was hired as a writer-performer to do what I did in The Premise, which was create and perform material.

FROUG: Did you go from that to "That Was The Week That Was"?

HENRY: No. I did two seasons of "The Garry Moore Show" in between.

FROUG: Writing and acting?

HENRY: Just writing. And I wrote a film in the interim with Ted Flicker called *The Troublemaker*, which he directed. It had all The Premise people in it, except for George Segal, and some Second City people were in it also.

FROUG: How did it do?

HENRY: Awful. It busted the back of Janus Films, who financed it. It didn't cost very much.

FROUG: What was wrong with it?

HENRY: Well, here we were, a bunch of unknown performers in a film that was heavily satirical. Quite far out for its time. I don't mean that it was a precursor, but it was sort of in the style of a lot of films that have been made in the past five or six years. Like the underground comedies, like Bob Downey's films. And we opened at the Beekman, which was then not a good theater. Crowther absolutely loathed it. Judith Crist loved it. And I sort of disagree with both of them. She liked it for the wrong reasons and he hated it for the wrong reasons. And it never got a good running start.

FROUG: After *The Troublemaker,* where did you go as a writer?

HENRY: I was still working for Garry Moore and then after those two seasons I went to work for "That Was The Week That Was" for a season and a half. I had worked on the pilot of it originally. I thought it was clumsy and rather bad. In fact, I may have even taken my name off it. Although I did write some material that was used on it. I've forgotten why I didn't like it, but I didn't. Although I loved the idea of it. And then Herb Sargent became the producer, and he and Leland Hayward hired me to write and perform, and that was a great last season. I loved it. It was the last live television there was. It was great fun to do. With all its problems and faults, it was, I thought, enormously rewarding.

FROUG: You were once quoted as saying that if you're writing for television, you're writing so that you can't offend anybody.

HENRY: Ideally, that's what they're looking for. Material that is inoffensive. Sometimes in the best liberal tradition, but really inoffensive. I mean, you can stump as *The Defenders,* say, did for years, for various perfectly reasonable causes. So reasonable that you really can't get into much trouble except with the most right-wing, hard-hatted weirdo. But, for the most part, if you're going for an audience of ten to twenty million or more per show, you try not to offend. Fortunately, less and less people are offended today, I think. The audience has gotten more sophisticated in a somewhat general sense. They have gotten more sophisticated to the extent that the medium in its electronic aspects has allowed people to do things they couldn't do ten years ago.

FROUG: In terms of technique they're sophisticated?

HENRY: In terms of technique enormously sophisticated. Oddly enough I think it comes by way of other things. I think "Laugh-In" is made possible more by sporting events than by any advance in the audience's concept of comedy. There's nothing really new in a comic sense on "Laugh-In" but their electronic technique is an inheritance from things that have been developed by television in other mediums, like public events and sports.

FROUG: In *Catch-22* you keep cutting back and forth to the dying gunner. Was that in the construction of the screenplay? Or was that unusual construction done in the cutting room?

HENRY: No, that's the way it was constructed in the script. And it really is Heller's construction, not mine. I mean I transmuted it to a certain extent. I switched events around and changed them and took things out and put things in, but it seems to me that had Heller written the screenplay, that's what he would have written. One does, in the novel, return to the dying Snowden, from time to time to time. It's the thread. Snowden is the correlative for all that dying and all that destruction and that's the way Heller uses him. It seems to me that it was built in. But *Catch-22* was shot as it was written.

FROUG: Were you happy with the film?

HENRY: Yes, I liked the film a lot.

FROUG: When did you and Mike Nichols first work together?

HENRY: On *The Graduate.*

FROUG: How did he happen to bring you into it?

HENRY: I was doing "Get Smart" out here and George Segal has been, since The Premise, a close friend of mine, and he was working in *Virginia Woolf.* We all used to spend a lot of time together. And they had a couple of scripts on *The Graduate* that they weren't satisfied with, and Mike sent me the book and asked me if I'd be interested. It was that simple.

FROUG: I had heard that Mike Nichols took *The Graduate* on the condition that he could bring you in as the writer.

HENRY: No. Larry Turman made a deal with Nichols to do *The Graduate* some years before it was done. I think a couple of years. Turman shopped it around. The studios weren't interested. Levine was interested. Then three writers wrote three scripts and then I came in on it. But, no, I was there long after it was set up. *Catch-22*, Mike and I did sort of as a package. About the time I started working on *The Graduate* we started talking about *Catch-22*. And then I started writing it toward the end of the shooting of *The Graduate*.

FROUG: When you were writing *Catch-22* you had a deal yet with a studio?

HENRY: Yeah. John Calley had bought it for Filmways from the previous owner, I don't remember who he was, and made the deal through Filmways at Paramount.

FROUG: Does it seem reasonable or fair for the film to be referred to as Mike Nichols' *Catch-22*, as opposed to Joseph Heller's *Catch-22*?

HENRY: Yeah. I think it's fair for a number of reasons. I mean, Joseph Heller's name is there, prominently. It's really a Mike Nichols film of Joseph Heller's *Catch-22*, which is the way, I think, the credits read. And that seems to me a fair description of what it is. Had it been Blake Edwards' film, or Sam Peckinpah's film, or Stanley Kubrick's film, etc., it would be a radically different film, in which case it would reflect the personality and the skills of whatever director had done it and it would be his film. I am subject to a certain amount of agreement with the auteur theory. Not quite as far as some critics take it, but I think it's consistent with what I think the esthetic of film is.

FROUG: In other words you feel that director apostrophed above the title is generally just, like Mike Nichols' *The Graduate*.

HENRY: Yeah. But one of the crude facts of the business is some directors are stars and that's part of what brings the audience in. Mike is a star. John Ford is a star. Stanley Kubrick is a star. There are a lot of stars among directors and it is certainly justified. In some cases it's not, but in some it is. And so part of that is the publicity, the promotion, the selling gambit. It's sort of up to the director whether he wants his name there or not. I know that the people who put money into a Mike Nichols film want it to say "A Mike Nichols Film" because he has proven that it means something. I don't know what I would do if I were the director. It's a matter of personal taste.

FROUG: In directing *Taking Off,* Milos Forman says that he didn't give the actors the complete script. He gave it to them page by page, or scene by scene. As the star of the picture did you ever see the screenplay?

HENRY: No, I never had anything to read. Ever.

FROUG: Is that an effective way for you to work as an actor?

HENRY: Oh, I think it's terrific. One, having been an improvisor, it's second nature. Some actors don't like it. But I think it's sensational and I think Forman's films are their own proof of the technique. He hates acting. I mean "acting," which is why he avoids, if he can, faces that are well-known; he likes for the audience to have no references, except what is happening there on the screen. He's only interested in behavior. It's interesting to go from someone like Nichols to someone like Forman because Nichols, too, is only interested in behavior, but he can't always get it because of the structure of some of his films. There is almost no behavior in *Catch-22,* which drove him crazy. The people don't behave because of the mood, because of the style, because there are so many events crammed into such a short space. His talents were stretched to their limit, I think, in finding areas for behavior. Because that's one of the things Mike does as well as any other director in the world. It's to get people to behave. But in a Forman film all you can do is behave because he constructs both the script and his system of shooting in such a way that nothing is important. Like life, the important things happen almost by accident, from moment to moment. And no one scene is the scene that says now I'm going to tell you what this is all about, I'm going to laugh, cry, or give a speech in such a way that everything is tied up in this one scene. His films are really an accumulation of every scene and every piece of behavior that happens. It's quite a different system.

FROUG: But he starts with a complete screenplay?

HENRY: He starts with a total screenplay, every single word. I know this secondhand, of course, because I, being an actor, never saw the script. But I know he'll come in with it completely rewritten on the page in his own illegible handwriting or completely rewritten in his mind. Or sometimes the actors will take him in a direction that doesn't exist on the written page.

FROUG: As an example, when you went looking for your daughter with a friend in *Taking Off* and you went into the bar and proceeded to get drunk, did you know when you started into the bar that you were going to drink too much? As the actor?

HENRY: I really don't remember.

FROUG: Did you know when you walked into the soda fountain and showed the lady the picture of your daughter and she showed you a picture of a girl that was sitting there—did you know what was going to happen as a consequence of that?

HENRY: I think in that case I did, because I think we did an entire piece from one side of the luncheonette so that there was a continuous master from the time I sat down and ordered coffee and showed her the picture until I saw the girl sitting there and went into the phone booth. So that whole hunk I knew about. But until the camera came around to the other kids, I don't think I knew about the Hells Angels. Unless there was a reason for me knowing what was going to happen, he wouldn't tell it to me. Like until I saw the finished film I didn't know what the hell I was doing watching Lynn come out of the bathroom and do that weird dance. I had no idea what that was about. I wasn't around the day they shot that and I hadn't read the script. And I didn't want to ask. I didn't particularly want to know.

FROUG: As a director, working off of your own screenplay, would you follow that system?

HENRY: Possibly. I really don't know. As a writer, I think in terms of the words meaning a great deal and the right word being at the end of a sentence and the rhythm of the sentence going somewhere and leading to something. On the other hand I am fond of improvisation. When it works it's sensational. There may be a way to mix the two things. I think Cassavetes mixes them with enormous success. I think Pakula mixed the two things in *Klute* where it looks to me as though Jane is improvising all her scenes with the psychiatrist and sometimes doing a little improvisation in the other scenes, but they are definitely scripted.

FROUG: Those scenes are different.

HENRY: They're different. She does them both sensationally, but there's a slight difference of tone that you can detect. It's a difficult mix. There are foreign directors who do it, but since I don't understand their language I can't really tell how well they do it. It looks terrific in the hands of people like Godard and men like what's his name who did *The Fiancés* and *Il Posto.* And some of the young Englishmen are using it a lot. That extraordinary film called *Kes* by that English guy. Did you see it?

FROUG: No.

HENRY: With the boy and the falcon? It didn't do well here but it's a remarkable job where he uses mostly real people. Wonderful picture. And it's terrific when it works. But a director really has to know where he's going.

FROUG: How do you think this mixture affects the screenwriter? When you're constructing a screenplay do you have in your mind that the actors may very well improvise around and above and beyond the material?

HENRY: It really depends on what kind of film it is. I don't think there's any law. I don't like actors screwing around with material that is positioned for a reason. I've never done a film that actors haven't found some things that are marvelous and have gone into the finished film, even if it's as small as the take in *The Graduate* where Dustin comes up with his own name. He's talking to the girl's father, and in the take that Mike picked, Murray Hamilton went blank on the name Benjamin and couldn't remember it, and he got to the end of the sentence and he just sort of stopped and Dustin said, "Benjamin." "Oh, yes. Benjamin." It's a wonderful moment. It wouldn't have occurred to me to write it, and had I thought of it, or had an actor come up with it, I would have said, no, it's abnormal. It doesn't sound right. But because it was that moment, and because Dustin is a terrific actor and Murray is, too, it was wonderful. There are other larger moments that work. Barbra Streisand and George Segal rehearsing in *Owl and the Pussycat* would, now and then, lead me into a direction that would cause me to rework a scene, or there are lines that George improvised and Barbra improvised that I put into the script. I just don't think there are any laws, nor do I think that the writer's area is sacrosanct in any way.

FROUG: In other words, you believe in a totally collaborative medium? The actor, the director, the writer?

HENRY: Ultimately, everyone's there to serve the director. That's the way I feel about it. If the director is a bad director, tough. It's too bad. But that's what everybody's hired for: to ultimately inform as best they can whatever vision the director has of the material. And whether it's the kind of technician that exists today that shoots the script page by page as it's written, and sticks as closely as he can to it, or whether it's a guy like Altman who, from what I've heard, goes off in ninety-two different directions, it's their vision. And it may sometimes hurt the screenwriter's feelings, because his material is disappearing as he saw it, but that's the way it goes. It's par for the course. It's the director's ultimate responsibility to see that the film is a good one. And he's got to do it the way he sees it.

FROUG: In *The Graduate* where the businessman whispers

in Dustin Hoffman's ear, "plastics," which has almost become the metaphor for our whole society, that was in the screenplay, I presume?

HENRY: Yes.

FROUG: There is a case, it seems to me, where the director must be locked into what is essential.

HENRY: The thing is with Nichols, because we're very close friends and because we think very much alike about certain things, I can write stuff like that and know that he knows exactly what I mean. I mean there are minor words in that scene, like Dustin comes down the stairs and somebody says how proud they are, and one of the ladies says, "Proud, proud, proud, proud," which I wrote. Proud. Proud. Proud. Proud. Proud. And I knew that the way I heard it, that's the way Mike would have the actor play it. It's not much of a line to write. But when it's said right it works. The same with "plastics." It's funny too, because I worried about "plastics" a long time, and I tried to find a word to replace "plastics" because I thought plastics was old-fashioned, and I wanted to find a word that conjured up transistors and something that had a more contemporary mechanical sound to it. But ultimately I couldn't think of anything better than plastics. I couldn't find a word that sounded as good. It's a dumb word . . . plas-tics.

FROUG: When you first went to work with Nichols on *The Graduate*, did you work jointly on the development of the screenplay or did you go off and write and give him a draft?

HENRY: I wrote a draft, then we talked, then I wrote another draft and we talked some more and then we both worked on the final version very closely. We really collaborated on the final draft.

FROUG: How far was the final draft from the first draft?

HENRY: Well, it was much, much shorter and a good deal closer to the book than my original draft, which is what usually happens, I think.

FROUG: The same thing happened in *Catch-22*?

HENRY: The same thing happened in *Catch-22*, but we didn't have the kind of collaboration we had on *The Graduate*. I mean, I was sort of finished by the end of the second draft. And then it was really a matter of cutting.

FROUG: You mean you were each busy elsewhere? Mike was busy elsewhere?

HENRY: Yeah.

FROUG: There was much publicity about how high the costs were running on *Catch-22*. How do you feel the screenplay contributed to that?

HENRY: Well, when I write a screenplay I don't think about the cost. I don't think one should in a first draft. You think about the ideal film you'd like to see. If I write, as I did, "The squadron takes off," and the shots that go with that, I can't sit there and say, Jesus, it's going to cost $250,000 for this shot. And of course, there are ways to do it more expensively or more cheaply. There are ways where you can take two planes and make it look like a squadron. You can shoot it in Malibu instead of going off someplace. It won't be as good but you can do it. The bombing of the field could have been done with a certain amount of fakery. It could have been done with some slides and some projection and other things, but it wouldn't look like it does. I was never asked to chop anything out or to cut anything down for cost. As I remember it, Marty Ransohoff originally budgeted the film, really off the top of this head. I don't mean this against Marty—he had nothing to go on, he didn't have a script, he didn't have anything, so his original deal was like $3.5, $4 million. When the first draft of the screenplay was written, it was apparent that that budget was a factitious one at best, so that one was sort of cancelled until it was worked out. Then the budget was $13, $13.5 million. The film ultimately came to around $15.5 to $16 million, which is not a bad overage for that expensive a film, and nothing near the $22 million that *New York* magazine and others keep insisting that it cost. I suppose that's to give them a good esthetic, that *Catch-22* should cost $22 million, but it didn't. In spite of the fact that they like to think it did.

FROUG: Why do you think they like to persist in that story?

HENRY: It's part of the hatchet. Part of the axe that's waiting for some people. It's a weapon to use against celebrities.

FROUG: Maybe it's part envy, maybe partly that Nichols deserted New York for Hollywood, which is probably the worst thing a New York director can do.

HENRY: Well, of course, these were film critics, folks who call themselves film critics, who were doing the complaining. And they should be, one would think, on the side of film. But there's sort of an endless cycle of resentment and glorification that goes with the relationship between critics and filmmakers since filmmaking is *everybody's* avocation.

FROUG: Are there any critics you look to for valid criticism of your work?

HENRY: I have not gotten very many good reviews in my life, for anything. No. Very few. So my personal relationship with the critics is not a completely salubrious one. I don't thrill to their names. I think Pauline Kael writes better than the others, although I disagree with her violently about many, many things. She certainly never said anything nice about me, and I have no personal friendship for her, but she writes more interestingly about films than the others, that's all. Sarris, whom I deplore, because he lies and he mixes the worst kind of gossip and scandal junk with his critiques, I think has taken film criticism into some interesting paths with the auteur theory which he carries to absurd lengths. I could show him ten films and he wouldn't know who directed them. But from time to time he writes interestingly about pictures. There are a few of them who really seem to like films and a great many of them who just seem to be sort of hatchet men. Strangely enough—I say strangely because it's unfashionable to say so—I think Canby writes well about films from time to time. Mainly I say that because he will take a clearly unpopular position about a film that comes out which is getting chopped to pieces by everybody else. And in the long view I think he's more right than wrong. He has had some notions about things I've worked on that are not exactly friendly, and he also has that thing about damning with faint praise which is harmful. But I think he writes honestly. I think Kauffmann, who has never said a good word about me as a writer, writes seriously about pictures.

FROUG: Aside from the cost factor, why do you think the critics attacked *Catch-22*?

HENRY: Well, they were attacking it before it was made. There's no way I think someone from the inside of a picture can adequately defend it, nor should they try to defend it. I mean you do the best you can. You're not out to create a flop or a piece of junk, although there are many films in both categories, but you spend so much time on a picture that you do lose sight of what it is from the outside. There's no way to objectify it, although you can look back on a film. I've been involved with films that I knew were bad while they were being made. There's one called *Candy* that I knew I was in trouble with, while it was going on.

FROUG: What happened with *Candy*?

HENRY: Everything was wrong with it. It was shot in Italy. It had a Swedish actress as the all-American girl. As *Candy*. It had a lot of foreign actors who had no concept of what the dialogue meant. I was writing the script as we were shooting, which is a terrible way to work. The director was French. He had no help on the production end, and he really needed it because it was a very heavy production. Actors were coming in and leaving every couple of weeks. I think some of them did remarkably good jobs under the circumstances. It was very expensive and the machinery of it was huge and cumbersome. Moves were made from Italy to the United States, New York to Hollywood, there was never any overall concept. I never had time to sit down with the director and say, "Let's decide what this is about," and everyone was sort of going off in nine different directions. There never was a beginning or an end to the film. It happens.

FROUG: Isn't it possible that the subject matter itself hinged so much on absurd and hilarious vulgarity and the attacking of the whole puritan ethic that you really couldn't show what was the essence of the book's humor?

HENRY: Well, a lot of it couldn't be shown at the time.

FROUG: With today's total lack of censorship in film, would it have made a difference?

HENRY: Probably not, given the same circumstances of production. The mix wasn't right. The wrong people were working together at the wrong time and the wrong place. *Candy* certainly can be made into a good film. Anything can be with the right people doing it, but it was just one of those things. Another bad movie.

FROUG: When you're at work, what are your writing habits? Do you have a discipline about your writing?

HENRY: No. I'm a deadline writer. Unfortunately, I fool around, make a couple of notes and think about things, and finally when the pressure gets really rough and somebody begins to yell at me, I start typing.

FROUG: Do you work out a step outline before you begin a job?

HENRY: Only with *Catch-22* did I do that, because I had to know where I was going. I couldn't improvise. It was too complicated. Once I had set the structure in my mind I had to know which sections fit into which other sections, or I would have gone berserk trying to fit the pieces together. But I don't know. The habits of television which are good on the one hand, in that you write every day, bad on the other hand, in respect to the fact that you are sort of forced to compromise with the time problem. That mix probably has created whatever habits, or nonhabits, that I have. But I do the work under pressure, I guess. And I'm also very easily distracted. There's too many things, too many movies I like to see. If I'm in New York, forget it. It's almost impossible. Which is where I like to live. But there are 900 films to see and a couple dozen Off Broadway plays, and thirty-two museums and galleries to wander through. I have a deep, deep envy of the drive and the concentration that is possessed by some men like Doc Simon, who just goes and sits at that damn thing and forces himself to do it. Maybe he doesn't have to force himself to do it, I don't know. Day after day after day and the material piles up and it's an invaluable asset and I don't have it. I wish I did.

FROUG: How long do you spend writing a first draft, on an average?

HENRY: It depends on the project. The thing I just wrote, *What's Up, Doc?*, I did the whole thing in three weeks. First, second and third.

FROUG: Drafts?

HENRY: Yeah. But really it's a first draft, cut and slightly juggled. I also had a story that already existed to work with, which helped, although I changed the story radically. In my mind I sort of like to think that the first draft is going to be pretty near the final, except it's going to be much longer.

FROUG: How long?

HENRY: Well, my scripts usually come in about a half to twice as long as they should be. The first draft on *Catch-22* was 265 pages long, something like that, which would have taken a good six hours of movie time. It would have been a little excessive, I suppose.

FROUG: How many pages was the final draft?

HENRY: About 160, 165.

FROUG: Does your procedure differ when you're working from a play, like *The Owl and the Pussycat*?

HENRY: I do the same thing on all of them, including *Catch-22*, which is I read the original material a lot of times, until I sort of know it by heart or it's in me somewhere, and then I don't look at it again until I'm through writing. Then

I go back and pick up the pieces that I missed, or dialogue or scenes I've forgotten and feel I should include. But I can't work with the book open. That's too peculiar. Ultimately your voice and his voice interfere with each other. Although ideally an adapter should be doing that, should attempt to find the tone of the writer whose original material it is. I mean, in the case of *Catch-22* I'm trying to do it as I think Heller would do it. In the case of *The Graduate* as Charles Webb would have done it. I know there are disagreements, of course. There always are and always will be between the original author and the adapter. It's perfectly normal.

FROUG: You are an inveterate moviegoer. Do you think that seeing a lot of films is a good background for the writer?

HENRY: I think it's invaluable. For an actor or a writer or a director. There's an awful lot of people who succumb to certain contemporary films because they are illiterate in a film sense. Some films become immensely popular simply because the young audience doesn't know that it has been done twenty times before—better. There are great films, going all the way back to the start of film history, and it's just a shame that they can't be seen. It's not the audience's fault. Unless you live in New York, you can't see them; there's no place you can do it. But for someone who is seriously interested in films I can't imagine not wanting to see as many as he could see.

FROUG: How about reading? Is a literary background helpful, do you think?

HENRY: Yeah. I do. Ultimately filmmaking is about life. And there is as much—I know this is contrary to the concepts of the present generation—but there is as much to learn about life in literature, and in a slightly different sense, as there is in life. And that's what those guys have done. They've distilled experience and developed an esthetic to deal with it. All the rules that apply to the creation of any kind of artistic product or the rules that are broken in the creation of it are as applicable to films as they are to books, paintings, drama, sculpture, or anything else.

FROUG: Your work as an actor was enormously helpful, obviously, to you as a writer. Is acting especially helpful to young filmmakers, do you think?

HENRY: Certainly, if you look over the list of directors that one thinks are great directors, you'll find as many actors among them as many non-actors. I can imagine putting Fellini into almost any film. I can't imagine putting Antonioni into a character role. But they're both great directors. There are an awful lot of good directors who are terrible actors. But if you are going to become a director or a writer, the experience of acting gives you that much more technical information to go on.

FROUG: It worked for you, as an actor.

HENRY: It worked for me accidentally. I wanted to be a writer long before I wanted to be an actor. And acting was always sort of a pleasant afterthought. I wanted to act, but it could never have, nor ever will, take the place of writing.

FROUG: You created and were head writer of one of the most successful comedies in television, "Get Smart." It lasted how many years?

HENRY: Five.

FROUG: What do you feel was the major difference for you in writing "Get Smart" as opposed to, say, *The Owl and the Pussycat*?

HENRY: Well, "Get Smart" is a cartoon. And *The Owl and the Pussycat* is a situation comedy with, hopefully, somewhat real people behaving in an outlandish but somewhat real way. It works sort of from character. Whereas "Get Smart" is really straight out satire, in some cases parody, and is much more hard-edged and cartoony. I tried to do another one called "Captain Nice" but it was the wrong time and the wrong place. And I'll try and do another one someday soon, too, because I like the tone. I think it's great for television. "Get Smart" was successful because it was funny in that way, and Don Adams was perfect for it, and was the motor that made it run. The supporting cast was terrific. My theory about it, which is a trivial theory at best, is that it combined visual—slapstick comedy for the kids, the younger kids—with, at times, a rather sophisticated verbal satire for adults. And the combination sort of captured two different audiences. It was a theory after the fact. We wrote it as we laughed at it.

FROUG: How long did you stay on it? How long did you write it?

HENRY: I stayed with it two seasons as story editor and wrote a number of them. I don't remember how many. And worked on all of them.

FROUG: How far do you go as a screenwriter in designing the visuals for your films? Do you write in master scenes? Or do you put in camera angles?

HENRY: I put in as few camera angles as my conscience allows me. Because it's mostly a lot of junk anyway that nobody pays any attention to, and I almost never describe anything because, unless it's some peculiar prop you've invented where you really need a description, there's no point in it. All that garbage about the camera is very boring to read. And ultimately when you get on a set, the set is constructed in such a way that the director may be forced, in order to follow the action, to put a lens on that can't possibly accommodate the junk that you've written to describe the way you think the scene is to be shot. You really cannot decide until you're inside that room, or till you're out on that street, what it's going to look like. So all of it is mostly filling time until you can think of the dialogue. Also it holds true, it seems to me, for character descriptions, which in most scripts, not so much anymore, are terribly overwritten. You know, he comes down the stairway, pausing a third of the way down, a look crossing his face to indicate that he knows that in the other room someone is dying. I mean this stuff isn't playable most of the time, and if it is the director is going to work it out with the actors, and have a certain amount of confidence in them. But more times than not the description gets in the way of what you're trying to write about in the script. Also, it's like the guys who do the story board—cartoons that are drawn, shot by shot, to indicate various angles the scene can be shot from—which a great many directors use, and which can be an invaluable aid for purposes of reference. And if a good artist makes the story board, they're a great help. But ultimately you have got to look through that camera and see what that camera sees before you can decide that that's an angle that's going to work.

FROUG: Which of your screenplays do you feel was the most successful?

HENRY: I can't talk about the screenplays. Only films.

FROUG: Why do you separate the two?

HENRY: Because they're radically different. The step between a screenplay and a film is just a whole, gigantic step. There are certain directors whom one can name who will always make a junky film no matter how good or bad the screenplay is, and there are certain directors who will always improve the screenplay, I think, whose vision is stronger than the screenplay. I mean, it doesn't seem to me that there's any point, for instance, in discussing the screenplay to an Altman film, because he clearly changes things so radically. Only he can say what his relationship to the screenplay is. Then there are directors, good directors, who seemingly slavishly follow a screenplay, but even then there are so many people who get in between the screenplay and the completed film. I mean, I never read the script, but I assume that *Casablanca* is written that way. Nevertheless, the step between that and the final editing of who is looking where, of when you go to a guy's face—and there's no way of seeing what he's seeing in that close-up until you hit the next shot. He could be looking at (you know the old Eisenstein trick) a bowl of food, a naked lady, or a dying child and the face still works. Same face every time. That's that magic process that goes on in the editing room. And it has very little to do with the script. The script is a point of departure, no matter how closely or how loosely it's followed, I think.

FROUG: In translating a novel or a play into visual terms, what is the chief problem you find?

HENRY: Well, you've got to know what you think you're writing about. I mean what the damn thing is about, first of all. In some cases you never quite decide and then you get in trouble. As a professional adapter, I steal as much as I can from the source. That's what I'm there for. The problem is to figure out the structure, clearly. But sometimes figuring out the structure varies radically from one job to another. I mean on *Catch-22* I knew the structure before I started typing because I made the structure up first and wrote it down on half a million index cards.

FROUG: Do you use the index card system?

HENRY: Just on that. On *The Owl and the Pussycat* I started and improvised from the very first page and just let it go where it went. It's weird. There's a great interview that every student should read, an interview in *Paris Review* of Pinter.

FROUG: The "Writers at Work" series.

HENRY: Oh, it's a terrific interview. And I love what he says, because it's so true, that thing about how he went crazy once because a character opened a door and came into the room and he didn't know who the goddamned character was and it took him something like three weeks to get the guy out of the scene. It's a great way to write, of course, if you're Pinter. It's a great way to write because he's a superb writer. If you can let the characters take over instead of having to force them around. If you really know who they are. If it's that kind of film and you're improvising freely enough, they can control the situation through you. It's like being a medium. And ultimately you decide whether you're doing the right or the wrong thing.

FROUG: When you're constructing a screenplay, do you consciously have a first-act curtain, a second-act curtain, kind of structure in mind? A beginning, a middle, and end? You talked earlier of a beginning and end. What about the middle? So many films fall apart because they have no middle.

HENRY: Yeah. I don't know what the middle is. Whether it's really the second act in the theatrical sense, or whether it's just whether you find those changes in gear, which I'm often accused of not finding. When you relax the pace, move back into second gear, give them a breath. If it's just a series of climaxes you can go crazy. You do have to find some way to moderate the tempo so that it's not all one crescendo, or one diminuendo. There have to be changes of pace to give the audience time to stop and start again. But then I don't know. I see films that I love and it's very hard to apply any particular rule to them, because the really good guys work out of inspiration. The really good directors, who in my mind I always think of being primarily responsible for the material, work out of a kind of genius that doesn't think in terms of any rules. I know how Nichols thinks because obviously I've been close to him. I don't know how Fellini does it from day to day. I don't know how he preserves that peculiar style he has. The impetus of the film, it's really a mystery. You can sort of see how Bergman does it. You can kind of see how Kubrick does it, or Antonioni even, but some of them are really strange. The really good ones, all of those I've named, have sort of private notions and ways of seeing things that draw them in directions other folks just don't have at their disposal. I don't know how writers work because I rarely ever talk about the specifics with other writers. We talk about finished film. And then it's just not talking about screenwriting. It's really talking about film-making and it's a different process. The reason I think the Writers Guild is a mass of neuroses is because they know, all of us know in the back of our minds, that you can deliver a mass of film shot at random to a brilliant director and he's going to make something out of it, make something very interesting out of it. Never needing a writer. So, that puts us at a slight disadvantage. Because it doesn't work the other way around. Of course, I may change my mind tomorrow. There's that, too. The process is almost impossible to talk about. As it is and as it should be. I don't like to use the word "artists" a lot. I mean, I think of artists really as guys who paint pictures. If you read interviews with the great ones, the great contemporary artists anyway, you cannot really make head or tail out of what they say. If they're actually talking about the process of creation. It doesn't make any more sense than Einstein trying to explain how he thought of the theory of general relativity. Those moments can't be articulated. That's a gift from someplace else. So the best you can get is a kind of metaphor for it.

David Giler

1967	TOGETHER* *(Story and Screenplay)*
1968	DIVIDED WE STAND* *(Story and Screenplay)*
1969	MYRA BRECKINRIDGE *(Joint Screenplay)*
1970	RESIST* *(Story and Screenplay)* CASUALTIES OF WAR* *(Screenplay)*
1971	THE SKIN GAME *(Rewrite-uncredited)*
1972	THE POSTMAN ALWAYS RINGS TWICE *(Screenplay)*
1974	THE PARALLAX VIEW *(Joint Screenplay)*
1975	THE BLACK BIRD *(Screenplay)*
1976	FUN WITH DICK AND JANE *(Joint Screenplay)*
1981	SOUTHERN COMFORT *(Joint Story and Screenplay)*
1985	THE MONEY PIT *(Story and Screenplay)*
1986	ALIENS *(Joint Story)*

*Unproduced

Bernie Giler, prolific television and sometimes moviewriter (*Tarzan's Greatest Adventure, Tarzan's Three Challenges, Gunfight in Abilene*) was a rare character on the Hollywood scene, a man who was comfortable with both his ability and his limitations. Outgoing, always affable, often laughing, Bernie's good humor was infectious. During the period we worked together on a "Playhouse 90" film I was producing in 1956, he would brag to me about his son, David, who, at 13, could beat him at chess and, according to his father, would someday be a "terrific writer." "Much better than me," said Bernie.

David Giler is now twenty-eight and a successful screenwriter. Like his father he doesn't take much of what goes on in the movie milieu very seriously. He's too sophisticated to be awed by kings, in a world where the crown changes hands every ten minutes.

David was born July 23, 1943, in New York City. When he was five his father moved the family to Los Angeles. (David has two younger sisters.) Bernie was in the vanguard of the mass migration of writers from New York to Hollywood after World War II.

David attended a variety of grammar schools and Hollywood High School, that unique temple of learning where students think of becoming actors in much the same way students in other communities think of becoming doctors and lawyers. David, a bright, normal kid, decided to become an actor. Bernie, a practical, normal father, reacted accordingly: "My son an actor! My God!" he once said to me.

David attended San Francisco State College for one year, San Fernando Valley State for two years, and the University of Uppsala, just outside Stockholm.

But simultaneously, Bernie was giving his son another kind of education. He was tutoring David in "the fine art of TV writing." One day I asked Bernie how his son was doing. "The kid's coming along great," he said. "His stuff is better than anything I've ever done."

Bernie's appraisal was essentially accurate. In a town not noted for its generosity, David Giler, it is widely believed, is a talented young man who will one day join the top rank of screenwriters.

I saw Bernie at lunch shortly before he died in 1967. Though he knew, as we all knew, that he had terminal cancer, his good disposition was intact. Because it would please him, I inquired about David. Bernie's eyes lit up. "The kid's terrific. After all, look who he had for a father." You might say Bernie Giler died laughing.

David and I arranged to meet at his office in the Writers Building at Warner Brothers studio in Burbank (he has since moved to MGM), an old but comfortable two-story bastardized Spanish remnant of the era of Bogart, Cagney, Bette Davis, et al.

At Warners the tired buildings and seedy furnishings are offset by magnificent trees, manicured lawns, and gardens outside the windows. If the San Fernando Valley is Los Angeles' answer to the Mojave Desert, at least such studios as Disney and Warners maintain a facade of lush beauty. (Universal, a Valley studio with a no-nonsense operation, blacktops or cements everything in sight except the bungalows of the high-salaried elite.)

But regardless of the name over the studio gate, seasoned writers learn to keep their offices bare. When you report for an assignment, the rule of thumb is bring only what you can stuff in one briefcase. You may be leaving soon.

David Giler is tall, lean (six foot one, one hundred sixty pounds), and handsome. He wears large metal-framed glasses which don't hide laughing brown eyes. He is brash, direct, and sure of himself, and he seems to have put his life into an amiable perspective. His self-mocking arrogance is rich with humor of the absurd. Our interview was often punctuated with uproarious laughter.

As I was about to leave I asked him what his hobbies were. The question perplexed him.

"What are my hobbies? I haven't even thought about that. I guess I don't have any. I go to the movies."

David is married to actress Nancy Kwan, who has an eight-year-old son by her former marriage. His name is Bernie.

"Isn't that terrific!" says David, laughing, like his father.

in girlish anticipation, Leticia empties the drink on Rusty's face. Rusty chuckles, and rips off her dress revealing the magnificent slip underneath. He then silences her by grabbing her and kissing her brutally. The sound of cigarette burning through silk to flesh is HEARD. Leticia howls with pain and delight, then nails him with a right to the midsection followed by a clean left to the jaw, sending him over coffee table and on to the floor between two barrel chairs.

FILM CLIPS - WESTERN BAR FIGHT

Showing similar action from the best bar fight between two Western stars that 20th ever made.

BACK TO SCENE

In time to see Leticia sailing over the couch, the result of a blow from Rusty who pursues this advantage by leaping over the couch after her. Neither is visible behind the couch. We HEAR lascivious laughter from both of them.

FILM CLIP - WESTERN BAR FIGHT

Hopefully from another movie. At any rate, heavy action; furniture broken over heads, bodies sailing through windows, etc.

BACK TO SCENE

Screams, cackling, ripping, tearing, and heavy breathing are heard from behind the couch. We SEE Leticia's hand reach out and grab a heavy vase off an end table. After the sound of glass shattered over skull, Leticia emerges from behind the couch looking ravaged and in high good humour. She runs for the stairs, making the second step before Rusty nails her with a flying tackle. He releases her to get up, and laughing coquettishly she kicks him in the face.

CUT TO:

EXT. BEACH

Myra, aided by a million violins, approaches the mournful Mary Ann. The two of them,

FROUG: David, did you start as a screenwriter, or did you work your way "up" through television?

GILER: Through television.

FROUG: What television shows did you write?

GILER: Well, the first one that I wrote was "The Gallant Men," a series at Warner Brothers. Actually, my father had the job. I was going to school in San Francisco and I got sick with mononucleosis in the middle of the term. I was lying on my back for six weeks. My father was quite busy with five or six TV assignments and I was just lying there. So he said, "Why don't you try this, and see how it comes out?" I wrote it and he liked it. (After he made some changes, he liked it better.) And he gave it to his producer and the producer liked it. Suddenly I had a television credit, and some money, and that was how I began.

FROUG: After "The Gallant Men" did you do more TV writing?

GILER: Yes. But I was more interested at that time in becoming an actor and eventually a director, and more interested in theater, really, than film or television. My father presented the fine art of writing for TV as a trade—rather like plumbing. As something which, once learned, I could always have to fall back on if I failed at everything else. Most people find that a strange sort of attitude, but I think it's a very good way.

FROUG: How long did you stick with television?

GILER: I wrote some other things for my father. Scenes here and there. Until one day I had an idea of my own, which became a "Kraft Suspense Theater." The first real lesson where I found out how you are deceived and rewritten and all the rest of that.

FROUG: How old were you then?

GILER: I was nineteen. I did some other television shows. I was not really very much interested, until I sold a pilot idea to MGM and they gave me an office at the studio. I had a terrific scam going in those days. I was still going to school. If I did one television show every six months, I could collect unemployment for the rest of the year. So then I could go to school. It worked out very well.

FROUG: Where were you going to school?

GILER: At that time I was going to San Fernando Valley State College. Eventually, I went to Sweden to the University of Uppsala. I was there for almost two years. When I came back I was broke, and I went to work on "The Girl from U.N.C.L.E." and "The Man from U.N.C.L.E.", and out of that experience I decided that I was really more interested in writing. I was really going to try and make it a career, and television was not the place to be. It was hopeless. There was just no hope.

FROUG: Why?

GILER: I haven't really formulated this idea very clearly, but it seemed to me that in television there was just no possibility of doing anything that was remotely interesting. Because of the sort of self-censorship of producers. All of them are former writers, or, in fact, are still writers. And they exercise a great deal of self-censorship on their shows, and probably justifiably, because the networks make such outrageous, such silly demands on them. But the ideal television show seems to be on a topical "relevant" subject, dealt with in the most shallow, blandest possible way. Something that will come out with proper conclusions, and all the rest of that. The way you look at television, it's very difficult to take it seriously.

FROUG: How did you make the break, having decided to leave the television field?

GILER: I had an idea for a movie and I was going to start to write it, and before I wrote it, I sold it to Raymond Stross. But it was a short-lived association between Stross and me. He financed the writing of the treatment, so I want to Canada and watched them shooting *The Fox.* Stross is a weird guy. Anyway, I later sold that same story to Jack Lemmon's company, Jalem.

FROUG: In other words, Raymond Stross didn't go forward with it, but paid for the treatment.

GILER: He had a reading period of one or two weeks before exercising the screenplay option. He didn't exercise it, so I sold it to Jalem.

FROUG: What was the title of it?

GILER: It was called *Together.* It was not for Jack Lemmon to do, himself. At that time his company was becoming a fairly large-scale independent company. They had just done *Cool Hand Luke.*

FROUG: What happened to it then?

GILER: Then I wrote the screenplay. It was not made. I was under contract to them. And I wrote another screenplay that was also not made.

FROUG: What was that screenplay called?

GILER: *Divided We Stand,* I think was the final title. Not mine. Mine, at the time, was called *Beatniks, Commies and Fruits.*

FROUG: Why wasn't it made?

GILER: Well, I don't know. It was difficult to find directors for both of those projects, actually.

FROUG: You mean they turned down the screenplays?

GILER: They were comedies, both of them, and there really does seem to be a genuine shortage of comedy directors. Particularly for these kind of comedies. The screenplay was meant to be very funny. It was a very broad piece, with a very serious underpinning. So for the serious director it wasn't serious enough, and for the comedy director there wasn't that much comedy. It sort of fell someplace in between. Which is an area I like to work in. And I have a great deal of difficulty getting those pictures made.

FROUG: Yet most writers say that all comedy must have its

basic roots in serious drama in order to work.

GILER: I think that's the absolute truth.

FROUG: How old were you when you sold your first film story to Raymond Stross?

GILER: Twenty-three.

FROUG: How much did you get for it?

GILER: From Stross I didn't get very much for the story, but for writing the screenplay for Jalem I think I got $15,000.

FROUG: So that was enough to keep you going and keep you away from the television trap?

GILER: Yeah. No expenses in those days.

FROUG: You were single then? Living alone?

GILER: My biggest expense was getting back to Sweden to register for school in the fall so I could maintain my student status and stay out of the Army.

FROUG: After the Jack Lemmon screenplays were written and unproduced, where did you go?

GILER: *Myra Breckinridge.*

FROUG: I have made the supreme sacrifice and have gone to see *Myra Breckinridge* in preparation for this interview.

GILER: I've actually seen *Myra Breckinridge* myself! *JESUS!*

FROUG: Tell me about it.

GILER: That was really a disaster. That's such a whole long and difficult story.

FROUG: Well, let's try to put it in some sort of perspective.

GILER: I must tell you this, to start off and give my own defense of *Myra Breckinridge.* I'm very proud of that script but it has nothing to do with what's on the screen whatsoever. Gore Vidal liked it a lot and he and I have become very good friends since then.

FROUG: I can give you another point of view that might be of interest to you. I know people who worked on the pre-production phase of the film. And every one of them told me that your original screenplay of *Myra Breckinridge* was absolutely marvelous.

GILER: Well, that's good.

FROUG: How did you get the job to begin with?

GILER: These two screenplays that were written for Jack Lemmon were liked enough so that I wasn't really having trouble getting jobs.

FROUG: They were being circulated around town by your agent?

GILER: Yeah.

FROUG: Was an agent helpful to you in the beginning as a young writer?

GILER: Yeah. My first agent was at Ashley Famous. That was terrific. Because I was about nineteen. I'd written a "Kraft Theater" which was very well received. It got a big full-page notice in the *Saturday Review*. I hated it. I thought it was terrible. Anyway, he took me to lunch at Scandia and said, "Well here you are, you're a young guy and you can go out there and make some serious money, and at the same time you can go to school." I said, "That sounds terrific." So I signed right up. Then I disgraced myself on my first interview so he would barely talk to me after that.

FROUG: What did you do?

GILER: I went on an interview for a TV series, "Mr. Novak."

FROUG: Which I used to produce. But apparently you came along after I left to produce "Twilight Zone."

GILER: Yeah. You weren't there. It was with Lou Morheim, the story editor. Well, I was about two years out of high school so it was perfect. Obviously they figured this was the right place for the kid to go. Just out of high school, send him right over there.

FROUG: A series about a high school teacher.

GILER: Exactly. So I told this story and they really liked it. But then they wanted to know what I thought about the show. I had only seen it once. The night before. I did a natural waffle. I said, well, interesting and all that. Then Morheim said, let me ask you just one question. I was not about to get seduced by this, but he kept asking. So finally I did criticize the show and we got into a big argument. Which ended, I think, in a rather embarrassing moment for him, because he decided to disprove something I'd said. He picked up a script and read from it, and read exactly what I'd said. It was a view of higher education. I said they tended to look at it as some vast insurance policy. He said absolutely not true and then read something where Mr. Novak was telling somebody that college was like a vast insurance policy. So I didn't hear from those guys again. Nor my agents at Ashley Famous. And then eventually I went to the William Morris office.

FROUG: Now, having circulated your two unproduced screenplays around, one came into the hands of Robert Fryer, the producer of *Myra Breckinridge.*

GILER: Both of them.

FROUG: He read them and decided to hire you.

GILER: Yeah. That was a pretty courageous move for Bobby, because at that time, of course, *Myra* was the hottest project in town. And Vidal had done a screenplay which had apparently not worked out. And the infamous Michael Sarne had also done a screenplay which was being handed around various places for people to appropriately chortle over. Neither of these were very good. Bobby, and Jim Cresson who works with Bobby, and I were talking about something else, and *Myra* sort of came up, and it is one of my favorite books. I'm an enormous admirer of Gore Vidal. So I read it and I liked the book very much and we talked about it. From that conversation came would I be interested? Would I be *interested*! Of course I'd be interested in working on the screenplay. This was not too long before production that they hired me. I'm told you could hear Richard Zanuck's voice echoing down the hall, *Who?*, when my name was mentioned. So, Sarne was told I was going to do a polish job on his screenplay. Bobby actually told me to write the whole thing over again. Which I did. Then everybody banded together, Bobby and Vidal and some other people, to try to get rid of the director, for the third time. And for whatever reasons Mr. Zanuck had, Sarne stayed on. The situation was openly hostile between the director and the producer, and me and the director, and everybody and the director.

FROUG: There was a great deal of publicity in the trade papers almost every day, and Sarne gave an interview which was one of the most incredible attacks on a producer in public print I've ever read. Because he did it by belittling Fryer.

GILER: Right.

FROUG: He said he was an innocuous man, that he was inoffensive. Something to that effect.

GILER: Exactly. Well, Sarne had all the power there.

FROUG: Because of Dick Zanuck?

GILER: Yeah. Fryer quit. Zanuck had made it impossible for Bobby to work, because there's only one thing you can do with a director. With a director either you fire him or he's in full control once the thing starts. So if you're not willing to fire him, there's nothing you can do. For example, Bobby wanted to shoot my script, Zanuck wanted to shoot an amalgam of both.

FROUG: Yours and Sarne's.

GILER: Which was a disaster. We tried to put that together and that really didn't work. Sarne thought it worked fine. He was pleased with that. He started shooting that, and then he started bringing some of his old pages from his former script on the set and shooting those. Obfuscating the script. Doing anything he could. I mean he had no real affinity for the material. I'm not talking about my script. I'm talking about the book and anything else. Not that my script and the movie had anything to do with it. That's why *Myra*, the movie, is so different.

FROUG: Did he ever express what he was after to you as the writer?

GILER: Yeah. He had some sort of an idea of doing a parody on Los Angeles, American vulgarity or something like that, which actually the book takes on pretty well, but does it in a much more subtle fashion than Sarne wanted to do it. Sarne didn't have any ideas of his own. I mean, he never did. He just had this giant, enormous ego.

FROUG: He wanted to be in total control?

GILER: Yeah. And he was allowed total control. He was in fact given it, which emasculated Fryer, made any writing that had to be done on the piece sort of worthless, and made it very difficult for the actors. Now Raquel Welch under the best of circumstances would have been tricky as Myra, but under those circumstances, it was impossible.

FROUG: Did the other actors complain about receiving a different script than they had read?

GILER: Oh, yeah. There were constant complaints. I mean it was such insanity, the whole thing. Not only because of Sarne, but because of what the actors wanted. Everybody was very nervous about the book, nervous about the taste-level involved and all of that. It was one of these situations where I felt like the lone defender. That's really the role I earmarked for myself. I really did like Vidal's book and my screenplay was very faithful to the book. It really could have made a marvelous movie. But I felt like all the people that were involved in it, except Bobby Fryer and Jim Cresson, were involved for all the wrong reasons. Because of its sensational elements.

FROUG: How did Mae West feel about the changes?

GILER: Well, Mae West never read the book. I don't think she ever read any of the scripts. She just wanted to deal in her own areas and make everything conform to that, which is the way she always worked. I mean, the pictures had always been hers. She'd written them. She told me with some pride that nobody had ever asked her to change a word on any of her screenplays. Well, that's of course because she wrote them for herself. Who was going to ask her to change it?

FROUG: According to the publicity, she wrote her own scenes, in effect.

GILER: Well, in effect, not. She wrote scenes that were sent to me, and later to Sarne, and they pretty much were never shot. A lot went on to show she was really writing her own scenes, but in fact she wasn't. Only lines here and there.

FROUG: A line such as she delivers to the tall, aspiring, young actor, "You're six feet, seven inches, eh? Never mind the six feet, let's talk about the seven inches." That sounded like pure Mae West.

GILER: That's absolutely her.

FROUG: Did Sarne have trouble with John Huston? Huston seemed to be playing a parody of himself.

GILER: Nobody could really figure it . . . everybody was waiting for the big explosion. But that never happened. I don't understand why. It was a simple take-the-money-and-run job, I guess, for Huston. Two or three days before we started shooting we were in Huston's suite at the Bel Air Hotel, and Raquel was on the phone to Zanuck about something. She was very upset when she got off the phone, started to cry, and all that stuff. Huston took her to comfort her and said, "Save your tears for something that's worth it." So he knew where it was right in the beginning. And then Sarne gave out an interview in which he said that Huston was really a shameless old hack and couldn't act worth shit, but that he was such a great fan of Sarne's that Sarne had chosen him to be in the movie. So we really thought that Huston was going to blow up then. And we were actively hoping that Sarne was really going to blow it and be thrown off.

FROUG: Sarne kept running over budget and over schedule, according to the trade papers, and Fox kept imposing new "absolute" deadlines by which time he was either to be finished shooting or the production would be shut down. Fox even put out news releases to that effect.

GILER: Right. And, at the same time, they kept saying to us, well, if he *really* falls behind we'll have to get rid of him. But they kept him right on. Vidal and Fryer offered to pay Sarne off, the first time, at his full salary, it wouldn't cost Fox a dime. Nope, they insisted on Sarne. Then Bobby got as far as offering to finance the shutdown of the picture while they got a new director, and they still wouldn't listen.

FROUG: What was Dick Zanuck's hangup with Sarne, do you know?

GILER: No one knows. One of the great mysteries.

FROUG: And young Zanuck's supposed to be a tough guy.

GILER: I think there's less there than meets the eye.

FROUG: Were the flashbacks to the old Hollywood movies in the original script?

GILER: Oh, sure. That's the one thing everybody agreed on, except Fox. They didn't like that idea because of the expense involved in the rights to the film clips. But as Vidal pointed out in one of his scripts, in a little postscript for those in management who had neither heard nor seen a movie before *Dr. Dolittle*, the film references were an integral part of a character "grown to be loved by millions."

FROUG: In what ways, specifically, do you think the film differed from what you had in mind?

GILER: I thought it should have been funny, for a start.

FROUG: It certainly wasn't. It was a bloody bore.

GILER: It was a bore from start to finish. I felt that it really should have been done rather classically. It should have been played like *Philadelphia Story*, for the most part. It does lay itself out rather neatly, in a classical structure, so that the outrageousness of it, played in a rather restrained manner, will come across in any event. And the more you play that down, instead of making it all outrageousness so that none of it means anything, then when it does become outrageous, it will really be outrageous. Also it wasn't about any of the things I thought it should be about.

FROUG: What was it about in the original screenplay? As opposed to Sarne's version? I couldn't find out what the movie was about.

GILER: I agree. I don't know what Sarne's movie was about at all. I have some idea what *Myra Breckinridge* was about. It had to do with the way *kitsch* becomes admired, great art, and the idea of free-floating sexuality. Basically the book deals with an awful lot of things. It's very complicated to talk about now, but Vidal's premise, in there and in a lot of other things, the thing he is concerned with and has been for a long time, before it was fashionable, was the idea of the overpopulation in the world and the changing of the idea of sexuality in order to deal with that problem on another level besides basic contraception, and all the rest of that. It's sort of a pan-sexuality. A freeing of the theater-of-the-mind sexuality. And Vidal's very much interested in that. And knows about it. *Myra Breckinridge* is a tragedy. Basically, on one level the story is about a man who grows up with these great visions of heroes, masculine heroes, and so on, and is oppressed by them, crushed by them in a certain way. He grows up with the great heroes of his youth, which are movie heroes, and you get these oppressive, crushing women like Bette Davis, Dietrich and all those, and at the same time the all-American tough guy, like Wayne and Cooper and Cagney, Bogart and all the rest of those. And the character then is really in love with these men, or emulating them or worshipping them, and at the same time wanting to destroy them. Then he becomes all-conquering Myra Breckinridge. And that's when the book began. When Myra Breckinridge comes to wreak revenge. It's just a sensational book and it was one of the great wastes of material. It should have been an enormous success with the built-in publicity of the book being read by about 20 million people. People were waiting to see it. If it had been anything at all. If it had been funny, if it had been shocking, in a positive way, it would have been a huge hit. A runaway hit. They managed to find the one way not to make it a hit.

FROUG: Which is to make it simply boring?

GILER: Make it simply boring. God knows, even people who hate the book, of which there are many, none of them think it's boring. It's a very strange book. Most of the people who have read it only react to the rape scene. It's like none of the rest of the book exists.

FROUG: The dildo scene?

GILER: Yeah. Because it really raised the flag, that scene.

FROUG: It had a kind of side effect, David, which you are aware of, in that it became a cause célebre for every censorship group in the United States. It became a symbol of what's wrong with Hollywood, of promiscuity in modern films.

GILER: I could never figure out why, because it didn't have that in it. There was damn little sex, really. There was certainly no explicit sex.

FROUG: In some circles it is believed *Myra Breckinridge* was, in part, responsible for the downfall of the Zanucks.

GILER: Well, I shouldn't be either shocked or surprised or unhappy about that. I mean, they were responsible for it. I'll say that. They did not let Bobby do it the way he wanted to. They backed Michael Sarne all the way. Good, bad, or indifferent, that's what they did. And while you admire that in the head of a studio, in this one case they just backed the wrong horse.

FROUG: You think that they were carried away with the auteur theory?

GILER: I think so. And I think it was a case where they felt that here was this book which was outrageous and basically dirty. (I think they all thought it was dirty.) Bud Yorkin, who was going to do it originally, with Vidal—their script was astonishingly clean. I mean, Doris Day could easily have played Myra Breckinridge. But Fox wanted to have it more outrageous than that, so they thought, "Ah, here is this young, hip guy, English," right? He can do it. And he's got a great act, Sarne, in an office. He comes on fairly strong and he's reasonably impressive, particularly to illiterates, so he's very impressive. I really don't think that a lot of studio executives distinguish between say *81/2* or *Joanna* or, I think it's just "those kind of movies," so here is one of "those kind of directors." He looks hip, he's got all the right kind of credentials, let's give him this project. He can do it. And hip movies were in then.

FROUG: Now you've washed *Myra Breckinridge* out of your system, did it help, or hurt you, for future jobs?

GILER: Well, I think it helped me a lot. That is, until the movie came out.

FROUG: Because you had been hired to do a major project?

GILER: Hired to do a major project, and I had my script to show. And there was so much controversy about it. And people who read my script and gave it to others liked it and because the movie was so bad, I was defended. Rex Reed went on television telling people I had written a great script. And Vidal was very good about it and said terrific things about the script. So it helped me. My agent made the decision about keeping my name on it. I don't know if I would have done that. I have five projects on the shelf, and that's my only credit, so I probably would have removed it, but at the same time I would have very ambivalent feelings about wanting to see my name on the screen, period.

FROUG: You've just finished a screenplay here at Warners called *The Skin Game*?

GILER: Well, that was really a patch job. I did two other scripts here before that.

FROUG: What two other scripts did you do?

GILER: I did one called *Casualties of War* for Jack Clayton, who is a really brilliant director. It was not made for budgetary reasons, apparently. I think, really, it had to do more with the subject matter than anything else.

FROUG: What was the subject matter?

GILER: Small-scale atrocities in Vietnam. Last year they were willing to take chances on those kind of films, but this year nobody is.

FROUG: They feel it's already passé?

GILER: Well, this was last fall when the decision was made

not to make it. And it was rather an expensive picture at the same time.

FROUG: You find yourself back under the aegis of Dick Zanuck again.

GILER: He arrived at Warners just in time, as my screenplay came out.

FROUG: *Casualties of War*?

GILER: Not *Casualties. Resist.*

FROUG: That was the second screenplay you did?

GILER: Right. That's what I came here to do originally. John Calley sort of had an idea he wanted to do a movie about deserters in Sweden. And so I went back to Sweden and did research on it. I decided to do it as a comedy. And I was going to direct it myself—I thought. It was decided that I was not going to direct it, eventually.

FROUG: When the new administration came in?

GILER: Well, I don't know that they had anything to do with it, per se. I know that this company has gotten burned by first-time directors, a lot.

FROUG: Warners went on a youth kick, the likes of which hasn't been seen in Hollywood, ever, under John Calley.

GILER: Well, they did some very interesting things. I mean, most of the companies that went on a youth kick seemed to pick just the worst people you could ever imagine, and here they had some really terrific stuff that was produced. One of them is being made now. It was originally called *The Crow Killer*, by a young writer named John Millius, a terrific writer, and that probably will bear no resemblance to his script, either.

FROUG: Why not?

GILER: Well, because his script is very original, very unique, and very difficult to understand in a certain kind of way, and very easy to understand in another kind of way. It was a sort of a homage to John Ford Westerns, with a rather complex system of motivations. And an interesting idea about violence. Very violent. And I think it made the director and the actors uncomfortable with all the violence and what seemed to be sort of just killing Indians for the sake of killing Indians.

FROUG: Who was the director?

GILER: Sydney Pollack. And Robert Redford is the star.

FROUG: And so another writer was brought in to rewrite?

GILER: I think three other writers were brought in to rewrite it at various times. [Edward Anhalt did the final rewrite and the film is being released under the title *Jeremiah Johnson*. See Anhalt interview.]

FROUG: So you did two screenplays here at Warners, both now sitting on the shelf, and then they came to you with *The Skin Game.*

GILER: *The Skin Game* was a picture that was ready to go with Peter Stone's original screenplay.

FROUG: Who is an established Hollywood writer.

GILER: And Broadway writer. I didn't like it very much and I did not originally want to do it, and then I thought I could make points with the studio, because I was then trying to get off the ground as a director. They came back to me a second time and asked if I would do it. And I liked the people who were doing the picture. They were terrific people.

FROUG: Who were the people?

GILER: Harry Keller was the producer, Meta Rosenberg was the executive producer, Paul Bogart was the director, and James Garner was the star. And they were all terrific. And they all had a unified idea of what they wanted the movie to be, and everybody got along with each other, and it was really sort of pleasant. My job called for some two weeks' work, a patch kind of thing. It was an interesting job, because what I tried to do was maintain the tone of the piece, and to keep it the way they had it, while at the same time I wasn't really crazy about it.

FROUG: Did it end up being just two weeks?

GILER: Two weeks and I would occasionally come in to help them pick up something. I wrote rather a lot in that two weeks. More than I thought I would.

FROUG: What percentage of the screenplay would you say you wrote?

GILER: A third, I'd say.

FROUG: Will you receive a credit?

GILER: No, I don't want a credit. Because I don't really think it's mine; it's Peter Stone's. [EDITOR'S NOTE: Stone removed his name from the film. The writing credit, his pseudonym, is "Pierre Marton."]

FROUG: What project are you on now?

GILER: I'm about to start at Metro on *The Postman Always Rings Twice.*

FROUG: A remake?

GILER: Yes. I don't really consider it a remake because it's another case like *Myra Breckinridge.* A book I've always loved. It's a great idea for a movie, but the original movie, which I just saw recently, however good it may have been in its time, has not held up at all.

FROUG: Who was in the original?

GILER: Lana Turner and John Garfield. That movie really couldn't do any of the things in those days that make *Postman* terrific. The relationship between the two characters. It's a bizarre combination of sex and violence. You never know when they get together whether they're going to go to bed or beat each other up. It's really a strange book. The movie was really the plot and all the sort of things that were under the surface were totally ignored. All the things that make it other than just a simple melodrama.

FROUG: When you construct a screenplay, do you think of the classic beginning, middle, and end? In the sense of posing a problem, complicating it, and then finding a resolution?

GILER: Most of my scripts, actually, you can divide up that way, but I don't consciously think about it. I like to have some clear idea what the story is going to be, and after going through a period of thinking and talking about the decline of plot and all that, I have decided that I really do like plots and stories.

FROUG: When you first come across an idea, do you make a step outline before you do a screenplay?

GILER: No, not anymore. I did in television days. You have to.

FROUG: What do you do in features? How do you begin?

GILER: I make a lot of notes in general, on scratch paper, whatever. Generally, I try to start. Just start.

FROUG: Do you know your ending when you start?

GILER: No, not usually. I have some vague idea what it's going to be.

FROUG: What do you know about the characters?

GILER: General ideas. In *Resist* it was really strange. I had a tough time with that in the beginning. And I wrote a scene someplace in the middle of it. I had an idea which I thought would be a terrific scene. And I wrote the scene and from that I got the idea of the character and all the rest of it and started to develop it so I went back and started over.

FROUG: So in that case you started with a middle scene of the picture.

GILER: I think the scene finally occurs on page twenty-five of the script. It was a very extended scene, and it was through that scene that I finally got into doing it. That's not the way I've worked in the past. I usually start in the beginning and go right through.

FROUG: Are you confident that you won't find yourself writing up a dead end?

GILER: It hasn't happened yet.

FROUG: Do you have any plot points along the way that are set in your mind?

GILER: Yes. Usually I do. I have some sort of general idea. When I finally started to work on *Resist*, for example, I had the idea in mind, at the beginning, that the deserters were not like anybody thought they were. Everybody thought the deserters were committed and serious revolutionaries, gut-level activists. In fact, they were mainly gas-station attendants from St. Louis, with no political ideas, not a clue. Most of them had joined the Army, most of them were in Germany, not in Vietnam, but if they knew about the war in Vietnam when they started, they didn't care, and eventually they became very committed on a sort of, in most cases, certainly not all, shallow level. So I had the idea. People had just taken these guys absolutely seriously, and were determined to prove that these were really seriously committed men. And they weren't. So I started with that. That's already a character.

FROUG: And was that a preconceived notion or had you done a lot of research?

GILER: I had done a lot of research. I'd been over there in Sweden, hanging around with the deserters.

FROUG: During your two years at Uppsala?

GILER: No, after that. Warner Brothers sent me back over there specifically to do that last year.

FROUG: When you start a screenplay, have you usually done a good deal of research?

GILER: Well, it depends on what it's about. In the case of *Resist,* the only kind of research I needed to do was to talk to the deserters for a while because I had been in Sweden for so long and I really wanted to do something about Sweden as well. I would never have done a story about the deserters if it wasn't for the fact that it was in Sweden.

FROUG: What about the other screenplays?

GILER: One of them stemmed, in part, from Dwight MacDonald's article on the New Politics Convention in Chicago.

FROUG: Is that the one that was originally called *Beatniks, Commies and Fruits?*

GILER: Yeah. This was sort of an idea I had about the whole kind of fragmentation of the left wing, the insanity and disorganization. And at the same time the right wing is convinced there is some sort of enormous plot going on, which, usually, they are responsible for. And the whole Statue of Liberty bombing plot. That was the basic idea.

The thing that started me off. The MacDonald thing and the thing I read in the papers about where they had arrested a group of people who were going to blow up the Statue of Liberty in New York. A year later came a small article in the paper that the charges against all of these people had been dismissed, because the instigator of the whole thing was an FBI agent, a double agent.

FROUG: It was a right-wing plot?

GILER: Yeah. So here's the FBI saying here are these people that pose a danger, a threat, but it's very hard to get them to come out in the open and pose that threat. I mean they're secretly posing that threat. So the FBI has got to move them out there to seriously make a threat so they can crush them. At the same time, the reverse idea on the left is that it's better to be out in the open and make a big noise and get crushed or martyred, or whatever, than sit there and do nothing. Those two elements always make for revolutions or actions.

FROUG: In other words, the absurdity of both extremes.

GILER: Actually they're not extremes. The left-wing point of view is actually a practical argument, rather than a theoretical one. And then there was another element, the element of bureaucratic covering up. And what eventually happens in this story is the FBI has organized this group of lunatics, this communist group, to bring off some sort of caper that will alert the country to the dangers of these kinds of people, and they were hopelessly disorganized in the beginning. But eventually, through the leadership of the FBI, they get organized. The FBI has an idea that one of the ways to get them really inflamed and get them going is heavy police brutality. So the communists are having some sort of demonstration to support the Bolivian tin workers, or something, and they're just stomped on by the police and they get really angry. Then they're going to go forward with the caper, right. And the caper turns out that they're going to kidnap the chief, the head of the FBI, or the "Bureau," as it's referred to.

FROUG: You can't refer to it as the FBI now, it's against the law, isn't it?

GILER: Yeah. Even Bureau is too much. Roger David of William Morris said I'd never get this off the ground.

FROUG: Because you call them the Bureau?

GILER: And also there's sexual references to J. Edgar Hoover. Not as J. Edgar Hoover, but as the chief. So what happens? They set out to kidnap J. Edgar Hoover in this elaborate, hopelessly complicated plot which, of course, could never work except for the fact that the FBI is continually helping them to bring this thing off. So, in fact, they finally do kidnap the chief, and they put him in this giant bag, which they keep putting food into. He's naked when they kidnap him. So they actually have the chief. They've got him. Success is assured. The double-agent guys, the FBI guys, cannot believe it. They just don't understand how it happened. But what finally happens is that they decide at the FBI, the Bureau, that if they admit that the chief has been kidnapped, it'll look bad for everybody. Not only will it look bad for everybody because the chief has been taken, but if the chief comes back, these FBI guys who instigated the idea are through, forever. They decide that the best idea is to really cover it up. To say that the chief has died in his sleep. And one of the guys says, "Well, they're going to show up with the chief and then what'll we do?" And another FBI double-agent says, "Nobody in his right mind will believe that if a group of freaks show up with this guy that he's the head of the FBI, and that these lunatics kidnapped him." The final scene is where it appears in a sidelight in the news. David Brinkley has a humorous anecdote about a bunch of freaks showing up today at police headquarters claiming they had kidnapped the chief. That the chief was not dead and that they had him. Of course, nobody believed them.

FROUG: I think I know now why Warner Brothers didn't want to go ahead with it.

GILER: It started at Jalem. They bought it, they developed it, and they couldn't get it together. Tommy Smothers wanted to do it once, and we almost got it off the ground out here. Warner Brothers was interested in it until somebody pointed out, I guess, that they also do the FBI television show, which is a much greater source of revenue than my movie looked to be. So that didn't happen.

FROUG: What do you think is the best way for a college student today to begin as a filmwriter?

GILER: Just to write an original screenplay.

FROUG: Are there any educational requirements you think are particularly helpful?

GILER: Literature courses are helpful. And English courses. I'm a fantastic reader. I don't agree with the kind of romantic approach to art and writing, that it bursts out of you, and that kind of stuff. I don't agree with that at all. I think most people feel they have great ideas, and that screenplays come from Ideas, capital I, and that they do a lot of moralizing and stuff like that. And I don't think it's like that at all.

FROUG: What do you think it's about?

GILER: Screenwriting, in a sense, is like any other kind of writing in that it basically involves words, writing a line, literary style. It's a bastard art, in a sense, in that no one reads what you write, except people who are going to destroy it. But it still makes a difference. I think screenplays should be more readable. And, of course, it's more exciting to write that way, more fun to write that way.

FROUG: Do you write master scenes?

GILER: Yeah.

FROUG: You don't include the camera angles?

GILER: Only if it's a point that I want to make. There's no reason to do it otherwise because no one pays any attention to it. And it makes the script much less readable.

FROUG: How long do your first drafts usually run?

GILER: My first first draft was 183 pages. And they've got

progressively shorter since then, till the last was about 138 pages and I cut it down to 120.

FROUG: Is 120 still an average shooting script?

GILER: Yeah. A little less, even.

FROUG: Do you write elaborate descriptions in your screenplay of the set and scene, etc.?

GILER: I write my descriptions in another voice from what the script is written in.

FROUG: They're almost asides to the reader?

GILER: Yeah. They are, in fact.

FROUG: In order to make the script more readable, and therefore more salable?

GILER: Also to amuse myself while I'm writing. Most people don't read the descriptions. Other writers read them.

FROUG: Do you write lengthy descriptions of your characters?

GILER: No. Absolutely not. I don't like that idea, as a matter of fact.

FROUG: What do you say about your characters when introducing them?

GILER: As little as possible. I mean, just as much as you need to know. I think characters are defined in terms of their actions, rather than in terms of what you say about them.

FROUG: Do you think the writer will ever have more control over his work?

GILER: No, I don't think so. The way that the thing is set up now the director has so much financial control that he just has got the power. Although it's sort of starting to shift back to the old balance. We were talking about the auteur theory before. It seems strange that a bunch of French critics could have as much effect on the giant corporate establishment over here as they have. André Bazin and all those guys, at the Cahiers in the fifties. And they have changed their opinions on it radically.

FROUG: *Cahiers du Cinéma*?

GILER: Well, not the magazine itself, but the guys on the magazine then are all now filmmakers. They didn't really understand the way movies were made in the thirties and forties, in the great days. They looked at these great movies and just assumed that they were made by great directors, because that's the way movies were made in Europe. In most cases the movie was written and developed by the writer and the producer, and the director came in two weeks before and shot it. Somebody else edited it, and that was the movie.

FROUG: In America?

GILER: Yeah. I mean they had a lot of directors in those days who did terrific work, but who simply just didn't understand scripts and were not capable of working on a script. And when left to their own devices, today they destroy themselves. They develop horrible scripts. You have to look back on the classic examples like Howard Hawks. Howard Hawks' movies are marvelous and each one different from the rest, but they all bear Howard Hawks' personal stamp. But the great Howard Hawks movies are the ones written by good writers, and if you look at the later ones in which he seems to be reading his own reviews and clearly in control of everything, they declined. The great ones were written by writers like Raymond Chandler or Borden Chase, or Nunnally Johnson, or Dudley Nichols and Hagar Wilde. There is a famous Robert Riskin-Frank Capra story. When Riskin handed Capra a sheaf of blank pages and said, "Here, give *that* the Capra touch." Frank Capra made wonderful movies, and directors have triumphed over their material in a lot of cases. And it's very difficult for a script to triumph over a director and become a good movie. But I'd suspect that there are probably more good scripts lying around than there are good movies.

Nunnally Johnson

1932 A BEDTIME STORY *(Joint Screenplay)*
MAMA LOVES PAPA *(Joint Screenplay)*

1934 BULLDOG DRUMMOND STRIKES BACK *(Screenplay)*
THE HOUSE OF ROTHSCHILD *(Screenplay)*
MOULIN ROUGE *(Joint Screenplay)*
KID MILLIONS *(Joint Story and Dialogue)*

1935 THE MAN WHO BROKE THE BANK AT MONTE CARLO *(Joint Screenplay)*
THANKS A MILLION *(Screenplay)*
BABY FACE HARRINGTON *(Joint Screenplay)*
CARDINAL RICHELIEU *(Contributor to Screenplay)*

1936 BANJO ON MY KNEE *(Screenplay)*
BOWERY PRINCESS *(Original Idea)*
THE PRISONER OF SHARK ISLAND *(Story and Screenplay)*

1938 WIFE, HUSBAND, AND FRIEND *(Screenplay)*
JESSE JAMES *(Story and Screenplay)*

1939 THE GRAPES OF WRATH *(Screenplay)*, Academy Nomination
ROSE OF WASHINGTON SQUARE *(Screenplay)*

1940 TOBACCO ROAD *(Screenplay)*
CHAD HANNA *(Screenplay)*

1941 ROXIE HART *(Screenplay)*

1942 THE PIED PIPER *(Screenplay)*
LIFE BEGINS AT 8:30 *(Screenplay)*

1943 THE MOON IS DOWN *(Screenplay)*
HOLY MATRIMONY *(Screenplay)*, Academy Nomination

1944 THE WOMAN IN THE WINDOW *(Screenplay)*
CASANOVA BROWN *(Screenplay)*
THE KEYS OF THE KINGDOM *(Joint Screenplay)*

1945 ALONG CAME JONES *(Screenplay)*

1946 THE DARK MIRROR *(Screenplay)*

1948 MR. PEABODY AND THE MERMAID *(Screenplay)*

1949 EVERYBODY DOES IT *(Screenplay)*
THREE CAME HOME *(Screenplay)*

1950 THE MUDLARK *(Screenplay)*

1951 PHONE CALL FROM A STRANGER *(Screenplay)*
THE DESERT FOX *(Screenplay)*
THE LONG DARK HALL *(Screenplay)*

1952 WE'RE NOT MARRIED *(Screenplay)*
MY COUSIN RACHEL *(Screenplay)*

1953 HOW TO MARRY A MILLIONAIRE *(Screenplay)*, Writers Guild Nomination
NIGHT PEOPLE *(Screenplay)*

1954 BLACK WIDOW *(Screenplay)*

1955 HOW TO BE VERY, VERY POPULAR *(Screenplay)*

1956 THE MAN IN THE GRAY FLANNEL SUIT *(Screenplay)*

1957 THE THREE FACES OF EVE *(Screenplay)*

1959 THE MAN WHO UNDERSTOOD WOMEN *(Screenplay)*

1960 FLAMING STAR *(Joint Screenplay)*

THE ANGEL WORE RED *(Screenplay)*

1962 MR. HOBBS TAKES A VACATION *(Screenplay)*,
Writers Guild Nomination

1963 TAKE HER, SHE'S MINE *(Screenplay)*
THE WORLD OF HENRY ORIENT *(Joint Screenplay)*,
Writers Guild Nomination

1966 THE DIRTY DOZEN *(Joint Screenplay)*

Many years ago the editor of a show-business paper stated, "Nunnally Johnson is the answer to every producer's prayers." For nearly forty years, during which time he wrote almost 100 motion pictures, Johnson proved himself the most reliable screenwriter in the business. More importantly, what Nunnally wrote got shot—his screenplays became movies.

If Darryl Zanuck was the master builder who erected 20th Century-Fox and made it a formidable edifice on the Hollywood skyline, it was Nunnally Johnson, as much as any other man, who provided the brick and mortar.

Zanuck gave tacit recognition to it when he prodded Johnson into becoming a producer as well as screenwriter. But it was Johnson, with a score of productions to his credit, who called a halt to the producer half of his dual life.

"I don't want to be producer of other people's movies," he said.

Zanuck next gave him director status and Johnson directed nine films (*Night People, Black Widow, Man in the Gray Flannel Suit*, etc.)—all creditable, if not inspired, efforts.

Zanuck finally offered him a $1 million contract, no options, an unheard of writer deal in the prewar days of the major studios. (By 1945 Nunnally Johnson-written films had grossed over $100 million, so nobody accused Zanuck of going soft in the center.)

Johnson turned it down. He departed Fox for another studio where he set up his own production company with a couple of executive-type partners. But the films they produced were not, generally, up to the Nunnally Johnson-Fox standard.

Nunnally was first and foremost a screenwriter.

For at least a dozen years, the tall, lanky country boy

from Georgia was the highest paid writer in America, at one time receiving $150,000 for eight weeks of work—roughly $18,645 per week.

And his wry barbs were the talk of Hollywood. His witty irreverencies for the high and the mighty of movies became legendary. (Having never won an Oscar, Nunnally and a friend designed and had their own cast, which they then presented to themselves in an ersatz ceremony. Their "Oscar" was nude and wore a derby.)

Johnson was born in Columbus, Georgia, December 5, 1897, in modest circumstances, the son of a railroad man. (His southern drawl is, to this day, so thick that the secretary who transcribed the tape of our conversation had serious difficulty understanding many of his words and colloquialisms. "He is obviously a super-charming southern gentleman," said Pat, somewhat defensively, I suspect.)

After high school he got a job as a cub reporter for the *Columbus Enquirer Sun.* He served in World War I as a second lieutenant in the field artillery.

After the war he headed for New York and the big time. He worked on the *New York Tribune,* the *New York Post,* and the *Brooklyn Eagle.*

During the *Eagle* period Johnson was married twice, both times to girl reporters on the paper.

He covered most of the big stories, the murders, the love-nest scandals, the highly publicized trials and tribulations of the Roaring Twenties. Perhaps no era in American history has received so much notoriety—and Nunnally Johnson helped create it.

"He walks, talks, thinks like a reporter," said a friend. But by the late twenties Johnson had become a phenomenally successful magazine writer (fifty-two short stories in *The Saturday Evening Post* alone). And he had his own newspaper column.

In 1932 the movies were in the throes of one of their periodic upheavals. Sound was in, the silents were out, and words were Hollywood's latest craze. Johnson was a wordsmith of proven prowess and Hollywood recruited him. He migrated to California.

In Hollywood he married for the third time, this time happily and permanently, and begat children and grandchildren, some of whom are working successfully in the business: daughter Marjorie, married to editor and director Gene Fowler, Jr., is also a successful film editor; daughter Nora wrote the novel *The World of Henry Orient,* upon which producer Nunnally Johnson based the movie.

Looking back from the vantage point of sixty years of writing, Johnson still retains much of the wry, sardonic humor that highlighted his years of glory. He laughed often as he reminisced. But being the dean emeritus of screenwriters is not a role Nunnally accepts cheerfully. There is still a touch of the aging fighter in him, the former champion impatient for another shot at the title. Even at seventy-five and not in the best of health, Nunnally Johnson's tongue is sharp and his mind, perhaps less nimble, is alert and restless. He wants to "get on with it."

Our conversations took place in his elegantly furnished living room. We were surrounded by leather-bound volumes of his screenplays and by the warm sounds of a household filled with family and children outside splashing in the pool on a beautiful, sunny day.

I told "Mr. Johnson" (how do you call a dean emeritus anything else?) that I had recently attended a screening of *Roxie Hart,* for which he had written the screenplay as well as produced, and I thought it remained one of the half-dozen funniest American comedies ever filmed. Yet few people know of it and it had come and gone rather quickly back in 1942.

"Well," he growled, "I didn't like it all that much. The director went and threw in all those foolish things, overplayed it, you know. Just went way overboard. The script was a whole lot better."

As we shook hands at the door of his Holmby Hills mansion, the tall, lean southerner, now somewhat stooped, breathing with difficulty from a recent bout with emphysema, summoned every ounce of his innate dignity and said, "I take pride in being a screenwriter."

BENHAM
You mean the great mouthpiece!?!

JAKE
Get Billy Flynn and you can write your own ticket.

BENHAM
And use it?

JACK
The streets of the city are congested with women that Billy has saved from their just desserts.

ROXIE
(slowly)
And you think he'd take ME?

JAKE
Billy would take an ape-woman if there was enough publicity in it.

ROXIE
(thinking)
He's good-looking, too, isn't he?

JAKE
Sex appeal rises from him like a cloud of steam.

Obviously tempted strongly by their seriousness, she studies first one and then the other before ...

ROXIE
And you don't think there's any chance -

JAKE
(wearily)
I'm telling you, honey, this county wouldn't hang Lucretia Borgia.

ROXIE
I wouldn't want to get in any jam, you know.

BENHAM
This is money from home, my dear - there is no other way to describe it.

FROUG: John Ford once said that you were the inspiration for the founding of the Directors Guild. What did he mean by that?

JOHNSON: Well, I imagine it was a clowning remark, but I was skeptical about the position of the director from the time I came out here. That has little to do with the fact that when I had a director on a picture that I was producing, this director seemed to me almost useless, and I was quoted in *Time* and *Life* and in various articles as saying that the director was only useful to see that the actors didn't go home before six o'clock. Now I said that about this particular director, but *Time* and *Life* made it a statement about all directors, and this was pretty embarrassing to me because, while I may not give the director top marks for the whole thing, I certainly wouldn't say such a thing about such men that I've worked with as Henry King, John Ford and people like that. I had to spend the next week or two sending apologies to these men. And Ford said that this remark made the directors realize that maybe they had better get together, and form something of a union, like the writers. I remember when this union, this guild, was formed, a friend of mine told me that at one of the meetings my friend Mervyn LeRoy got up and proposed a resolution that no members of the guild would ever work with me again. Another of my friends, Eddie Goulding, seconded this motion. But of course nothing came of it, and less than a year later Eddie was directing a picture for me.

FROUG: With you as the producer as well as the writer?

JOHNSON: Yes. And I said, "Eddie, what became of that idea that you would never work with me as a director?" He said, "Where did you get that, old boy?" I said, "I was told that you had seconded this motion in the Screen Directors Guild." He said, "Dead drunk, chum, dead drunk."

FROUG: You've written more than fifty major motion pictures and directed nine of them. You've also produced many of your screenplays, and yet you've maintained in all of your interviews that you are still essentially a writer.

JOHNSON: Well, of course. I was a writer before I came out here. Arrogantly put, I was a reporter. I wrote a column for six years, and short stories, and that was my business, writing. Out here the other things, directing and producing, were adjuncts to writing. Zanuck put me into those positions. Now, the directing I asked for because the picture was to be made in Berlin, and I had been the producer on a picture made in London and my position was so uncomfortable as producer. I had to be there, and I had nothing to do except look over the director's shoulder, which was uncomfortable for him, and uncomfortable for me, and a pure waste of time. And so I asked Zanuck if I could direct the next picture. In this case he said it's okay with me if Gregory Peck agrees to do it.

FROUG: This was *Night People.*

JOHNSON: *Night People.* Of course Peck had a right to pass on this. He was a star. You know, he had to take care of this career, and he had to protect it. Anyway, Greg said okay with him and I went ahead with it. But I remember the first scene I directed. It was on top of a building in Berlin and it was a scene which was actually near the end of the picture, and it had four or five people in it. And I got them lined up in their positions. Greg was to enter the scene. Everything was ready. And just before I said, "Camera," I looked up and I saw Greg looking at me and our eyes met and I knew exactly what he was thinking. He was thinking to himself, "Was I crazy to let this man direct this picture?" I was wondering the same thing, you know. But then we went ahead and we got along very well. As a matter of fact I directed him in another picture later. *The Man in the Gray Flannel Suit.* But I have a belief, and I've had it all along, that the director maintains a kind of mystery. There's so little to do really that you have to make up some mystique. Now there's some proof of this because if you'll notice every now and then this actor is going to direct his next picture. There was an agent I knew that produced a couple of pictures and now he's going to direct his next picture. Now the point of this is that you see all these people who are going to direct their next pictures. They don't say they're going to write their next picture or they're going to score their next picture, they see that's a rather soft touch, directing a picture. That's not to say that good directors don't make a great contribution. But as long as they can read and they have some experience, it's awful hard to go wrong in directing a picture. I know. I did it. And I don't think, as a matter of fact I know, I wasn't an unusually good director. But I wasn't dedicated enough for that. I mean, to be a good director, like George Roy Hill, you have to really give more to it than I was prepared to give. And when they give more to it, then they manage to make a contribution, to improve it in some way. But what they are improving is something solid to begin with. It's largely a cosmetician's job. I won't take a script of my own. Take a script like *The Gunfighter.* Bill Bowers' script.

FROUG: You produced that film and Henry King directed it.

JOHNSON: That's right and he directed it beautifully. And it was acted beautifully. Greg Peck got the spirit, the feeling of the thing from the very beginning, and between the two of them, they turned out quite a good picture. The only thing a producer could do in that case I didn't do, and I was blamed for.

FROUG: Which was what? For letting them put a mustache on Greg Peck?

JOHNSON: That's right. For a year or two after that Skouras, [Spyros Skouras, late president of 20th Century-Fox] when he had occasion to introduce me to somebody, would say, "Nunnally's the man who put a mustache on Gregory Peck." As a matter of fact, I had nothing to do with this. I was about as surprised as anybody when I saw it in the first day's rushes. I was pleased by it and I saw immediately what they were after.

FROUG: Authenticity?

JOHNSON: They wanted a Remington effect, you know. And they got it in Greg. I don't know whether it was Greg who had the idea or Henry. I knew then, but I can't remember now. But that was the only "producer" touch. And Skouras would say, "You know, you cost that picture a million dollars." Well, it was kind of flattering to me— that I could cost anybody a million dollars, but the thing was I didn't believe it one second. I didn't believe hardly anything that Skouras said. But this, in particular, I thought was nonsense.

FROUG: But the function of producing for you was really a boring job in which you stood by and watched the creators work?

JOHNSON: The function of a producer to me is that he makes *one* decision that is greater than all of the other decisions put together, and that is the decision to make this picture. After that he has ordinarily very little to do. The director has, I think rather properly, taken on a good deal of the passing on the production and the wardrobe and the location. These are things that concern the director. He has to work with them. The producer in most respects simply goes along with it. There may be producers who are very firm and overrule the director, but I don't really think he should. Unless it's a matter of money. Then he has to exercise some decision on the thing. But I've seen a producer producing one picture, I don't know what in god's name he does. Once the picture starts he just sits there and scratches himself. I don't know what else there is for him to do. He looks at the rushes but what's he going to say? Sometimes he can say, well, I think this character's getting a little broad, or a little funny, or something, but for the most part once the picture gets started on the set, you've lost control. The control is in the hands of the director. And I think for the most part that's proper. He's the captain of the ship. But if it goes wrong, or is going wrong, there's hardly anything you can do about it.

FROUG: But to follow that metaphor, the screenwriter has built the ship, and once he has completed it and it slides down into the water, the director takes over as captain and the screenwriter also has almost no function.

JOHNSON: That's right.

FROUG: There seems to be no way he can protect his ship once he turns it over to the captain.

JOHNSON: There isn't. That's not true on the stage, of course. You may give up your own property in the movies, but by god you're paid for it. But on the stage I don't see how those fellows live. I've had, at times, several disastrous experiences with it. I could see what the circumstances were. I did three plays, three musicals, scripts of books, a few years ago, and one ran about three months, the other got out of my hands completely, and I suppose it took me something over two years to do those things.

FROUG: What were the names of them?

JOHNSON: *Breakfast at Tiffany's*, which was just lifted out of my hands, one called *Henry, Sweet Henry*, which was from a picture I wrote.

FROUG: Which was written by your daughter, originally, as a novel, *The World of Henry Orient*?

JOHNSON: Yes, that's right. And one called *Darling of the Day*, I believe it was, which was actually another version of a picture I had written, called *Holy Matrimony* with Monty Woolley. In any case there was two and a half years and I got a total of about $10,000. If you get an advance it isn't much on the stage, but very few people get any advance. I don't see how they exist, and I don't see how the stage goes on, because who wants to go in there and starve to death? The fact is, the movies have got more dynamism, got more ideas, they have just passed the stage so thoroughly, so completely, that there's just no comparison anymore. I said this to Walter Kerr five years ago, and he has since agreed with me.

FROUG: That films have far outstripped, creatively, the stage?

JOHNSON: I can only take the discussions you hear now. Everybody talks about film. Who talks about the stage?

FROUG: Do you think that the movies today are, as we used to say in Hollywood, "better than ever"?

JOHNSON: I think they're more thoughtful. I think some of them are aiming higher, which is the only way you can judge a thing, than they were. Yes, I believe on the whole that there's better quality, besides the fact that there's so much nonsense. But there's so much nonsense always in a mass thing. But I would hate to be in this business right now, because I don't understand what makes a story, or what makes a hit. It's something beyond me.

FROUG: Does anybody really know what makes a hit?

JOHNSON: No, I don't believe they do. I'd have to fall back on those things that I did or saw done, but I'd feel uncomfortable in the present period as I'd feel uncomfortable driving a foreign car, that I had never touched. I saw *Harry Kellerman* the other night. I don't care how good a movie is, if it has a title like *Who Is Harry Kellerman and Why Is He Saying Those Terrible Things About Me?* I know that fellow is not a secure man who wrote that. Because nobody puts down that kind of nonsensical title if he thinks his thing is good. He's grabbin,' grabbin,' grabbin' for some kind of interest in the thing. And sometimes it's justified and most of the time it's not. There was a great deal of razzle-dazzle and I don't know whether this picture is a hit or not. If it's a hit, people want razzle-dazzle. If I had been making this picture, if I had been writing it, say a few years ago, I would have found some reason why the audience would have been concerned about Hoffman.

FROUG: Whether he killed himself or not?

JOHNSON: To begin with, I'd have to have some feeling about this man. To make an audience concerned with the fact that he is being harassed by telephone calls. As it was, to me, it was just like hearing that there was a man in Kansas city being bothered by telephone calls. I'd say, "Why that's a pretty bad thing but it doesn't disturb me in the least. I have no relationship with this thing." Grover Jones, who was a writer at Paramount when I first came out here, who'd written silent pictures, and he had a pretty elemental idea of picture storytelling; he'd say, "When a man came out and patted the dog, he was a hero. If he came out and kicked the dog, he was the heavy." Now that's a pretty simple idea, but goddamn it, you do have to have that sort of thing. If Dustin Hoffman had come out there and patted the dog first, I'd have gone right along with him, and I would say who is this sonofabitch that's threatening him, and I would have had a sympathetic feeling about him. As it was, I didn't care. They were just showing me various camera tricks and beautifully done, too, and elaborate sets and so on. But on the whole I do think that even if they miss, I think that they are missing on a higher level than they did twenty years ago, say where they only missed if they tried to make another *Captain Blood*. These guys do have a go at it, and I think that's the only way the movies will reach an art form.

FROUG: Of all your films, which is your favorite?

JOHNSON: If people wanted to examine my head, I'd say I liked *Bulldog Drummond Strikes Back*.

FROUG: That was your first, wasn't it?

JOHNSON: No. I had done about four or five at the time. But even for a year or two or three after that, I just liked it.

FROUG: You told me that you recently saw a screening of *The Grapes of Wrath*. And you also reread the screenplay. And that the picture followed the screenplay exactly.

JOHNSON: Yes, that's true.

FROUG: But it's most often called John Ford's *Grapes of Wrath.*

JOHNSON: Well, there's nothing to be done about that. I can't spend the rest of my life saying this is Nunnally Johnson, because actually it's John Steinbeck's idea. That's the man who wrote the original. And we just hope that I reflected his book, his story.

FROUG: Was Steinbeck pleased with it?

JOHNSON: Yes, he was. The result was we became friends until he died. And let me tell you this. That's a rare thing. Because, as I say, I've done closer to 150 screenplays and the authors of the books (these were almost all adaptations of course), well, you get no thanks from them ever. No matter what it is, they don't like it. I long ago got used to that, so it didn't matter. I don't think I've had more than two or three people who were friendly with me after the picture. John was one. We were very close friends all the rest of his life. And Desmond Young, who was delighted with *The Desert Fox*, was a friend until he died. Maybe people shouldn't be friends with me. They die.

FROUG: You were quoted once as saying, "As a producer, I couldn't work with writers."

JOHNSON: Well, that was true. This was an incapacity on my part. Zanuck wanted me to produce more pictures. I had two or three different stories in the process of work with writers. There are some people who can handle that, who can read the script and say you ought to do this or you ought to do that. I found that I was just an incurable meddler. I would begin rewriting and I would begin doing it myself, and that's very improper. It reflects on the writer who is doing it and it generally screws the whole thing up. I finally went to Zanuck. I had reached a point where I was just helpless, and I told him, I said, "Look, I think I will leave here now." And he said, "What's the matter?" And I said, "I can't handle these writers. I just don't know how." Zanuck was able to—he was very skillful about handling writers. He laughed. And he said, "Well, do like Griffith." He was another producer at Fox. Darryl said, "He doesn't know a goddamn thing. He just reads the script, then he says, 'Not right, try again.' He doesn't tell them a goddamn thing. And they go out and rewrite." Darryl said to me, "I don't think he knows when he gets it. But he says, 'That's better, thanks.'" Darryl said, "Why can't you do that?" I said, "I can't, I just can't."

FROUG: One of the producer functions, as I've understood it, is to work with the writer before the director comes in.

JOHNSON: Well, it was at Fox. And I imagine it is in most cases. I think John Ford almost dies because he can't write. It just runs him nuts, that he has thoughts and ideas and has never trained himself to put them down on paper. And I've found this true of so many directors. They're just so thwarted. That's why they often try to pretend that the writer didn't exist. That this stuff on the paper came on there through some chemical action of the director's eyes, as they ran down a blank sheet. The town is full of legends of John Ford mistreating his script. You know, tearing out twenty pages and saying, "Now, we're three days ahead of schedule." Or saying to somebody, "Goddamn it, this fellow has been reading the script." All of these things belittle the script. And, of course, it's a perfectly clear indication that he hates the fact that he didn't write the script. He would like to, he wanted to. However, that's the same with all directors, or most of them.

FROUG: In order to advance themselves they must denigrate the screenwriter?

JOHNSON: I think screenwriters were given this position. I would trace it all the way back to the beginning. Most of the discussion of movies was by newspaper critics, reviewers, and it was often the publisher's niece, or a sister-in-law who needed a job, or something like that. Harold Ross, the late editor of *New Yorker* magazine, told me once, "Reviewing movies is for women and fairies." But those people who were writing movie reviews, let's say in New York, they saw half a dozen or a dozen newspapermen lifted up and brought out to Hollywood for large sums of money. Large compared to what they were getting. Dudley Nichols, Ollie Garrett, Jim McGuinness—I can't remember them all now. Herman Mankiewicz used to come east and sign a half a dozen of them at once and bring them back. I cannot help but believe that these people writing about movies resented this. Ollie Garrett, you know, wasn't getting as much as the movie reviewer on the paper was getting. And now suddenly these reporters were getting $350 or $500 a week out in Hollywood. And I think that was one of the reasons why the newspaper reviewers celebrated the director. Not the writer. I think it was jealousy. But also, in addition to that, the credit system was such that you could not make any goddamn intelligent credit. You know, screenplay by so-and-so and so-and-so based on an idea by so-and-so, additional dialogue by so-and-so. Why, there could be seven and eight writers. Nobody was conscientious to name all those people every time they wanted to refer to the script. It was easier to say Stephen Roberts' picture, or Norman Taurog's picture, or something like that. And presently it became that was a mystique about directors, because they'd come out here and they'd go on the set and a director is a showy fella. He's out in front. Where's the poor writer? He's up in some office by himself writing the thing. He doesn't put on any show. The director is there, a traffic cop, carrying out the signals that are on the paper.

FROUG: Getting back to your reference to what the New York reporters thought of you, reporters who were lured to Hollywood, I have a quote here from Harold Ross. He said, in 1946, referring to you, "He is one of the six humorists in the country. Johnson is also sickening from my standpoint, for he has been sucking around the diamond merchants of Hollywood for the last fifteen years, and hasn't written anything. There is a misspent life."

JOHNSON: That's one view. My wife went down to Palm Springs and signed at a golf club as a guest membership, and the woman who signed her in looked at her name and said, "Nunnally Johnson. I always read him in the *Evening Post* and in *The Saturday Evening Post.* My goodness, whatever became of him?" Nobody really knows who writes screenplays.

FROUG: It's a curious paradox because the screenwriter is unknown and yet at one time you were called the highest-priced writer in America. On one job you were paid over $18,000 a week. Why do you think the screenwriter is paid so well and yet remains so anonymous?

JOHNSON: Well, because he's not merchandised like an actor. It's not easy to get a good script. I may not have been good, but I was reliable. I nearly always came up with something that could be the basis of improvement, say, but it was never where somebody said, "Look, we can't do a goddamn thing with this crap," and throw it out and say, "Let's get somebody else." It never happened like that. I remember one time Johnny Hyde, my agent, was talking to Sam Goldwyn, who wanted me for some picture, and Johnny quoted him a price that Goldwyn thought was exorbitant, and Johnny, who had handled a good many people over at Goldwyn, added up what Sam had already paid for the scripts that weren't useful, that couldn't be done. Johnny's argument was if you get me in the first place, you don't go through all of that. That doesn't mean that my script is going to be usable without any additions. It's not perfect.

FROUG: Yet, in almost all your credits, you have sole screenplay credit. There are no collaborators.

JOHNSON: I wouldn't have any collaborators. And I've withdrawn from pictures when anybody else was put on them.

FROUG: Why is that?

JOHNSON: I didn't want that kind of thing and I was able to

do it until I got a little indifferent. I had done a script called *Keys of the Kingdom* and I left Fox about that time and the script was turned over to Joe Mankiewicz to produce, and Joe futzed around with it a little bit and then they told me he had asked for sole screenplay credit. And I said, "I never argue about a thing like that; turn it over to the arbitration at the Guild." I can't see how Joe (he's a friend of mine) could have done that much work. Certainly not the sole credit. Anyway, the arbitration committee said it would be Nunnally Johnson and Joe Mankiewicz, or Joe Mankiewicz and Nunnally Johnson, co-credit, whatever it was, and I was too indifferent to protest. And I think that was the first time since I left Paramount in the early days that I ever got co-credit on anything. I don't think I've had but maybe two or three in my whole life.

FROUG: Very few on your credit list. They're almost all sole screenplay credits.

JOHNSON: Now there was *The Dirty Dozen*. I think if I had had enough energy to protest it I would have, because Aldrich has kind of a staff writer, kind of an amanuensis named Heller, I think his name is. People who saw the picture—I never saw the picture—said they thought it was my script. They didn't see what had been done. But Heller claimed sole screenplay and this was nonsense. So again I said, "Look, turn it over to the Writers Guild for arbitration, that's their business." And they gave him co-credit. I think if I had objected and pointed out what I had done that I could have got sole screenplay credit. I have nothing against Heller but I just think that I deserved it in this case. It was too elaborate a job I had done. A very elaborate job. But there again I was just too indifferent to make any protest. In the early days, I think I would say only three fellas in this business had regular solo screen credit. There was Bob Riskin, Dudley Nichols, and myself. There were teams all over town. Teams of writers. And the way circumstances were, often they had to give credit to another writer who was on the picture before, or came on later. It was so mixed up they would give co-credits. If I inspired the Screen Directors Guild, Barney Glazer is definitely the man who inspired the Screen Writers Guild. Do you remember Barney Glazer?

FROUG: No.

JOHNSON: Benjamin F. Glazer was a producer at Paramount. And, oddly enough, no matter what the picture was, Barney's name was on it as one of the writers. And I think his name was on *Bedtime Story.* Wally Young, Nunnally Johnson, and Benjamin F. Glazer. And he hadn't anything to do with this. Well, this happened so often, not just with me, for god's sake, but a dozen others, that his victims met to see how they could stop him from taking credit, and the result was the Screen Writers Guild.

FROUG: That was the reason for the Screen Writers Guild?

JOHNSON: One of the first purposes was to have a fair system of credit for pictures. It was just a mess before then, and I think the first thing the Guild did was to draw up some kind of ground rules, as to who was entitled to credit and who was not.

FROUG: Which became the current arbitration system?

JOHNSON: They had an arbitration for situations like with Joe Mankiewicz and myself, when there was a difference of opinion between two writers. And I'm sure that the arbitration committee is a pretty busy outfit. I'm not sure that they do their job very well. I don't think that they could have read *The Dirty Dozen* scripts, or they wouldn't have come up with the decision they made. But it doesn't matter a great deal now. I'm through with it.

FROUG: You've retired from writing screenplays?

JOHNSON: Yes. I'm through with it.

FROUG: I know you have cards that you pass out. Our mutual friends have told me to get one. [Johnson hands me a business card.] Ah. That's it. The card says, "Retired" in the center, "No Business" in the left-hand corner, "No Money" in the right corner, "No Phone" in the lower corner, and there's no address and no name on it. May I have this?

JOHNSON: Sure.

FROUG: There's another quote of yours from twenty-five years ago that I think is pertinent and prophetic. You said in 1946, "Someday there will be true writers writing directly for the screen, and who knows but one of my kids will be among them."

JOHNSON: Well, I think that the time has come when what is called an original screenplay will be submitted and the writer will have the same distinction, say, as the playwright. Tennessee Williams doesn't adapt things. He writes his play and brings it in and I think that's the way it's going. But then, as some guy pointed out to me, Shakespeare did adaptations. Nearly all of his plays were adaptations of somebody else's stuff. Because I was saying that I didn't regard myself as a writer in that sense. I regard myself as kind of a cabinetmaker. Because I was using other people's material so much—99 percent of the time. Well, this guy said Shakespeare did that. So I thought I was in pretty good company, and I didn't argue the point anymore.

FROUG: You won the Writers Guild Laurel Award in 1959.

JOHNSON: That's for the body of your work. You stay in it long enough and you get the Laurel Award. You stay in long enough and you keep employed. I must say I'm proud of it. I was pleased to get it and I was pleased when I was told it was the first time it was ever awarded unanimously. There were no other contestants that year. I suppose they'd given out of people.

FROUG: If you were to single out in your mind some particular advice for young screenwriters, for whom this book is really aimed, what would you say is the most important thing to keep in mind, as beginning writers?

JOHNSON: I'll tell you what a fella at Paramount told me when I got here. This is facetious, of course. But I think there's a little truth in it. He said, "The best asset that a screenwriter can have is a slightly faulty memory." And that's not bad.

FROUG: How does he use that slightly faulty memory? By distorting the truth?

JOHNSON: Well, you've got the basis of it, but you have to make a contribution yourself. That's true of all writing, I think. There are very few entirely original efforts. There are variations. I mean, it's good if they turn out to have an instinct for drama. That is, dramatic writing. I was on a newspaper. You know what they say there: who, where, what, why, and when. Tell it at once. Theoretically, when you write a newspaper story, you write it so it can be cut off after any paragraph, but you've still got a story. Well, I found when I got here that drama called for exactly the reverse. You don't let them know anything till the last minute.

FROUG: You withhold who, what, why, where and when?

JOHNSON: You withhold. And I've made probably a lot of half-assed suggestions about writing, about screenwriting. I've said that maybe if a writer had to pay by the word for the words he puts down, he'd be a little more careful. He ought to write it with the same care that he sends a night letter or telegram.

FROUG: Then perhaps one of the things that a young writer should beware of is telling too much? I find that in students' screenplays frequently.

JOHNSON: Yes. They do that because they don't know what to do next. They think that adding a few words keeps them busy, you might say, psychologically, until they get another idea. But I think if that scene is worked out in their minds before time, they'll avoid that. When I was going to produce *The World of Henry Orient,* I asked Nora to do a screenplay from her book. I hired her. And she did a screenplay which was unusable.

FROUG: This is your daughter.

JOHNSON: Yes. It was a hard thing to do, but I explained to her and I think she understood. I said, "Look, you can't be faithful to the book. Or, if you're faithful to the book, it's only where it's coincidental. You've got to be faithful to the audience. Don't say this is right out of the book. It doesn't matter if it's right out of the book, if it's not very interesting to the audience, who you've got to think of at all times." It used to be you'd say, "If you do that they'll be reaching for their hats." This was the days when people wore hats and you had a view of your audience with everybody down there like this.

FROUG: Reaching for their hats under their seats.

JOHNSON: Yes. If you didn't keep going, these fellows were on their marks, get set, go, and they were out of the theater. They'd be reaching for their hats. Well, it's not a bad idea to keep in the back of your mind. They may not be that quick to leave, but you can press their patience. You can go too far. You know, I was down in my home town, Columbus, Georgia, once. My mother was quite ill, and I remember one afternoon the minister of her church and his curate, if that's what you call it in the Methodist Church, came by to see her. They were both comparatively young men, one about forty and the other about thirty, and they sat down and talked to me on the porch. And they began talking about sermons. And they began asking me about the techniques I used, and I realized that the word of God had to be presented, too. And I said, "Well, there's one rule: if you don't think it's going good, make it fast. Or if you have any doubt about it, cut it." And they looked at each other and said, "That's true. If I had stopped that sermon five minutes earlier last Sunday . . ." They agreed. They talked about it like two showmen. Everybody has to use some technique to get the thing across.

FROUG: So the same rules apply to any form of storytelling, really. If in doubt, cut it?

JOHNSON: If you've got to have a scene and no good idea comes to make it entertaining in itself, make it short. Cut it down to nothing. You've got to do that. There's one other thing which I think is very damned important. When Heywood Broun was a critic in New York, he was writing about Ed McNamara, who had once been a cop but was on the stage in *Strictly Dishonorable.* And he played a cop. He always played cops. But Broun wrote that McNamara played the cop as if he had been studying other cops, not other actors playing cops. And I think the truth in that is very, very important, because we inevitably come up with stock characters. Fussy old maid, or the chitter-chatty girl's sister, you know. But if the writer will try to *remember* a sister or a girl, maybe he doesn't get as many laughs as he does by copying another thing, but he'll get a great deal more truth. And it will be a better contribution to his play. Get your own person. In the course of time you accumulate knowledge of people. Base your characters on real people rather than other pictures.

FROUG: When you start out to develop a character, you start with people you know, and you put different pieces of different people together?

JOHNSON: Well, sometimes I may think of the actor that I want to play it and whether I'm going to get him or not. Whether I have even asked for him, I have a knowledge of what he can best do. Now within the framework of what I'm saying, the reality and the actor, I have just to make a mixture of the two together and see what can come out. I based the Betty Bacall character in *How to Marry a Millionaire* on Betty Bacall. That was Betty. That's the way she acts, and in this particular case I didn't have any great obligation for reality. We were putting on a charade. Betty Grable is not going to be anything but Betty Grable, there's no need of asking her to do something else, you know. So you try to keep it within her baby-blue-eyes kind of comedy thing. And as for Marilyn Monroe, god only knows what she would turn out. I didn't think she was a very good comedienne, but I managed to do one thing which I think made her liked more in that picture than any other. I made her nearsighted. I put her in glasses and she was very self-conscious about this. I always liked that scene where she and David Wayne, they're both astigmatic, didn't even know what each other looked like.

FROUG: It did give Marilyn Monroe more sympathy than I have ever seen.

JOHNSON: It was the first time that Marilyn was not self-consciously the sex symbol. The character had a measure of modesty. She didn't think she was the end. In other words, you also base your characters on what the hell the material is around you.

FROUG: We were talking about withholding information. Does that help you sustain dramatic tension?

JOHNSON: That's it. Dramatic tension is a most important thing. It's what's going to happen, or what can happen. It's just like *Rififi* or some of the best Hitchcock, and that is what *may* happen. Not what's happened. People fighting aren't very good, but if a man is walking along the edge of a roof, trying to get away, that's where you watch him. The best I was able to do it ever was in *Woman in the Window*, where Eddie Robinson was trying to get rid of a body. A man he killed, almost by accident. He was attacked and he resisted and he killed a man. But the circumstances were such that he felt that he wouldn't have a chance, with the police or in court.

FROUG: No one would believe him?

JOHNSON: No one would believe him. So he takes the body and puts it in his car and sets out to get rid of it. Well, that car, just driving, was suspense. Nothing happened. He nearly runs through a red light and he looks over. There's a cop on the motorcycle over there and the cop grins at him, "Well, boy, you nearly made it." He grins back and goes on. But it's what is *going* to happen, what *may* happen, *not* what's happening. Don't give way to violence. The threat or promise or prospect of violence is eight times as good as violence.

FROUG: In the course of your career you've written comedy, suspense, melodrama, almost every kind and style of screenwriting.

JOHNSON: I have, and I think that was a mistake.

FROUG: Why?

JOHNSON: Because I think that people who specialize—well, it's this: people forget what you're doing. When somebody recommended to Kenny Hyman that I do *The Dirty Dozen*, he said, "You know he writes comedy. You always see his name on those Jimmy Stewart pictures, something like that."

FROUG: *The Grapes of Wrath* wasn't a comedy.

JOHNSON: Well, the people don't remember all those things. And I think that sticking to one thing, the way Hitchcock stuck to one thing, his thriller pictures, I think in the long run that's better. I think it is true of actors, too. For instance, it's all very well to have people say Dustin Hoffman plays different characters and all that kind of stuff. But he'll never live like Clark Gable, who played one character all the time. He'll never be as big and he'll never be as important. Look at *Midnight Cowboy.* You give a man a tricky voice, a limp, a dying disease, and no shave, and I can play the part. There's too many gimmicks involved in the thing. The other fellow didn't have all those gimmicks and had a better performance.

FROUG: Looking back on over 100 movies, and earning up to $18,000 a week, the problem, you feel, was that you would have been better off if you were typed?

JOHNSON: I should have been typed. I'm not kicking about the thing, of course, but the first serious picture I ever did was *The House of Rothschild*, and I had done comedies. Zanuck called me in. It was still 20th Century over at Goldwyn, and I said, "Are you sure you called in the right man?" I said my characters are liable to fall in a flour barrel. I mean, that's the kind of stuff I've been writing. "Well," he said, "have a go at it anyway." Happily, it worked out all right. It was the first dramatic writing I had ever done. I sometimes think I should have stuck to comedy.

FROUG: What would have been different if you'd stuck to comedy?

JOHNSON: Well, I wouldn't have got *any* kind of an award. They don't get them.

FROUG: Comedy writers don't often get awards. Although Ring Lardner, Jr. did with *M*A*S*H.* He won the Writers Guild Award and he won the Academy Award. So it can happen.

JOHNSON: Yes, but most of the time the big sugar goes to the deep-dish affairs.

Edward Anhalt

1947 BULLDOG DRUMMOND STRIKES BACK *(Joint Screenplay)*

1948 THE GENTLEMAN FROM NOWHERE *(Story and Screenplay)*
THE CRIME DOCTOR'S DIARY *(Joint Story and Sole Screenplay)*

1950 PANIC IN THE STREETS *(Joint Short Story Basis)*, Academy Award, Writers Guild Nomination

1951 THE SNIPER *(Joint Story)*, Academy Nomination

1952 THE MEMBER OF THE WEDDING *(Screenplay)*

1954 NOT AS A STRANGER *(Joint Screenplay)*

1957 THE PRIDE AND THE PASSION *(Joint Story and Screenplay)*
THE WONDERFUL YEARS *(Screenplay)*
THE YOUNG LIONS *(Screenplay)*

1958 IN LOVE AND WAR *(Screenplay)*

1959 THE SINS OF RACHEL CADE *(Screenplay)*
THE RESTLESS YEARS *(Screenplay)*

1961 THE YOUNG SAVAGES *(Joint Screenplay)*

1962 GIRLS! GIRLS! GIRLS! *(Joint Screenplay)*

1963 A GIRL NAMED TAMIKO *(Screenplay)*
WIVES AND LOVERS *(Screenplay)*
BECKET *(Screenplay)*, Academy Award, Writers Guild Award

1964 THE SATAN BUG *(Joint Screenplay)*

1967 HOUR OF THE GUN *(Screenplay)*
IN ENEMY COUNTRY *(Screenplay)*

1968 THE BOSTON STRANGLER *(Screenplay)*

1969 THE MADWOMAN OF CHAILLOT *(Screenplay)*

1971 JEREMIAH JOHNSON *(Joint Screenplay)*

1972 QBVII *(Screenplay)*
THE KILLING ZONE* *(Screenplay)*

1973 LUTHER *(Screenplay)*

1975 THE MAN IN THE GLASS BOOTH *(Screenplay)*

1978 ESCAPE TO ATHENA *(Joint Screenplay)*

1981 GREEN ICE *(Joint Screenplay)*

1984 THE HOLCROFT COVENANT *(Joint Screenplay)*

*Unproduced

It is a fair indication of the anonymity of the screenwriter that Paul Anka, a somewhat less than *au courant* teen-pop idol, is listed in the latest issue of *Who's Who in America* ("World Wide Notables") while two-time Oscar winner Edward Anhalt, adapter of *Becket*, *The Member of the Wedding*, *The Madwoman of Chaillot*, etc., is not.

I single out Anhalt for comparison not so much because of the name similarity as that Eddie has received as much press and public attention as any screenwriter is apt to get. Newspapers around the country have done extensive articles on him. *Time* has done a feature story on him. He is frequently interviewed and quoted. But it is highly doubtful if any but the most studious film historian has ever heard of his name.

Fortunately, the income of the Hollywood screenwriter, unlike that of the actor, the director, and, occasionally, even the producer, is unrelated to his lack of public recognition. Until the bottom fell out of the movie market quite recently, Anhalt contentedly plugged along writing two screenplays a year, year in and year out, at between $150,000 and $200,000 per script. At those prices a man can stand a lot of anonymity.

In the Writers Guild of America, west, "Newsletter," Anhalt is nearly always referred to, affectionately, as Edward *von* Anhalt and, in fact, the fictitious "von" marvelously gathers together a lot of what goes into the total portrait of the man.

In the first place, Eddie looks like his name ought to be von Anhalt. He is short, thick-necked, powerfully built, and shaven-headed. He is the very model of a mini Prussian general—or a miniature Erich von Stroheim.

In the second place, Eddie's position in the marketplace is baronial; he is an elitist, not only in the Guild, but in the studios where his reputation as the man you bring in when everything else has failed remains unblemished. ("By actual count, when I came in on *The Young Lions,* it was the fourteenth attempt by nine writers.") Anhalt sells screenplays when equally talented and established fellow writers are hanging on the ropes.

Lastly, Eddie, a hard-working and dedicated member of his union, describes himself as the Guild's "token reactionary." He is known for his sometimes right-wing and often controversial views in council meetings. He delights in telling the story of the time when the real Prince Edward von Anhalt (no relation) of Munich came to Hollywood. ("This guy actually exists. He's young, he has long hair, he looks like a hippie. And he isn't even Jewish!")

Anhalt, the non-von one, was born March 28, 1914, in New York City. His mother was a teacher and his father manufactured gambling equipment. He attended private schools in New York and studied journalism at Columbia University.

In 1935 he won a Rockefeller Fellowship to Princeton, where he studied propaganda techniques under the former head of Austrian Radio who had fled the Nazis.

In the same year Eddie became a filmmaker. He wrote, directed, produced, and was cameraman and editor of a 16mm film called *Problem Child,* which he sold to Bell Telephone for educational use. ("I was a premature auteur.") The following year he made *Thunder of the Sea* for the World Lutheran Congress, a study of the founding of Lutheranism, and it is still being shown in churches throughout the world.

In 1937 Anhalt became an assistant editor at Pathé News and was awarded another Rockefeller Fellowship, this time to study documentary techniques under Van Dyke, Steiner, and Rotha.

He was cinematographer on Pare Lorentz's *The City* and had a one-man exhibit of his still photographs at Columbia.

In 1938 Anhalt went to work for CBS where, along with producer Worthington Miner and then-program director Gilbert Seldes, he helped establish TV drama. ("We invented a thing called television programming—and lived to regret it ever since.")

He was cameraman on the first television production of a stage play, *Stage Door*, and, in 1940, wrote and produced television's first documentary, "Fifty Thousand Airplanes."

During World War II he was assigned to the O.S.S. Bomb Damage Assessment Section. "My job was to see how much the Air Force was lying about the bomb damage it was inflicting. I reported they were lying considerably—and they transferred me out."

Eddie and his wife, Edna, began to write pulp-magazine stories while he was in the Army. ("How much were they paying captains in those days—$280 a month!") They sold to *Amazing Stories*, *Argosy*, *Detective Story*, all under the joint name of Andrew Holt.

By 1942 the Anhalts were in California and the movies began buying up their pulp fiction. ("They were making 600 pictures a year in those days. They'd buy anything.")

After the war, the team of Edward and Edna Anhalt became established in the film capital, and by 1950 they had won an Academy Award for their story *Panic in the Streets*.

But in 1955, after twenty years of marriage and a string of highly successful pictures, both the team and the marriage dissolved. Their last picture together was *The Pride and the Passion* for Stanley Kramer. ("It was a case," says Eddie, of "too much pride and too little passion.")

Anhalt wrote his way to the top of his profession, taking any job, gaining a reputation for turning out shootable material. He wrote seven pictures for producer Hal Wallis. ("I had to write two Elvis Presley pictures in order to get him to let me write *Becket*.")

Anhalt is a man in a hurry. He walks with short, quick steps. You have to move to keep up with him. He drives hot sports cars fast. During one period he had three crack-ups in two years.

He carries a tape recorder in his car, dictating ideas to his secretary as he rushes to and from appointments. At one time he had a press agent and a staff of researchers on his payroll, not to mention agents, attorneys, and business managers.

His office is in Los Angeles' Marina del Rey yacht harbor aboard a new thirty-five-foot sports fisher. When Eddie travels to Catalina Island for an afternoon or for a weekend, he cruises at speeds over twenty knots.

Our interview took place in two sections. The first was at a mutual friend's apartment (his former P.R. man), and it was punctuated by telephone calls for Eddie—his secretary, his producer-director on *The Killing Zone*, Gilbert Cates, the Guild office. ("I *live* on the telephone.")

Our second meeting was aboard Eddie's boat-office and he apologized at once for having to rush off to another meeting shortly due to a last-minute change in plans.

Anhalt lives on Amalfi Drive in the Pacific Palisades, one of the most beautiful residential streets in America, overlooking the Pacific Ocean.

He married Jacqueline Richards in 1957 and they have four children "collectively."

Chasing after Anhalt can be an exhilarating game. He continuously tosses one-liners that are Groucho Marxian, at their best, and marvelously vulgar, at their worst. His sense of life's absurdities is acute and incisive. He is droll, dry, and a very funny man.

But on the subject of screenwriting Anhalt is both serious and knowledgeable. He cares deeply about his craft, he continues to study it, and he ceaselessly talks about it with his students at Loyola University.

"I teach because I learn as much from them as they do from me."

JOHNSON (CONFIDENTLY)
Not more'n half a mile.

BEAR CLAW (APPROVINGLY)
~~(nodding)~~
~~Close as you can guess 'em.~~ You're GUESSIN' CLOSE.

JOHNSON
That's how I see it. An' he knows where we are. That's why he's heading uphill.

BEAR CLAW
Well, since you got old Mr. Elk figured out, you intend to go up after him?

Johnson turns and smiles.

JOHNSON
No. I'm goin' around this ~~mountain~~ HILL and wait 'til he come down.

Bear Claw mounts his horse.

BEAR CLAW
You're learnin'.

127 ~~MED. TRAVELLING SHOT~~ - JOHNSON AND BEAR CLAW

THEY ~~riding~~ RIDE slowly through the deep woods AT THE BASE OF THE HILL, rifles across their saddles. THE SLOPE ABOVE THEM IS SPARSELY TREED.

BEAR CLAW
You track well, Pilgrim. Kinda like it, don't you?

JOHNSON
~~Maybe.~~ YEP.

BEAR CLAW
Figures. Human man, he likes trackin' and killin. An Injun, he figures it's natural. Thant's why a human man is meaner than an Injun.

JOHNSON
Don't see ~~no~~ THE difference.

127 CONTINUTED:

BEAR CLAW
Injun's lived here all his life. His people lived here before him. He knows what's goin' to happen every day. How hungry him and his family has to get before he sets out on a hunt. Human man comes here and it's somethin' new. He don't fit in, has to learn, has to be twice as tough, twice as mean. Huntin' and killin' ain't natural to him, he enjoys it.

JOHNSON REACHES OVER SUDDENLY AND STOPS BEAR CLAW'S HORSE. THEY BOTH LOOK AHEAD.

128 ~~FULL SHOT~~ POV - BULL ELK AND TWO COWS

THEY stand~~ing~~ on the ~~far edge of a meadow.~~ SLOPE IN THE CLEAR.

JOHNSON~~'S VOICE~~
~~(over)~~
Wind's right but ~~it's all open between us and them.~~ They'll ~~just~~ SEE US AND run soon as ~~we step out of the trees.~~ MOVE TOWARD THEM.

BEAR CLAW~~'S VOICE~~
~~(over)~~
Trick to it. Get off and walk on this side of your horse.

129 ~~MED. SHOT JOHNSON AND BEAR CLAW~~ BACK TO SCENE

THEY DISMOUNT EDGE TOWARD THE ~~ELK~~ ~~edging out into the meadow~~ on the far side of their horses.

JOHNSON
~~What if~~ They'll see our feet WON'T THEY?

BEAR CLAW
Elk don't know how many feet a horse have.

Johnson peers over the saddle of his horse. He starts to move toward the horse's neck, BRINGING HIS RIFLE UP.

BEAR CLAW
~~(continuing, harsh whisper)~~
No ~~damn fool!~~ Slide her up over the saddle.

FROUG: Do you find when you go to work on a project like *Becket*, a stageplay where everything takes place inside three walls, that you have an especially difficult job making it visual?

ANHALT: I've done six or seven plays, or more, I guess, and I don't have that approach to make it visual or make it cinematic. I just forget that. What I become involved with, as I did particularly with *Becket,* is to get away from the concept that the audience is a collaborator with the play. In other words, I believe that the essential difference between the cinema and the theater is when you go into the theater there is a covenant between you and the proscenium arch, which is agreed upon tacitly, to the extent that going to the theater in itself is an event, a social event, a psychological event, and you are there to help the playwright and the actors do what they do, and without your help, it doesn't work at all. But at all times, you are aware that you're in the theater and you're going through that mutual process. On the contrary, when you're going to a film, a film is never really successful unless you forget where you are, completely, and are totally and absolutely involved in a very realistic sense with what's going on. I never have a sense of reality in the theater. I have a sense of something else, which is theatrical. So *Becket,* to me, was a magnificent collaborative experience with Tony Quinn and Laurence Olivier when I saw it in New York in the theater, but I never for a moment forgot where I was. Now, if you put *Becket* on film and you don't forget where you are, it simply doesn't work. For example, in the final scene between Becket and the archbishop. In the play they were mounted on papier-mâché horses, and they played the scene mounted on papier-mâché horses. Well, in the film, we had real horses and we had a real beach instead of just an impressionistic set. The same content couldn't work in both places. To begin with, in spite of efforts to the contrary, to me the theater is always declamation. Nothing wrong with that, but I always have the feeling, even with superb performers, that I'm being addressed. The particular problem with *Becket* was to take it out of the context of being a tapestry and make it a real, live thing. So to do that, I changed the dialogue considerably, plus, of course, doing scenes which were off-scene in the play. For example, the accusation of Becket by the king's man and his arrest and all that was off-scene. I did that on film. And the excommunication scene was off-scene. I did that on film. But it wasn't out of the need to visualize. It was simply out of a need to make it real.

FROUG: *Becket* was enormously successful, both from a critical as well as an audience standpoint. Let's take another play which you adapted for the screen, the almost equally famous *The Madwoman of Chaillot,* which didn't work, apparently, either from an audience standpoint or from a critical standpoint. Why do you feel the one succeeded so enormously, where the other failed?

ANHALT: Well, *The Madwoman of Chaillot,* to begin with, is a fantasy and a satire. For some reason, fantasy and satire simply don't work on the screen. I'm not offering it as an excuse. What I did with *The Madwoman of Chaillot* in the screenplay and what you saw on the screen is not the same.

FROUG: Why wasn't it? Were you rewritten?

ANHALT: More than rewritten. What happened is that John Huston and I started on the film together, and then in my absence Huston had some sort of quarrel with the producers and left. They were desperate to start the film, which they had scheduled and the actors were set and everything, and they took Bryan Forbes on. No, Bryan did not rewrite my screenplay. What he did was take the play and shoot both of them, so that the thing is enormously repetitious. Danny Kaye plays the same scene twice, once my scene and once the play scene. Why he did that, only god knows. But anyway, that's the way it came out, and when I first saw it, which was at Warner Brothers, it ran about two and three quarter hours. The management at Warners then were the Hymans, and everyone sat and applauded vigorously, and I went to Ely Landau, who was the producer, and I said, "Ely, this is a disaster." He said, "But look how everybody loved it." I said, "They love it. They've all been paid to love it!" So I offered to go to London. I said, "I know how to cut it (I used to be a film editor); let me sit down and do it, for free." But he didn't want to. And it was released that way, more or less. And it was a disaster. I'm not saying that it wouldn't have been a disaster otherwise, because maybe there was no way out of it. But the cheap attempt to bring it up to date, to put in student riots and so forth.

FROUG: They were not in your original screenplay?

ANHALT: I had them off-scene. I played those riots off the part of the prospector, and I played him for fun. I played him as Howard Hughes, who was busy collecting graffiti while these riots were going on. It wasn't done that way. There was an attempt to modernize it. Now, Bryan was in Paris when the riots occurred, and so was I, separately. And I was enormously impressed and moved by the riots. But you can't bring in peace up to date (the play was written in 1942 during the war) by arbitrarily seizing on events of today and sticking them into a concept that goes back thirty years. The play itself dates terribly. It's a middle-class play and, generally speaking, I think the things that are being terribly successful now, give or take *Love Story* and *Airport,* are not middle-class. So the audience, speaking only in present-day film ways, became very impatient with *The Madwoman.* I don't think it would have worked even with my screenplay, but it would have worked better. Essentially it would have been defeated by the fact that it dealt with attitudes that are no longer heterodox and, therefore, seem archaic. And yet, they presume heterodoxy.

FROUG: In what way can the screenwriter come to control his own work better so that we don't constantly have the situation of the screenplay versus the picture, and sometimes the twain never meet?

ANHALT: Well, I think by writing original material and refusing to part with it unless you have control, or some amount of control. I don't think that on the screen you probably will ever get the control that the playwright does because the expense of making a film is so enormous, as opposed to doing most plays. The other way is for the individual screenwriter to achieve such status that he's trusted. Now, until things fell apart recently, when I worked for major studios I was trusted to the degree that very frequently I was, in fact, in charge of the project. On several occasions, I actually produced the film without taking credit. As you know, I used to be a producer. And there are a few screenwriters who got themselves into that position. They are no longer in that position, as far as I know.

FROUG: Do you think that film is essentially a director's medium?

ANHALT: I don't think you can make a generalization. I think some directors, even though they may not have actually written the screenplay, are a greater factor in the film than the screenwriter is. On the other hand, in most cases, I would say that the screenwriter is. It's significant that in the case of those directors who are called auteurs, they *are* authors. Fellini is a writer, Milos Forman is a writer. They work on their screenplays.

FROUG: Have you generally had a close collaboration with the director on your pictures, or has there been a wide disparity between the style of working? You've written twenty-six features.

ANHALT: That doesn't include all the "B" pictures.

FROUG: How many would you say were in the "B" picture class?

ANHALT: Oh, I must have written forty "B" pictures.

FROUG: Some under the name of Andrew Holt?

ANHALT: And some under my own name, which I've omitted from the records, and some in collaboration with my ex-wife, and so forth. But in any case, yes, I've always collaborated very closely with the director, when he would let me. As a matter of fact, I can only think of two occasions when I didn't collaborate and that was quite recently. One, I did not collaborate with Bryan Forbes on *The Madwoman*, although I must say, in Bryan's defense, I was in Switzerland when they started to shoot *The Madwoman* and he asked me to come down to Nice to work with him, and I couldn't do it because I was doing something else. So I must have collaborated there. And I did not collaborate there. And I did not collaborate with Peter Glenville on *Becket* because I didn't like him.

FROUG: Why didn't you like him?

ANHALT: Because on our first meeting he said to me, "Now what school did you go to?" And I said, "P.S. Fifty-Four," which doesn't happen to be true, but I found him an impossible snob in a very bad way, and he just turned me off. I just couldn't deal with him without getting angry, so I chose not to. Fortunately, he had already written a screenplay of *Becket*, which was a disaster, so the producer was on my side.

FROUG: And the producer, in effect, imposed your screenplay on him?

ANHALT: Yes, and I would go up to Rome twice a week to see that it was imposed. I never dealt directly with Peter, however.

FROUG: Do most producers tend to back the writer, in your experience, or do they tend to back the director?

ANHALT: In my experience, where there has been a struggle, he is inclined to back the director. Because the director is the captain of the ship—he's there. And usually the writer is elsewhere and, in the end, can't physically do it. How do you take control of the set? I once had this out with Fred Zinnemann when we were doing *Member of the Wedding*. I was also the producer. We got into a disagreement about whether Julie Harris should ride her own bicycle. And I argued that if she fell off the bicycle, that would be the end of it. And he said, "But we can't have a double. It will look terrible." And I said, "Well, it may look terrible, but we can finish the picture." And we got into a real thing about it. So I finally took the command position which, in theory, was mine, and I said, "In that case, you get off the picture and I'm going to have the assistant take over." The assistant had a director's card. But it didn't work; they took me off the picture. So I'm very chary about quarreling with directors ever since.

FROUG: In *The Boston Strangler*, split-screen techniques and various kinds of multiple-image techniques were used. Were those written into the screenplay?

ANHALT: No. Those were the director's, Dick Fleischer's, idea and put in after the screenplay. I indicated them by indicating parallel actions in the screenplay. But the actual configuration of those things, the design, was done by Dick and the art director. I opposed it because I thought it was tricky and brought the picture down. However, I think I was wrong. It seemed to work very well in *The Boston Strangler*. At least, I thought it did.

FROUG: I often feel those techniques tend to get in the way of the story.

ANHALT: It's true. They've disappeared. They were too obviously a technique. It was used and that was the end of it.

FROUG: When your films are shown on television, such as *The Young Savages, Rachel Cade, The Young Lions, The Pride and the Passion, Not as a Stranger*, and so forth, do you receive a royalty payment?

ANHALT: Only the ones made after 1966. We get 1.2 percent

of what the production company takes in. I've gotten about $20,000 from *Becket*, I think, or maybe more, from TV runs.

FROUG: Your other picture which won an Academy Award, *Panic in the Streets*, was your original story?

ANHALT: Yeah, that was an original I wrote with my ex-wife. That was a time when not many originals were written, but that was a hot one. It took about eight hours to write. It was written in treatment form—thirteen pages. And it sold the next day. Every studio bid for it. It was one of those unique occasions.

FROUG: How much did it sell for?

ANHALT: I think it was $75,000.

FROUG: And then were you paid additionally for the screenplay?

ANHALT: We didn't do the screenplay. Dick Murphy did the screenplay.

FROUG: Why?

ANHALT: The producer had another property he wanted us to do and we saw the possibility of getting two credits, one for the screenplay and the other property and one for the original of *Panic in the Streets*. So between the two of us, we either elected to, or were conned into, doing the other property which, of course, was never made. It was called *Waltz into Darkness*.

FROUG: Do you find that the days of writing screenplays that don't get made is as commonplace today as it was a few years back? Can the economics of the industry support non-produced screenplays?

ANHALT: Well, of course, the writers are now coming so cheap because almost all deals are step deals.

FROUG: Can you explain a "step deal?"

ANHALT: That's where the producer can buy an idea from a writer and cut him off after he sees the fully developed story if he decides he doesn't like the way it turned out. He pays a very small amount for that initial investment. Or he can elect to go forward into screenplay and then, if he doesn't like it when it's finished, he can cut off the writer at that point and, if he chooses, hire another writer. I know writers who are now writing their first treatment for minimum.

FROUG: Which is how much?

ANHALT: It's about $2,500. And many producers today are able to get a complete screenplay from a great many writers, a first draft, for maybe $8,000 or $9,000. That's their basic investment. So I would say the chances of not making a lot of them are fairly good. Now, the chances of not making them on the level that I was not making them three or four years ago, no. *The Salzburg Connection* which, I understand now, is finally about to be made, was abandoned by Fox because the budget was about $6.5 million. But I spent more on expenses researching it than most writers get today on a screenplay.

FROUG: How much did you spend on research?

ANHALT: About $28,000.

FROUG: And how much were you paid for the screenplay?

ANHALT: $200,000. The same goes for *Man on a Nylon String*. But the budget came out at $8.5 million. That was for Steve McQueen's company at CBS, Cinema Center, so the picture was impossible at that price.

FROUG: And what were you paid for the screenplay?

ANHALT: The same.

FROUG: $200,000 and they abandoned it?

ANHALT: Well, it was better to abandon it than to spend $8.5 million or $9 million, whatever it was. Sometimes they don't. They made *Le Mans,* which I think cost that much. That started as a screenplay of mine that I called—I can't remember the name of it. Whatever it was, it was about racing, and Steve, who is a racing nut, hung on to it. It was called *The Day of the Champion*, that's right, with John Sturges as the director, originally. Steve stuck with it and he finally made the film. But they spent so much money on it that unless it's a major, major film, it's not going to get its money back. [It hasn't.]

FROUG: CBS had a great deal of trouble with that, sending to France not only supervisors and executives but, at one time, I was told, they had three writers simultaneously writing in different offices outside of Paris, each writing a complete screenplay.

ANHALT: I wouldn't doubt it. The problem with any racing film is that the only really interesting thing about it is the racing. You can't do more than twenty minutes of that. You get dizzy. So what do you do in between? The ones I've seen have always been dull because there are only three or four basic situations. There's also the feeling, I think, in the minds of most people that a man who races is somehow alienated from them. I can't see any great personality conflicts coming out of a race.

FROUG: A couple of years back, *Time* magazine reported that you had a staff of researchers. Do you still have them?

ANHALT: I have one. But what I did in those days was kind of scattershoot. I had people looking things up for me and trying to get me ideas, and so forth.

FROUG: *Time* also quoted you as saying, "If the writer has improved his status at all, he has probably become a producer or director." Do you still feel that way?

ANHALT: Yeah, I think so. I did it backwards. I was a producer before I had any status, and the production thing really bored me. It was a bookkeeping operation a great deal of the time. And except for casting and supervising of scripts, I found it not satisfying, not creatively. As far as directing, I've tried desperately to direct, but the only things I've ever been able to direct, or been offered to direct, are television shows. I did one television show.

FROUG: *A Time for Killing*, on the "Chrysler Theater"?

ANHALT: Yeah, with George C. Scott and Michael Parks. And then after that, I was offered other television shows to direct. And, very foolishly, I put them down in my mind. I didn't do them. I guess because, if I'm realistic, they didn't pay very much.

FROUG: I understand that you directed *A Time for Killing*

for scale in order to get your first chance?

ANHALT: Right, right. It cost me $2,500 to join the Directors Guild. I got maybe $2,000 for the show, so I experienced a loss. However, they paid me to write it. But in those days I was getting one-fifty for a screenplay.

FROUG: $150,000?

ANHALT: Yeah, or $6,000 a week. But television shows paid maybe tops $4,000 to direct. So in the time that I directed a television show, I could write a screenplay. I guess I was greedy. It was very stupid of me because had I done it, and done four or five successful ones—and *A Time for Killing* was very successful for me—I probably would have escalated into feature direction.

FROUG: Do the critics affect your work?

ANHALT: No, no. I regard film criticism, at least in the United States, as kind of a literary effort on the part of the critic. I'm very impressed by the quality, the literary quality, of the criticism, but I think a great deal of it is done for its own sake. And I wish some of the critics would become writers because they write so well, it seems a shame to waste it on criticism.

FROUG: What responsibility do you think the film director has toward the screenplay? Do you think he should have the freedom to change as he sees fit?

ANHALT: Well, I don't think you can make a morality of it. It seems to me the producer, although, frequently now, he is also the director, is in control of the material. If I were in that position and I liked a piece of material and was making the film, I would want to consult with the writer. As a matter of fact, on the film I'm now writing, *The Killing Zone*, the writer of the original material is Bill Woods, and I consult him constantly. He wrote the novel. It's not a question of morality. I would take his material and turn it inside out. As a matter of fact, I am, to a degree, but I do it with his knowledge and in consultation with him because, obviously, it's his material. And, by the same token, if I were directing a film, I would want to consult with the screenwriter. But I don't think that directors are obliged to do anything. He does what he wants to do.

FROUG: Do you feel, in adapting a play or a novel that is familiar to the mass audience, that you are obliged to preserve the original material as much as possible?

ANHALT: Absolutely not because I don't think it *is* familiar, except to a very small number of people, give or take a runaway thing like *Love Story* where it's in the *Reader's Digest* and it's been read by maybe ten million people, then you have an obligation only in the sense that you may get some kickback. But I've distorted very popular novels. *The Young Lions, Not as a Stranger* were very distorted on the screen, very changed. *The Boston Strangler* is turned completely inside out, and give or take Digby Diehl in the *Los Angeles Times*, who spent a whole page attacking it, nobody ever notices.

FROUG: In other words, you feel that the screen requirements are so different that, when necessary, you must change the story as you see fit?

ANHALT: No, I don't think that. I don't think it's a question of the requirements of the screen changing the story. In all the three cases that I mentioned, I changed the story because I didn't like the story that much. I wanted to change it, I rewrote. In the case of *The Boston Strangler*, for example, in Gerald Frank's book, which was real, DeSalvo was a guy who got his kicks by killing women. He killed fourteen women, and he was very open about his kicks. I've heard his tape, illegally, and he keeps saying in his confession that it was the only way that he could come. Well, I did that in the screenplay, but I found it dull. I found that if you strangle one woman, you strangle two. After you strangle enough women, then it just doesn't move anymore—which is one of the things that's wrong with escalating violence, dramatically. So I had to invent something that was more interesting to me and, therefore, presumably would be to the audience. I believe that people write for themselves. I really pay no attention to anything else. But to me, I had to make him more interesting, so I made him a dual personality. The good DeSalvo didn't know what the bad DeSalvo was doing, which is certainly one of the oldest devices in the world. But it worked on the screen, and not only that, the people who read the book never realized they weren't seeing reality.

FROUG: They assumed that that was the actual character?

ANHALT: Well, the screen has great authority. If you see it, you're inclined to believe it.

FROUG: More so than the novel?

ANHALT: I think so. Because with the novel, after all, you read it, you put it down and go to sleep, you eat, and you pick it up again and, after all, you are imagining it. You don't imagine anything on the screen. You see it. So when you see it you believe it, which is what the people who want to censor television have been talking about in the sense that if you see violence you'll believe it, and you're liable to do it. In any case, the trick in doing that is to reinforce it with a kind of documentary flavor. In *The Boston Strangler,* Dick and I reinforced the fantasy, our fantasy, with a great deal of reality, or apparent reality, which was tricky, but it worked.

FROUG: Do you feel that excessive violence in films and TV is a problem?

ANHALT: Well, I think it's a problem to those people who can be touched off by violence. And I wouldn't stop it or censor it just for that reason. But I do think that some people are touched off by it. I was involved in a case, a rather well-known case, in *The Sniper.*

FROUG: It was nominated, I believe, for an Academy Award.

ANHALT: Yeah, in 1950.

FROUG: Was that an original screenplay?

ANHALT: It was an original treatment. The screenplay was done by Harry Brown, who wrote *A Walk in the Sun*. *The Sniper* was a man who got his orgasms by shooting women. The studio said he was a pervert, and I pointed out to them that if the man had his orgasms by shooting men, he would be a pervert. But, after all, as a man who used women for that purpose, he was just a simple heterosexual and, for some reason or other, this appealed to them. And we got to make the picture. But what happened wasn't quite so funny. In Ottawa, Canada, a kid, I think, of nineteen, sat through the picture five times, went out and shot eight women. And, I have a letter someplace from his parents saying that nobody understood his problem until they saw the film, and the film understood his problem better than anyone, and so forth. But, in any case, the women who were shot (luckily the gun was a .22), none of them were killed. But they all sued, or most of them sued, the studio. And it went to the Canadian Supreme Court, and the court decided against the plaintiff on the grounds that the artist does not have the responsibility of what happens afterward. That attitude has gone through the courts here, too. It was a monumental decision, legally speaking.

FROUG: The decision was that art was imitating life?

ANHALT: That the artist, or the artistic entity, does not have the responsibility for what happens as a consequence of whatever it does. And that goes for pornography. You know, there's the illusion that some people, on seeing a pornographic film, will go out and rape somebody. That's, of course, nonsense, because the people who see pornographic films get their satisfaction from that, and they're the least likely to rape anybody. If you go to the porno theaters around here, you'll see that they're all masturbating. They're not interested in women at all. That's why they go.

FROUG: What are some of the techniques you employ to give depth to a character?

ANHALT: Same techniques used in the theater and in novel writing. They're not techniques, they're explorations of character, in one form or another. I can't really write about a character that I don't know. If I find a character that I don't know, I usually convert him or her to some character that I do know so that I can write about them.

FROUG: In *Becket*, those characters were laid out in the play. Did you use those characters, or did you add to them material from people you also knew?

ANHALT: No, I added material from people who have been in that kind of conflict, and from my own conflicts in that area. Which is, after all, a moral conflict that is not confined to the church or state relationship. I don't think I could write successfully about people that I don't know.

FROUG: Is there any central problem you've found in translating the novel to the screen?

ANHALT: Well, there's a great deal of going down from and going up to essential scenes in a novel—bridging—usually taken up with rather cerebral, internal investigations of the character, which are useless on the screen. Although they may clarify character to the writer, as far as action goes they're meaningless. So I developed a technique in dealing with novels which is somewhat primitive. But what I do is, I take the binding off the novel and then when I read it, when I read something that excites me, I put it on a bulletin board until finally I have maybe ten sequences that I find stimulating.

FROUG: Pages that you've torn out of a novel?

ANHALT: Yeah. And then, generally speaking, what I do is, I somehow develop ways of connecting those sequences, or I may add my own sequences. In any case, it's a mechanistic way of approaching it, and I don't recommend it as what everybody should do. But it just works for me, or it seems to.

FROUG: Do you begin a screenplay with a step outline?

ANHALT: Always. I use cards.

FROUG: Three-by-five index cards?

ANHALT: Three by five. And I write each sequence in detail on the cards. One card for each sequence. I usually end up with twenty-eight, thirty sequences per hour of film.

FROUG: In the course of planning your story structure, do

you shuffle those cards around?

ANHALT: Yes. I put them on the floor sometimes so I can see them from up here. Probably because I was a film editor. I think it's very good training for a screenwriter because I can tell the actual lengths of sequences in terms of film. Frequently, before I write them. I know pretty much how they're going to come out, in some strange way.

FROUG: In terms of film time and page count?

ANHALT: Yeah.

FROUG: How many pages do your first drafts usually run?

ANHALT: They usually run about 145 to 150 pages.

FROUG: And how much do you cut that to get a final draft?

ANHALT: My final draft runs between 128 and 134 or 135—almost always, unless there's an enormous amount of action in the film, I figure maybe 14,000 feet (6,000 feet is an hour, and an hour and a half is 9,000 feet) so for every ten minutes, you add 1,000 feet.

FROUG: How many drafts do you write before you get what you call a final draft?

ANHALT: Well, I've never written more than three. I rarely do anything radical after the first draft. Give or take minor changes. I've rarely written anything that I've looked at and said this doesn't work at all, because the cards seem to tell me this.

FROUG: Have you ever rewritten to accommodate actors?

ANHALT: Marlon Brando had a lot of problems about *The Young Lions*, a lot of internal questions that were never satisfactorily answered to him in the screenplay, and he would say, "I just can't do this." Particularly, there was one love scene, I remember, that he and I sat around and, somehow by playing the part (he'd play himself and I'd play the girl), we somehow got the scene out. That kind of thing. I've done that with actors.

FROUG: Where you've gone back and rewritten to accommodate their idiosyncrasies?

ANHALT: Well, not so much their idiosyncrasies, but their very strong feelings about the content of the scene, that it wasn't right for them or it wasn't right for the story. I have great faith in actors, in their instincts. If I ever direct again, I'd be very, very humble with the actors because I think that's their business. I think their projection of emotion is how they make a living. And they almost always, to me, have very good instincts. That's why I'm working at the Actor's Studio now, because that experience, I think, is important to a writer.

FROUG: Are you working there as an actor?

ANHALT: No. I'm working there as a monitor in the playwrighting course. But in the course of it, I do see student plays done by experienced performers, and I also go to the acting classes as an observer.

FROUG: In today's market, we're talking now about screenwriters getting $2,500 for a story and maybe $10,000 for a screenplay, can the writer make a living out of films?

ANHALT: Well, if he's successful with his first screenplay, of course, his price will escalate. It will never go to where it was before. At least not in the immediate future, although a few writers . . . I understand Waldo Salt is now getting $200,000.

FROUG: Because of *Midnight Cowboy*?

ANHALT: Well, because of *Midnight Cowboy*, but principally because he's a tremendously talented writer, which nobody gave him a chance to show in recent years, because of the blacklist and the reverberations from that.

FROUG: Do you have regular work habits?

ANHALT: Well, I'd like to but, of course, I actually don't. To begin with, I loathe writing. I assume most writers do, and I get up in the morning and invent incredible reasons not to write. And, ultimately, I run out of reasons not to write. There are no telephone calls to make, there's nothing to do, so I have to write. I find that being emotionally upset is very good for me because then I escape into writing. However, that can drain you, being in a constant state of turmoil. But generally I get down to it and then I begin to enjoy it, and then I'll write quite extensively until it becomes non-enjoyable. Then I stop, on the theory that not enjoying it is akin to not doing it very well.

FROUG: How many hours do you work at a stretch, generally?

ANHALT: Oh, maybe between two and three, and then I get tired.

FROUG: Do you work seven days a week?

ANHALT: Yeah. I never work at night. I find that my most productive hours are usually between eight and ten in the morning and maybe between four and seven in the afternoon. I think I'm still on infant feeding because I feel that I'll reward myself with lunch at twelve, so I'm aiming toward that; and later in the day, I'll reward myself with a cocktail, so I aim toward that.

FROUG: How many screenplays do you turn out a year?

ANHALT: Usually two.

FROUG: Do you dictate or do you write with a typewriter?

ANHALT: I write longhand and from that I go to tape. I read the scene. I also act out the scene, and if it doesn't sound right when I replay it, I do it over. Although I'm not a very good actor, it works for me. So I can play a number of parts. Brando taught me that. He does that—where he'll play all the parts and listen to himself. So I do that and then I transmit that over the telephone to my secretary, who has a telephone pickup on her end, and then she takes it off her tape onto the typewriter. Then once a day or so, we meet. She comes down to the boat or I go to her house, or whatever, and she gives me the pages.

FROUG: When you see the pages from the tape, are they revised heavily?

ANHALT: Not heavily, just in detail.

FROUG: How long does it take you to write that first draft?

ANHALT: Usually eight weeks.

FROUG: How many days or weeks do you allow yourself for the step outline before that?

ANHALT: Well, in contracts, I usually allow four. To me, the step outline is the most important part of it. And I would allow more if I thought there was a serious problem. For example, on *The Boston Strangler*, when I took the job, I knew there was a terrible problem because they had an awfully good writer on it before me, and he was a disaster. But I knew somewhere, intuitively, there was some solution to it, so I made them give me six weeks to do the step outline. Once you know that you can write, per se, writing is not a problem to me. The problem is construction and what's it about and what do they do, and so forth. If I have trouble writing a scene, it's because something is wrong with the scene. It's not writable. That's arrogant, but I find it to be true. The scenes that break down are the ones that could not be written.

FROUG: When you have trouble writing a scene, do you go back to the step outline?

ANHALT: Yeah. What the hell is wrong? I could write a scene and, no matter what I do, it doesn't come out right, and I'm not having any fun, which is the first canon. So then I go recheck the outline and usually find it's an unnecessary scene or should have been combined with something else, or whatever.

FROUG: Is the problem often that there's no conflict in the scene?

ANHALT: Yeah. Usually I've masked an expository move by having a synthetic conflict of some kind. That's almost always what's wrong, and it's apparent—it doesn't play. Now, a great many writers—I've observed this as a producer or when I've been in supervisory capacities—a great many writers don't seem to know that. It seems to be the major fault in screenwriters. Which is, that a scene types and reads jazzily and doesn't break down until you get it on the stage. That's what Brando found in that scene that was bad in *The Young Lions*. It simply falls apart. I think one of the advantages of the tape is that you can play the scene out and maybe hear where it falls apart before you commit it to the screenplay and before it gets on the stage.

FROUG: Do you find that if you have strong characters that they will tend to drive your scene forward for you?

ANHALT: Yeah. If you have strong characters and you enjoy them or hate them or love them or whatever, I think what Shaw spoke of actually happens. That is, the characters seem to be speaking themselves, they seem to be real. I just had a phone call, here while we were talking, from the director of this picture, Gil Cates, and he said, "You put in the flashbacks," because I'd said we won't have any flashbacks, and we had agreed on that. Well, what happened is, I got inside the man's head and I began to think in his terms—in his relationship with his girl—and he began to dream of his girl and think of her, and I had to do the scenes involving the girl. It seemed obligatory when I was doing it. It's not in the outline. I had not intended to do it. Then when I get finished—this, of course, is compulsive on my part—I committed it to the outline and put it in with the cards and looked at it and it seemed to work.

FROUG: The character drove you to this?

ANHALT: Right.

FROUG: Do you do extensive research before you begin to write?

ANHALT: I can't conceive of doing a screenplay in an area with which I am not familiar without exhaustively going into it. When I did *Not as a Stranger*, I must have seen ten surgeries.

FROUG: And you did a picture about call girls . . .

ANHALT: *The Almost People.* To do that, I went to the local whorehouses, of which there are many right in this area, incidentally. I must have talked to twenty hookers of various kinds, and I went into the whole economics—you know, the various social aspects of the business. And the same with the restaurant business. The lead is a man who is the second in command of a chain of restaurants, so I have a friend, Jack Bartell, who runs the Tail o'the Cock chain, and I went with him for a couple of weeks, and wherever he went I went, listened and took notes, and learned about the restaurant business.

FROUG: And carried your tape recorder with you?

ANHALT: Yeah. But I didn't tape direct conversations. That makes people very nervous. Although I did tape the brigade commander's debriefing, secretly, on this army maneuver, and it really sounds like Bob Newhart wrote it. But anyway, I usually just make notes.

FROUG: Do you often get whole scenes during your research?

ANHALT: Absolutely.

FROUG: And dialogue?

ANHALT: Yeah. The one scene in *The Almost People,* which is unbelievable, actually happened, and is a scene in a whorehouse where one of the customers caught on fire. And there was a great deal of excitement. So I have it in the picture—not believable, but it happened. That's one of the problems, incidentally, of doing screenplays. Because it's real doesn't necessarily mean it's believable. What happened here was, this man liked to be tortured and, as you probably know, very few of the customers who go to the houses are straight. They're all strange in some way. They require special treatment. So this particular man liked to be tortured. So they would drop alcohol on his genitals, which burned him, and then he had a whole number with hot wax, and so forth. Well, anyway, while I was there, the girl dropped the candle which ignited the alcohol, and there was a great deal of excitement with blankets and fire extinguishers and so forth. And the madame threw a great line, which I used in the picture. She said, "My god, what's he gonna tell his wife? He doesn't even smoke!" But that might not work on the screen because it's too grotesque. In Germany it would work.

FROUG: With the reduction in the number of films being made, what do you think is the future for the screenwriter?

ANHALT: Well, I think if CATV becomes a reality, on a big

scale, if pay television happens, and I would say whether it happens or not depends on whether the manufacturers of equipment can put up more money for lobbying than the broadcasters and the advertising agencies, and I suspect they can—if that happens then I think it's a very good one because there will be enormous select markets to write for, to make pictures for.

FROUG: Why does the writer, historically, have less control than almost any other person connected with the film—the producer, the director has more control, the actor has more control.

ANHALT: Because the other crafts have to do with the actual committing of the story to film, which is something you can hold in your hand and project on a screen. Whereas the screenplay is essentially a blueprint for that piece of work. It's the relationship between the architect and the builder.

FROUG: And yet the builder wouldn't think of reconstructing from the blueprint in the sense that the director or the producer or the actor often feels free to do in film. A builder will inevitably slavishly follow that blueprint. Frank Lloyd Wright did blueprints but nobody dared tamper with them.

ANHALT: Yes, but Frank Lloyd Wright also supervised the building. In other words, he was like the writer who becomes the director; nobody dared because he was there and he'd kill 'em. It was also written in his contracts. However, the blueprint can be changed, frequently should be changed, and almost always is changed. And that's why the writer is in the inferior position, economically and every other way, because he's not there and it's not necessary for him to be there. It is necessary for the director and everybody else to be there. And also because the manuscript is not a plastic medium, it isn't real, it isn't dimensional. It's a piece of paper with some writing on it.

FROUG: And yet, ironically, even in film, in the beginning is the word, is it not?

ANHALT: Well, that is true. But the word, in a play, preempts everything else. On the screen, the illusion is—and the writers have collaborated in this illusion—that the dialogue is the word and the description is something else. So that the people who read screenplays almost invariably do not read the descriptive phrases or the internal descriptions and read only the dialogue. So a wise screenwriter will always put anything of significance in parenthesis after the character's name in the dialogue or nobody will read it. In any case, that's simply the reality. Now what the writer does about that, he bullies by status or he becomes very friendly with everybody. I think it's very important, at least in screen and probably in television, for the writer to belong to the same social circle as the director and/or producer. That's very important because they're a little awkward then about making changes without consulting him.

FROUG: Do you see the film cassette as being a livelihood for the screenwriter?

ANHALT: No.

FROUG: Why not?

ANHALT: I can't imagine anybody making a collection of films on cassettes, give or take people who collect classic films. I think there'll be so many channels that you'll be able to pick your films.

FROUG: Will the Writers Guild succeed in getting a royalty for the writer from cassettes or pay TV?

ANHALT: Well, the Writers Guild will try. There'll be a major strike. They'll be hard to strike because I don't know where the people are that we're going to strike. They've all disappeared. And, hopefully, if there is a strike, it will be run on a very professional kind of teamsters level.

FROUG: I see in the trade papers that you're writing what appears to be the longest movie ever planned. Could you tell us about it?

ANHALT: It's *QBVII*, Leon Uris' novel, which Screen Gems and ABC are doing, and the plan is to screen it one night a week, Monday through Friday, five nights in a row, an hour each night. It's done in the manner of "Forsyte Saga," the way the BBC did it, but all in one week.

FROUG: In the course of developing that, are you doing it with commercial act breaks? Does each hour episode have its own conclusion, or is it a cliffhanger?

ANHALT: I'm just writing a 400-page screenplay. But there are enough natural curtains. I'm not worried about that. I'll do it afterwards. If I start to worry about that I'll go crazy.

FROUG: When you construct a 400-page screenplay, an awesome job, do you look at it as simply a longer version of what you've always done?

ANHALT: Well, it's twice as awesome as doing a 150-page or a 200-page screenplay, but there's enough story in it, or at least suggested in the novel. Uris does things like, "And then Abraham Cady went to Sausalito where he spent the next ten years." That's two pages. Well, I'll invent what happens in Sausalito or wherever. I won't use Sausalito actually. I'm going to use Beverly Hills, and do ten years.

FROUG: Why have you changed Sausalito to Beverly Hills?

ANHALT: Because there are, I think, three major time spans in the novel, all three of which Uris handles in two pages of description. So I have a choice between the outskirts of London, Sausalito, and Hollywood. And since the character point that I'm developing has its basis in Beverly Hills, in his Hollywood experience, I'm going to do Cady's experience as a screenwriter in Hollywood in the fifties.

FROUG: How much research do you do, aside from the book itself before beginning writing?

ANHALT: I went to London and sat in the law court where at least 50 percent of the film takes place (in the Royal Courts of Justice) and listened to cases and talked to the attorneys and the solicitors and so forth. I read everything I could about the court, and then I took the route that I'm going to have Cady take in Europe, looking for the survivors of the concentration camp. I invented that route and then I followed it, going to the different concentration camps.

FROUG: How long have you spent preparing to write the screenplay?

ANHALT: I spent about four weeks in Europe, and probably three weeks of intensive reading. About seven weeks.

FROUG: And then are you working from your index cards to build a step outline?

ANHALT: Yes. I've already done the index card number with the producer, but now, because the network is involved, I have to do a formal rendering. In other words I'll have to put the index cards into English.

FROUG: Into treatment form?

ANHALT: No, I won't do that. That would be death. Because to describe what happens in the unliterate form of the treatment would be dull. So I prefer to do it in shorthand on the cards. I'll simply make it less shorthand-y than I would for professionals like myself or the producers.

FROUG: Are they going to spend the kind of money that a five-hour picture might warrant, or is it going to be reasonably low budget?

ANHALT: Low budget—$2.5 million. A lot for television, I guess, but after all, it is a film, whether it's on television or not. One of the problems is that they then intend to cut it down for theatrical release outside the United States and the United Kingdom, to a two- or two-hour-and-fifteen-minute picture, so I really am writing with both productions in mind. In other words, I'm writing it as I would if I were the film editor, trying to figure out how to do it.

FROUG: Is there any difference that you've noted in writing this feature for television as opposed to writing a feature for theatrical release?

ANHALT: I guess the primary difference is one that I hadn't thought of until the producers brought it to my attention, which is that since I'm working it out in parallel action (I'm starting with the story of Cady and then cutting to what's happening to Kelno at the same time in history, that is, the end of the Second World War), the producer said to me on television, "No one is going to sit through the story of Cady the way you have it, because they won't know that Kelno is coming up and the assumption is they won't know the property, most of them, regardless of the advertising and publicity. So you've got to hook them right away. So," he said, "what you have to start with is a statement of what it's about, what the conflict is, and who the major characters are. And where you are. In some sort of explosive way." So that's what I've done. I've already written that part of the screenplay because it seemed to me that that was the basic thing I had to do. So I opened up with that kind of statement in dramatic terms. And I wouldn't have done that for a theatrical film.

FROUG: You'd have let it build gradually, bringing in surprises as they develop?

ANHALT: Yes, because the audience is already in the theater. They've paid their admission and they're hooked, whereas on television they just find it dull if it's difficult or it isn't fast enough for them, or they don't know what it's about.

FROUG: In writing a five-hour movie for television, is your fee commensurate with writing a feature motion picture?

ANHALT: Well, my fees are down so drastically anyway, like everybody else's, it's commensurate in terms of the reduction of the whole economy. The whole economy of the picture business. I'm told it's still outrageous for television. In other words, with my reduction I'm still getting a great deal. Actually, in terms of, say, two years ago, in terms of what I normally turned in, I figured I should be getting $500,000 for this. Figuring that I used to get $200,000 for a 150-page screenplay, and this is 400. However, those are idle dreams. But I have been making deals for percentages, and they are percentages that I would say they could only steal say 50 percent of.

FROUG: So you might even end up with something?

ANHALT: Well, on "QBVII" I'll just end up with the cash. But it was irresistible, at least when everyone told me that your name will be on the television screen every night for five nights, and this has never been done before and you'll be a very important fellow to the networks.

FROUG: So the future is television?

ANHALT: Well, I think the future is television in the sense of pay television or cable television.

FROUG: In other words, you feel that the thing that hooked you was that you were moving into a new form. Like it or not, that's what's here.

ANHALT: That's it.

FROUG: I understand you were called in to rewrite *The Crow Killer*, which subsequently became *Jeremiah Johnson.*

ANHALT: When a script gets in some kind of story trouble, when they're in extremus, then they need help. I always follow the same procedure. I ask whoever is in charge what they're trying to say. And then, having digested that, I play the Coming Out of the Theater Game. An acquaintance comes up to me and he says, "What was the picture all about?" And if I can't tell him in three sentences, then I know it doesn't work. The answer to *Jeremiah Johnson* was; "This is the story of the inevitable destruction of every man's dream, and the spine of the film, the comment it makes, is that the measure of a man is the grace with which he survives that destruction." As soon as everybody, Sidney Pollack, the director, and his associates, came to this statement, then I reconstructed the film to say that.

FROUG: Do you like being a script doctor?

ANHALT: I like it providing enough doctoring is required to get screen credit. In this case it was.

FROUG: Do you feel a script is improved generally by the number of writers who work on it?

ANHALT: No. But sometimes it's unavoidable. John Milius, the original writer, was committed to one kind of story and the producers weren't.

FROUG: Did you like the original screenplay?

ANHALT: I thought it was brilliant but I don't know how many people would have paid to see it.

FROUG: Why not?

ANHALT: Because the real Jeremiah Johnson killed 247 Crow Indians and then ate their livers and that's not nice.

Stirling Silliphant

1954 FIVE AGAINST THE HOUSE *(Joint Screenplay)*

1956 NIGHTFALL *(Screenplay)*
HUK! *(Novel and Screenplay)*

1957 DAMN CITIZEN *(Story and Screenplay)*
MARACAIBO *(Novel Basis for Screenplay)*
THE LINEUP *(Story and Screenplay)*

1960 VILLAGE OF THE DAMNED *(Joint Screenplay)*

1965 THE SLENDER THREAD *(Screenplay)*

1966 IN THE HEAT OF THE NIGHT *(Screenplay)*,
Academy Award, Writers Guild Nomination

1967 CHARLY *(Screenplay)*

1969 MARLOWE *(Screenplay)*
THE LIBERATION OF L.B. JONES *(Joint Screenplay)*
A WALK IN THE SPRING RAIN *(Screenplay)*

1970 MURPHY'S WAR *(Screenplay)*

1972 THE NEW CENTURIONS *(Screenplay)*
THE POSEIDON ADVENTURE *(Joint Screenplay)*

1973 SHAFT IN AFRICA *(Story and Screenplay)*

1974 TOWERING INFERNO *(Screenplay)*

1975 THE KILLER ELITE *(Joint Screenplay)*

1976 THE ENFORCER *(Joint Screenplay)*

1977 TELEFON *(Joint Screenplay)*
THE SWARM *(Screenplay)*

1978 THE SILENT FLUTE *(Joint Screenplay)*
CIRCLE OF IRON *(Joint Story and Screenplay)*

1979 WHEN TIME RAN OUT *(Joint Screenplay)*

1986 OVER THE TOP *(Joint Screenplay)*

1987 CATCH THE HEAT *(Story and Screenplay)*

The extraordinary frankness of Stirling Silliphant, which this interview demonstrates, is a fair measure of the man. He is, in the current vernacular, "out front." You know where he stands.

A conversation with Stirling can leave you both stimulated and exhausted. His mind races ahead seizing new ideas and articulating them with the ease of a trapeze artist who knows precisely when to leap.

It is an indication of Stirling's pace and organizational ability that he read and edited the transcript of our conversation (in its original form, over 100 pages) the same afternoon he received it, made meticulous notes and minor changes on every page, gave it to his secretary to read and comment on, telephoned me to discuss what he had done with the material, and returned the revised copy to me all within the span of four hours.

Yet there is nothing frenetic in Silliphant's modus operandi. The supercharged energy of the man operates within a sphere of serenity and self-assurance.

Pingree Productions (Stirling's own company) is the operational center of one of Hollywood's most successful and prolific writer-producers. Our interview took place at its headquarters at Paramount Studios in Hollywood. Stirling says he maintains offices in five studios, in addition to one on the Sunset Strip.

The atmosphere in Silliphant's suite is one of cool efficiency. A battery of secretaries quietly turns out the day's work. There is none of the hysteria one normally finds in the nerve center of a weekly television series in full production.

Pingree currently has a one-hour series shooting for ABC-TV ("Longstreet"), a film in release for MGM (*Shaft*), a subsidiary, Yaqui Film Company, consisting of a group of young filmmakers now writing and producing *The Teachings of Don Juan, A Yaqui Way of Knowledge*, another feature seeking financing for filming in India (*The Silent Flute*, to star James Coburn and to be directed by William Fraker), and a lawsuit against Avco-Embassy Pictures for $150,000 charging breach of contract over preproduction costs and screenwriter advances (to Silliphant, who was to write the screenplay) for a projected film titled *All the Emperor's Horses*.

If that schedule weren't enough to break the back of the average writer, much less producer, Stirling has just completed writing the screenplay of the best-selling novel, *The New Centurions*, for Columbia Pictures, is personally overseeing production of the "Longstreet" television series as executive producer, and has promised the network he will write a substantial number of the first group of episodes.

None of these activities, however, prevents Silliphant from traveling all over the world. ("I was out of the country five times this year, in India, Europe, Japan, Mexico. I have to get away from here once in a while.") Or lecturing at colleges and universities. No guest speaker who has ever addressed my classes has received a more enthusiastic reception.

In the face of this truly staggering schedule, I expected to find a weary and harassed writer-producer agonizing behind a desk piled high with the debris of overcommitment.

On the contrary, Silliphant's office has no desk. Instead there is a small conference table (spotlessly clean) with four chairs, a couch, a bar, a private bathroom, subdued colors, and soft lighting. There isn't a script in sight. Only the soft clicking of the secretarial typewriters can be heard, like crickets, faintly in the distance. The television and movie world is far away.

Stirling is of medium build, lean, wiry, appearing exceptionally fit. His casual attire is expensive Mod, as is his haircut, long, styled. Except that his hair is gray, he might easily pass for fifteen years younger than his actual age—early fifties.

Silliphant's manner is effortless, efficient, and professional. One gets the impression that he immediately computes a situation in terms of how much time he should allow it—and how much effort. For our interview he shut off the phones, set aside the afternoon, and talked about what he likes most—writing.

Silliphant graduated magna cum laude and Phi Beta Kappa from the University of Southern California. During his college days he wrote poetry in Spanish using a vocabulary of 15,000 words. After graduation he worked as a newspaper reporter, advertising man, and publicity manager for a studio, and wrote a novel before turning to screen and television writing. ("I wanted to write from the day I was born.")

His prolificacy on TV on two series, "Naked City" and "Route 66," is legendary in Hollywood. He wrote seventy-one original one-hour scripts for "Route 66," and most of them are on a level of quality far above the average television dramatic fare.

Until *In the Heat of the Night*, he was not considered an "important" filmwriter—but with the winning of the Oscar for that screenplay he became much in demand.

Silliphant drives a white Rolls Royce and his wife a Mercedes-Benz convertible. He has been reported as having a personal income of $500,000 a year and it's probably not far from the truth.

Stirling has gone through all of the Hollywood success syndromes, from adulation and awards to derogation and divorces. He has been the subject of no small amount of jealous envy from his fellow writers as well as overblown praise from overeager press agents. He has known more than his share of deep personal tragedies, not the least of which was the senseless murder of his teenage son.

Stirling speaks of "grinding and exhilarating" experiences which are part of the life process, and he has survived an abundance of both. Perhaps because of it, somewhere within the incredible drive for ever greater achievement and the contradictory force that has led him to seek asylum and peace through Eastern religions have found a "symbiosis"—a favorite word of Stirling's.

Silliphant is neither Glick nor Gandhi. He is a brilliant, determined, ambitious man moving at all deliberate speed toward his own private destination.

FAT WOMAN
I'm not going in. I'm afraid of him. He said he'd kill me if I called the ~~coops~~ cops.

SERGIO
He got a gun?

FAT WOMAN
Bedroom closet. ~~When you take him, you better take that too.~~

Sergio goes up the steps first.

FAT WOMAN
(calling after him)
Number twelve. We live in number twelve.

EXT. THE COURTYARD

The three officers enter the court, there's ~~look around. The apartments~~ On the second level ~~have~~ a balcony which runs all the way around the U-shaped apartment house.

ROY
Twelve must be back this way.

He ~~moves off toward one side and~~ passes a stairway surrounded by high ferns. A frail chalky man in a damp undershirt steps from behind the ferns, ~~and~~ points a cheap .22 revolver at Roy's stomach and fires. Then he throws the gun away and starts to scream insanely. Roy sits down on the stairway in amazement.

ROY
Christ! Not in the stomach.
Not again. Not the stomach!

Guns out, Sergio and Gus close in on the frantic old man, pick up the .22 he's dropped. The man makes no resistance. He ~~except to~~ starts sobbing as they cuff him to a stanchion. ~~and go to Roy.~~

Roy has opened his uniform and his shirt. He touches the tiny bubbling cavity in the pit of his stomach. ~~with one finger.~~ He unclamps his teeth, ~~and~~ swallows hard.

Sergio and Gus kneel beside him. Sergio crosses himself and kisses his thumbnail.

ROY
(whispering to Gus)
~~Gus,~~ It can't happen now. I don't want it to happen now. Please, not now. I'm just starting to know . . .

Sergio takes Roy's hand.

Gus shouts up at the people gathering above him on the balcony.

GUS
Somebody call an ambulance.

ROY
...know...know...know...

Sergio looks up despairingly at Gus

SERGIO
Ay, Dios mio. His hand is cold.

Roy leans over sideways, Sergio still holding his hand. ~~Roy lies now without moving~~.

SERGIO
~~(clutching his hand)~~
Gus, do you hear him? Do you hear what he is saying? He is saying "no" to death! No, no, no he is saying!

Gus feels for Roy's pulse.

GUS
He's dead.

~~Sobbing,~~ Sergio shakes his head, denying this. But Gus' look is conclusive. Sergio lifts his friend into his arms, ~~cuddles him,~~ rocks him gently.

SERGIO
Dios te salve Maria, llena de
gracia, el senor es contigo.

Gus rises, looks up through the tears welling in his eyes at the faces of people staring down from the balcony above.

GUS
Please, somebody...throw us a
blanket.

Sergio continues to rock the dead young man.

SERGIO
(softly)
Santa Maria...Santa Maria...

Someone throws down a blanket.

As it falls - like a dark shadow hovering for all time above the three officers - we FREEZE FRAME.

<u>THE END</u>

FROUG: Stirling, you have been quoted as saying, "If there is any joy to be had from writing screenplays, somewhere along the way I have failed to stumble across it." Do you still feel that way?

SILLIPHANT: Yes, more or less, because the only time I truly feel good is when I hit my last act, when you've got it going. I've discovered more and more that's what makes me happy, not the conceptualization period of screenwriting, which is the rugged, miserable period. Not the time when you're trying to get a fix on what the total film should be, what it should say, what it should look like, what it's about, because that's all pretty agonizing, that's a bad period. That's when you don't sleep at night, that's when you go to parties with your wife and you aren't really there, and I don't like to live in absentia. Most of the time, as a writer—and I do a lot of writing every year, so that means most of my time—I am never really *with* anyone else, never really there. That bothers my sense of being *in* the world, my personal *umwelt.* But the really happy period for me, and I guess I am one writer who does love to write, is the period of actual writing. Once the concept is formed, once you know who your people are, once you really have got that fixed, then to me there really is no joy like the joy of putting it down. Now, that comes very fast. I take a dim view of the bullshit mystique of six or seven months on first drafts. I have never spent more than four weeks on any first draft in my life. Two weeks is ordinary, but how much time is ahead of writing FADE IN is another matter. That could be a long time. Even forever—or never.

FROUG: How much time do you average in the gestation period of working out your story?

SILLIPHANT: Anywhere from two months to six months to a year or longer. In terms of actual research, never less than two months. Usually three to four months. By research, I mean totally immersing myself in my subject. As an example, *Charly.* Once I knew I was going to do the assignment, before we got to the story itself I knew that I suffered vast areas of ignorance about the brain and brain surgery and memory and genetic structure and DNA and retardation. All the problems indigenous to writing this particular film. I got every piece of information I could, whether it was from periodicals or books, whatever it was. I talked to many doctors, I went to different universities. I spent two weeks in Boston. Now, the more knowledgeable I became about the subject, the more the pace accelerated in terms of my learning process. Pretty soon I began to find there was very little known about the human brain, that this is truly an unexplored area, that the sources of so-called authority were infinitely duplicated in the available bibliography. Only when I had reduced it all to its basic sources and got it shaped back to its origin did I begin to have an overall understanding of where we were and what truly our understanding of the brain amounted to. Once that happened I was able to hypothecate a theory of my own in terms of what this surgery is that my fictional character, Charly, has, with some sense of authority, then to check that out with doctors and discuss that with them on a medical basis. Or take *The Slender Thread,* which dealt with suicide. I spent at least six months researching the field of suicide and again found the sources of information ultimately very limited. The terrifying thing is that when you really get deeply into a subject you find that very few people know much about anything, that we're all kind of parroting superficial two or three book-layers of information which someone has glazed over until we begin to pretend we're authorities.

When you really go into a subject, into a field, you find there were very few people in it who were geniuses or towering mentalities who really knew it at its core. I'm willing to make that flat statement about anything. If suddenly you wanted to do something about the Eskimo, I think you'd find only three or four people who have ever really gone into that subject. If you wanted to do something about the Yaqui Indian, you'll probably find that only one man, Carlos Castaneda, in the whole world, really understands the Yaqui Indian and his mysticism. Obviously, if you get into the study of English grammar, you're going to find thousands of books, but there again, they pretty well relate back to a few basic sources. This part of research I find fascinating.

FROUG: Going back to the source?

SILLIPHANT: Yes, going back to the source. Trying to get an overview of the whole subject—where it began, how it was discovered, where it's gone, where it may go, the attitudes of people about it. Now, none of this do you use in order to write, for instance, the character of a brain surgeon. Well, it's like writing about a writer. We're all different, as all brain surgeons are different. So what many writers tend to do is to write stereotypical characters—they have brain surgeons talking the way writers think brain surgeons talk. Not the way brain surgeons really talk—which is no way at all.

FROUG: By the way they've seen them in the movies?

SILLIPHANT: Now, that's an interesting point. In fact, when we were doing "Route 66", I wanted to do a story about heroin addiction. This was ten years ago before it got beat to death on television, almost twelve years ago. I felt that having only seen *The Man with the Golden Arm* and one or two other film things on the subject, that somehow I'd only seen bullshit. I didn't feel that if a man withdrew cold turkey from heroin addiction that he would climb the walls and carry on like Mr. Sinatra did. So I got in touch with the proper government sources in the Department of

Public Health and they in turn arranged for me to go to Lexington Hospital in Kentucky, probably the outstanding hospital in the world in terms of trying to treat narcotic addiction with, incidentally, an immensely discouraging rate of cure, something less than 8 percent. Not anywhere near the success that Synanon has had. So I spent two weeks in there before I wrote my story, *Birdcage on My Foot*, which had nothing to do with Lexington. It took place in Boston, but my central character was addicted to heroin, and I just had to know so many, many things. I was surprised, and delighted, to find that everything I had seen in previous films was essentially false, was some dramatist's point of view and highly colored and overtheatricalized. It's like all the things I was raised on—early Warner Brothers movies. All my social mores stem from watching Paul Muni and Humphrey Bogart and Jimmy Cagney. So in trying to grow out of that immensely appealing marshmallow of crappy learning I had, I've just had to reject everything and go back to the source. Now to bring that back to your question, the period of preparing to write a script I find very agonizing, even though the research is fun. It's like looking up a word in the dictionary and that word leads you to another word and pretty soon you forget why you looked up the original word. Well, I get carried away like that. We all do. That's fun, but then I have to keep reminding myself, "Hey, you're doing this for a reason, and you've got to learn something so you can unlearn it so you can un-write it and make it simple and therefore totally comprehensible." That's part of its fun. The conceptualization, what kind of film should it be. Should it be a nonlinear script in the sense there is no definite story progression? Should it be a tightly compact script that takes place in two days with a time clock built in? Should it be a multi-character script? Should it be an intensely personal, slice-of-life script? What kind of a movie are you going to make? These are the decisions which just rack me up. Because I don't know. I'm not only concerned with trying to do good and meaningful screenwriting, but I'm also concerned with writing a film that's going to make some money, because I don't care how good you are as a writer, if you have a reputation for turning out very fine work which always dies at the box office, pretty soon no one is going to be calling you anymore. So, once a year, once every two years, once every three years, you have just got to come through. Something's got to work. Otherwise the phone stops ringing. It's like Humphrey Bogart once said (as a matter of fact he said it to a lot of people, but he said it to me the year before he died when I was in publicity in New York and taking him around to the newspapers on interviews). We got talking about what was success and what was failure in the business. And he said, "It's very simple, kid. Success is still being around after twenty-five years. Just be a survivor. Out-endure the other sons-of-bitches. You'll be more famous than any of them. It's the guys who are still around who get the awards. They say, 'He must be doing something right. Christ, he's been in this business forty years.'" So I'm no longer depressed by the appearance on the horizon of some bursting new talent. I say, great. We need it. We need the inspiration and some new guy who will challenge all of us, but I want to see him ten years from now, and I want to see him twenty years from now. I want to see the guy who can do what Nunnally Johnson has done, what Billy Wilder has done, and what some of these great cats have done, you know? The Joe Mankiewiczs, who now, in terms of where the public head is, may seem to be out of it, but who have done over two or three decades really stunning and beautiful work. And I would much rather have that longevity, that long list of good things, than maybe even have done the greatest single film of all times. So you can see that this is not fun, this kind of thing. That's what I meant when I said I have never seen the joy in it. I don't know anything else to do, Bill, I mean that's the only job

I know, and the only thing that I can work at, and make bread, yet still feel I'm growing, still feel that every new morning there's nothing else in the whole world I'd rather be doing.

FROUG: How about producing? We're fellow board members of the Producers Guild. We're both hyphenates. What value is that to you? Controlling your own work?

SILLIPHANT: Well, I find it *doesn't* "control" it. There's no possible way for a writer to control his work. I think the most he can do is try to preserve as much of his original intent as he can, therefore he should wear as many hats as he's able. But on the other hand, sometimes the writer's original intent isn't all that great either. And it can be improved by a chance remark. Or a whole conceptual approach contributed by anybody on the creative team, whether it's the musical director, the editor, director, whatever. I like to be the producer now for what I write, only because I like to narrow the attendance in the committee meetings. If, say, producer, writer and director, which is the ordinary triad, are involved, I much prefer to have only two of us involved, that is, I as the writer-producer, with the director. To me that is the ideal collaboration. And whenever I have been able to effect that kind of liaison, I have always felt I was working the most effectively.

FROUG: You have said that the director and writer are back to back on the same coin, like it or not.

SILLIPHANT: Very true. An example. I've just finished a screenplay at Columbia for a book called *The New Centurions.* Any number of ways to go on that book. It's a very rich book in terms of its incidents and its scenes. It could really be a six-hour movie. Now if you have to take a 456-page book and bring it down to 125 pages, with all the characters in it, you're going to have to make a choice.

FROUG: The novel was written by a Los Angeles police officer?

SILLIPHANT: Yes. Sergeant Joseph Wambaugh. I have a

wonderful producer, Bob Chartoff, who permitted me to work closely with Dick Fleischer, the director. We were able to arrive at a mutual concept. We decided to do a nonlinear script, a sort of pastiche, a great number of short scenes with impact constantly hitting at you, so that the structure of the story, which covers a five-year period, seems to be formless, yet its form is within the changing aspects of the characters, and the multitude of experiences they undergo, which you, the audience, undergo with them. And, at the end, when one of the characters is killed, you've got the end of the story. Now the point of it is you could easily have decided that no, you'd be better off to take just one of the three characters in the book, tell *his* story, give it let's say, a hook, where he was caught up in an incident, a teaser, at the beginning and now we go back and see how he got to that point. That would be one way to go. Well, you could figure out twenty-five different approaches to this book. We chose this nonlinear structure in order to give us a large canvas covering a great deal of time, and never commenting, never lingering, just *whap whap whap whap*, sort of an electronic input thing, so that you're staggered by the multiplicity of characters and events, and you never really have time to absorb one before you get hit with another one.

FROUG: Within this framework of the nonlinear structure, did you still basically look for a beginning, middle, and end?

SILLIPHANT: No, not in *The New Centurions.* The only thing that really guided me was the technique of the film itself, which is the coming into scenes either at the end or the middle or the beginning, and getting out. See, when you're doing a story about police, you have to be very careful not to fall into all the other police clichés you've seen. Guys in police cars, guys pulling up in front of houses, getting out of the car, and walking up the lawn and ringing the doorbell. You would chew up endless miles of footage. What we have done is, by forgetting all that in time and space, we leap from scene to scene, into the high points of the scenes. We go from one scene into another scene where a man runs around the side of a building and someone shoots him in the face, and someone else comes out and says, "No, that wasn't the man, that's my brother," and the guy says, "Shit, I'm sorry, baby." End of scene. The whole thing might only be forty feet. But what you've just seen is hideous. Yet it's just a piece. And we wouldn't even follow up the result of what that meant until maybe twenty pages later when someone would say, "What ever happened to so and so that shot that guy in the face?" You'd say, "Well, he's up in Oregon now. He retired." And all these little things are not tied up neatly. They're spread and loose and unresolved, so just by following that technique, that advanced us.

FROUG: Are we, perhaps all of us in American films, being influenced by some of the early foreign films? For example, *Last Year at Marienbad*, where we began to recognize the possibilities of distorting space and time?

SILLIPHANT: No, I don't really think so, Bill. I don't think any of us are that consciously influenced by any single film because we all see too many films. We're all aware of the incestuous nature of our work. So that if you have any sense of professional integrity you don't say, "Yeah, man, I originated something," or "I thought of something brand new." There's no way any one of us is about to originate anything. All we can do, I think—and this is what I mean by getting the mystique out of screenwriting—all we can do, I think, is to be totally professional, totally devoted to whatever our latest project is, and try continually to refresh our attitudes in terms of where we are in the world at this moment in time and constantly reappraise our moral obligations to worldwide society, not just to our American society, and to try to tell our stories in the most contemporary possible terms. Now, obviously, if people, because of the nature of their private lives, have reached a sense of boredom with scenes that run ten minutes, and you elect, instead of giving them the ten-minute scene, to give them instead fourteen short scenes, then you're being influenced by the times, not necessarily by the past. On the other hand, you may elect to say people don't like ten-minute scenes anymore. Therefore I'm damn well going to give them a ten-minute scene anyway. And you may then be applauded as having started a new trend, when, in fact, ten-minute scenes were quite the vogue in previous films. All of this is a bunch of guys sitting around saying, "What can we do with this fantastic marvelous concept to really make it brilliant?" And that's what the screenwriter does. He, in my opinion, is the filmmaker in the purest sense. This is why I take terrible issue with the auteur theory, because auteurs really are writers who are using cameras. There is no reason why I cannot take up a camera instead of a typewriter, because I probably understand lenses and know more about cameras then most directors. Everything I see, I see only in the visual sense, not in the literary sense. I only think in terms of frames of film. Everything I see is a composition of arrangements, of elements within a photograph. It would be very simple for me to direct a film. But I choose not to.

FROUG: Why do you choose not to?

SILLIPHANT: Because I don't want to waste my time dealing with a lot of goddamned people. I prefer to work by myself. It's just my temperament. I don't enjoy manipulating crews of fifteen to fifty people, and worrying about other people, what they're thinking about, what are their problems, or trying to convince some actress to get into the mood for a scene I've written. That takes a special kind of temperament. I get no pleasure from that. I tend to be a shorthand person because I think visually. I just want to do it now, and I get terribly impatient and intolerant if the human factor gets in the way of my reaching for the effect spontaneously. With the typewriter I have no problem. It's me and the machine. And it's my instant picture being put down on paper, instantly. If I have to cajole and play psychological games and play a lot of bullshit roles, then it makes me very unhappy. But in terms of seeing a film that I write, I see it as a director sees it, right from the start.

FROUG: How far should the writer go in designing the visuals for his film? Do you write in master scenes or do you visualize shots?

SILLIPHANT: I'm glad you asked me that question, Bill, because it's something I have worked my way out of after fourteen years of writing. The bottom line is I only write a master sequence. But even those I'm trying to eliminate. I started out writing the sprocket holes originally, and as a result my scripts, now that I read them, are very ponderous, very heavily laden with atmosphere, the mood, the smell of the frangipani, and the clothes the people are wearing, and the way the musical score should go, and I guess I was beautifully naive about being a filmmaker on paper. I have found out that's all wasted motion. Because, number one, it's much harder for anyone to read it. You have to wade through it to get to the dialogue. Number two, it totally and instantly alienates any director. Even a bad one. A good one, if you're trying to get a David Lean or someone, they won't even talk to you after that. They throw the thing away. I have progressed to the point now where I have learned to write a shorthand script which somehow, maybe because of my specific choice of words, which are emotion-laden words, will in the very sparse and brief stage directions create a mood, so that in a sense it's a shorthand poem. Stage directions are very brief. I usually have no adjectives, no adverbs, frequently not even verbs. For instance, in *The New Centurions*, it says INTERIOR APARTMENT—SHITTY. That's all. One word. Then the dialogue starts. That's what I mean. I hardly call the word "shitty" an emotion-laden word, but it does convey its appropriate meaning at the precise moment. I have learned not to put under the character who is about to say some dialogue a stage direction, such as "softly" or "with great feeling" or "crying out." I drop all that.

FROUG: You feel the line speaks for itself?

SILLIPHANT: If it doesn't you'd better rewrite it. So I've eliminated all that. As a matter of fact, *The New Centurions* is, I think, an example of a script where nothing was written except times of day and places. It just says INTERIOR POLICE STATION; EXTERIOR STREET—DAY; NIGHT, whatever; and it just goes into dialogue. If there's a police car on the street, it just says PROWL CAR—ROY DRIVING, GUS KEEPING SCORE. That's all. And then into the scene. If the scene doesn't play in terms of the circumstances of where it's happening, when it's happening, why it's happening, you're not going to make it better by throwing a lot of words in. They simply don't cut it. It's in the *concept* of the scene where the real screenwriting takes place. Not in the words you put on the page. So I've tried to take all the words off the page, and if you look at a script of mine which works, even if it says EXTERIOR—STREET you start to cry—or laugh—because you know at that moment if the guy's in that street you're gonna cry—or laugh.

FROUG: Something's going to happen?

SILLIPHANT: The juxtaposition, the placement of him at that place at that moment of his life is where the emotion is, not the description about the fact that the shadows are long in the street, and that the lights are far off, and that the cry of the passing train is heard. All that shit is gone. I've even tried to go beyond that for myself but I've had no success in getting anyone to understand it, as in the case of *The Silent Flute.* That script is the way I would love to write scripts from now on. For example, it doesn't say FADE IN; it never says CUT; it doesn't say EXTERIOR. It doesn't say DAY or NIGHT. What it is, the opening thing for instance, the opening sentence, is "The dawn has brought no relief from night." Now the production guy looking at this says, "What is this, what the hell, how do I break this down?" He says, "The dawn has brought to relief from the night? What's that?" I say, "You *don't* break it down. You know it's dawn and you know it's hot and therefore the character has got to be sweating, because he's also running down a dusty mountain, right?" So the guy says, "EXTERIOR MOUNTAIN—DAY." I say, "No, you see the difference is that my thing conveys a mood, your thing is something else." "Yeah, but we got to have our thing to budget." And I say, "But it's all there. You have to read it, though. Read it and *then* you underline it so you can break it down, but I'm not going to do that anymore for you guys. *You're* going to do it." Now, it reads like a short story, except that it's in present tense. Every sentence is a shock, but every sentence is calculated to convey a mood and that is where the poetry of the writing and the imagery exists. The dialogue is put in the center of the page, the way dialogue is, but in this instance, much of the dialogue is in Thai, or in Japanese, or in Urdu, and we're going to use English subtitles. Because the things that I want to say, if I say them in English, you're going to break out laughing. For instance, since it's a metaphysical piece, if Coburn says, "Why don't you send me to look for the Book," and the monk says, "The man I send must be able to bind an elephant in a spider's web." Now imagine you're sitting in a theater and some guy with a shaven head and saffron robe says *that*, you break up laughing. But if the guy says it in Thai, then underneath you read the English, you say, goddamn, that's beautiful. That's groovy, man, I've got to write that down. So it's really a weird script, but to me it's the evolution I have sought in scripts because you can't put it down. It reads like the very lean stories Garson Kanin used to write for *Cosmopolitan*. They would just be all dialogue. *Boom, boom, boom*, like that. It went so fast you couldn't stand it. You were just turning the pages, and suddenly, *whap!* There'd be an emotional thing and you'd say, "Wow, what a scene that is!" Well, all I can say to learning screenwriters is, if you will think in cinematic terms, in visual terms, and whatever is on that page, if you're not interested in reading, or it gets in your way, take it out. Pretend you're the director. Pretend you're the actor. And I don't underline things anymore. I used to underline within a piece of dialogue. To show where I wanted the thing hit. Well, that's stupid, because that's the way *I'd* like it, that isn't the way some *actor* likes it. George Maharis in "Route 66" taught me that. Maharis could take a phrase which should be hit on the third word and he'd hit the eighth word, or the first word, and he'd create some wild, wonderful, new way of saying something I'd never heard before. So if the writer puts that damn underline on, the actor has to work his way away from that into his own thing.

FROUG: So what you're about is putting down on paper only what's going to be on screen?

SILLIPHANT: Just his simple humanity. The things that reveal either his special human nature or his universal human nature. As an example, we had a "Naked City" with Rip Torn and Tuesday Weld. It was a story of a young southern guy and his southern girlfriend who come up to New York and kill fourteen people. And at the end of the thing when the police shoot him and he dies on the floor of Grand Central Station and the girl is holding him in her arms and crying and Paul Burke says, "Why?" she looks up at him and screams, "For the hell of it!" Now, those five words are about as revealing as anything. There's no big Freudian number about why they went around and killed so many people. They had a ball doing it. They loved it. Well, that's a special kind of revelation about people. By taking the weirdest of people, in terms of antisocial, abnormal, reprehensible behavior, somehow that cry of hers was human. She did it because they had a ball doing it, and why ask? That shows you where she is, man, and that's a pretty sad place. But that's *her* story. The only way you can reveal character is through what they do and what they say, because we aren't privileged to show on film what they think unless you choose to have voice-over or something. So you're really limited to those two things. Their behavior and what they say. I try in my own writing to make the things they say very revealing of them, or in the things they do not say.

SILLIPHANT: You once said that Norman Jewison emancipated you totally from the writer-versus-director animosity in your working relationship on *In the Heat of the Night.* Could you elaborate on that?

SILLIPHANT: Norman was very kind. And very clever. He has the ability to deal with people, which I suppose we all have, but some of us are less willing to use it than others. When I submitted my first draft, he was so flattering about it he disarmed me completely. Because as you know, Bill, having been in it yourself, you are, as a writer, terribly nervous, anxious, your ego is involved, your masculinity is involved, your whole existence is involved in what people think about that thing you've done. And it's in that first approach. It's in the way a man makes love to a woman. I mean, you just don't come in and push a woman down and enter her. You come in and you court her. Well, some producers just come in and they enter the writer. They say, "I just read the worst piece of shit. Jesus, how could you write that kind of crap?" And right away you're in terrible shape with that man. You can pick the hostility off the wallpaper. If, on the other hand, you're dealing with a reasonable, intelligent person, you like him to play a few games with you. And Norman is absolutely brilliant at this. He said, "Stirling, in all my time in this industry, this script is probably the most perfect first draft I've ever read." And I said, "Well, Norman, that's beautiful, but there's got to be a few things. I mean, there's just got to be." He said, "No, not a thing. It's perfect the way it is. The way I want to shoot it." Well, he gave me one week of this beautiful, wonderful euphoria. I went around telling everyone, "Do you know, this man is going to shoot my script just the way I wrote it. First time it's ever happened. He's beautiful! God, he's a great director." Then, I kept feeling there had to be something that had to be done to it. And I called him and said, "Norman, couldn't we have lunch? And maybe just kind of run through it all a little bit, because I feel that maybe there are a *few* things I'd like to do. Because it is just a first draft."

FROUG: The writer's insecurity at work.

SILLIPHANT: Right. He had me. Because he let me do it to myself. And he said, "Yes, sure." So we went to lunch. He allowed here and there maybe there were a couple of things and I was eager to do them. And I said, "When can we get together?" And he said, "Anytime." So I was the one who forced myself into rewriting. It turned out he had planned it all along. Well, six months later I was still working on that script. And he was fantastic about that. He made you *want* to change it. He challenged you. He would just guide you from one thing to the other. That's a talent—and Norman has that great talent.

FROUG: You wrote an excellent article recently in the Directors Guild magazine under the title of "In the Name of Symbiosis," I believe, and you explained symbiosis in terms of the writer-director working relationship. The definition you gave of symbiosis was "the living together of two dissimilar organisms, especially when this association is mutually beneficial."

SILLIPHANT: Well, that's what it is. Because, you see, the writer does his thing. And now the director has to come in and take that primary step and create film from it. So there may be phrases which a writer adores, absolutely gorgeous phrases, which the director also adores from a literary standpoint, but which he knows, from the standpoint of a filmmaker, are going to destroy a mood, are suddenly going to remind people of the writing behind the character. And sometimes the writing can be so overpowering, so overbearing, so exquisite, that it transcends the actor saying it.

FROUG: As a Frankenheimer camera angle often overshadows the action on the screen?

SILLIPHANT: Precisely. It is the kind of arty pretentiousness which a really fine writer, a fine director, should not permit to be evident within his work. He should really remove himself from it. This is what I meant by the process, the very difficult process of "un-writing." And I find, in my own work, I tend to be, try to be, extremely poetic, in the sense that I like imagery. And I like to reach for very oblique things. I don't like filler dialogue, or ping-pong dialogue. I'm a big Pinter fan. Because Pinter covers his tracks magnificently. In a Pinter piece, every time someone says something, even if it's the most obvious kind of commonplace, you feel as though some immense announcement has been made. That's the kind of dialogue I love, where someone will say some dumb thing, which is earth shattering, and yet in the simplest words. Well, I tend to want to do that, but with Shakespearean words. So I will lay in what I think are fantastic combinations of words which I have labored over for days to put six words together, to say something that's never been said that way before, and maybe it'll work. Sometimes it does. Well, in a whole movie if somebody that you have accepted as a certain kind of character suddenly comes out with this quotable Noel Cowardish or George Bernard Shawish, or Pinterish thing, you say, "My god, what a great piece of dialogue. It sticks up there like a mountain." And you have to say, "No, baby, that's got to come out. That's too good. That throws the whole thing off." Well, I wish I had that problem all the time with things that are too good. But you know what I'm trying to say. You've got to go for the total. And not for the brilliance of the parts, because the brilliance of the parts doesn't always make a great total. And the emphasis really has to be on the screenplay. And I have taken years to learn that. And if you really think about it, how many films have you seen where there might be two or three absolutely super scenes, and yet the film as a whole fails? And yet other films, which absolutely wipe you out, if you went back and thought about it, the scenes didn't seem to be at the time that outstanding, the dialogue actually wasn't that magic, but the whole damn thing works. In a sense, to me, *In the Heat of the Night* is an example of that. Because I must tell you I did not like the script. The final script. I didn't even like the first draft. I felt that it was less than many "Naked City" scripts I had written. As a matter of fact I can think of at least twenty different television scripts I've written which I think are monumental in comparison. But *In the Heat of the Night* had a curious kind of special and slick mediocrity. With one exception, there was one scene Lee Grant played—as a matter of fact, she won the award that year as Best Supporting Actress, and what no one realized is that she only had three scenes in the whole movie. Now what are the scenes? She comes into the police station and Poitier tells her her husband is dead. Big deal. Another scene where he goes to her and says something else. And another scene where she went to the mayor. But it was the one scene, and one other scene in the whole movie I considered on a par with some of our "Naked City"s. There was a scene in which a brother brings a sister in and accuses one of the cops of raping her, and she is telling Steiger what he really did and how he came by and picked her up and took her out to the cemetery and how he put her on the tombstone because it was the coolest place in town, and he boffed her. And it's in the way she tells it. It's kind of a good scene. Those two scenes, plus the scene in which Sidney Poitier does the analysis of the dead body. Outside of those three scenes which are kind of good, the rest of it is very, very ordinary. But it is in that consistent ordinariness that it all worked. Every scene had a slight unpredictability, a slight surprise, and yet it didn't go off into areas which would shock you. It would take you out of saying, "Yeah, let's see what's going to happen in that scene. This is the scene where the white guy's telling the nigger that so and so, and this is the scene where the nigger tells those white sons-of-bitches." And it had just enough of that. But to me it was a copout. Because it was like pushing the button called *Mother*, or the button, *American Eagle*. You get conditioned responses. It was to me a conditioned-response film. It was a sure thing. And that's why I regard it as less than challenging. I couldn't understand all the acclaim, if I can use that word.

FROUG: You won an Oscar for the screenplay; that's pretty good acclaim.

SILLIPHANT: Yeah, it really blows your mind, because it isn't that good a film. I don't understand why. I can understand why it was the end of a period, really, in Hollywood, with the Academy, where they had to comment, like liberals, on the tragedy of the black experience in our society. That was the year they gave Best Adaptation to my picture and Best Original to *Guess Who's Coming to Dinner?*, both black subjects. But I think it was the end of the "Let's Reward the Brave Producer for Making a Daring Film About Black/Whites." Well, since that time, the films that have been made make these films seem like exercises in child life. And those films are no longer applauded.

FROUG: Such as *The Liberation of L. B. Jones*, which you also wrote?

SILLIPHANT: Which came much later and, in my opinion, could have been, although it didn't turn out to be, a far better film. Actually, it had things in it, it had scenes in it, which were truly literature of the screen. In terms of writing. I'm not commenting about direction.

FROUG: What happened to keep it from achieving any kind of success? It was critically panned and it did poorly at the box office.

SILLIPHANT: Because it achieved what I had set out to do. I wanted to make a film that was offensive to everybody. I am so bored with the polarity and the postures of our society, the people who have their little sides, and I wanted to say, "Hey, come on, this is all wrong. You're not a white, you're not a black, you're not a racist. You're not this. Let's cut out all those labels." And so this film was really directed to the lost lonely human being who has no side. And therefore it was offensive to the whites, to the blacks, to the police, to the non-police, there was no one this film wouldn't offend. And that was my deliberate intention, and it proves once again that's no way to make money at the box office.

FROUG: Stirling, how do you go about selecting what material you're going to do? What do you look for in material before you decide you're going to take on what's going to be at least six months and possibly a year of your life?

SILLIPHANT: Well, Bill, I have to believe in it. I have to care for it passionately. And I don't want to be typed. The minute I achieve a kind of ability within a certain genre of filmmaking, I try to leave it and go off into something I haven't done, or maybe can't do. I guess what I'm interested in is failure, and I really mean that.

FROUG: You mean the chance to fail?

SILLIPHANT: Yes, I need the chance to fail. If I don't, then there's no hope for me. Then I will simply be repeating myself. I'll just be piling more money into the bank, and that is truly a fruitless and pointless objective. That really isn't why you do it. So if it isn't for money, then what is it for? The reason I took *The New Centurions*, for example, is I had not really done a police story since "Naked City." That's 1964 when we were cancelled. Going on seven years ago. And we started the show almost eleven years ago. In 1949 there was done first a play and then a film, which to me is the number-one police story I had ever seen, and that's Sidney Kingsley's *Detective Story.* To me that stands as the definitive work on precinct and plainclothes officers ever done in America. Now *The New Centurions* could be the definitive policy story of the next two decades, in terms of the patrolman, and I saw it as a chance to do a landmark film. A breakthrough film. And a film I care about very passionately. That's why I begged to get that assignment, and was very lucky to get it against terribly stiff competition. The reason I took *Charly* as an assignment was that I had never done a film of that nature, almost into science fiction, but not quite. A film of a man who is mentally retarded. That struck me as an immense challenge in an area where I was uninformed. If I can get work that takes me into things, where I learn as a human being, and where I am challenged to become emotionally informed, then synthesize that and dramatize that. It has to be that kind of thing, or sometimes just a pure, commercial piece of junk will fascinate me into trying to do something magic with it. This, incidentally, is the French system. The French auteurs take as their basic stories, Truffaut particularly, sometimes comic strip situations, but by endowing them with depth and a new look and a unique perspective, somehow make them into screen literature. Take John Fowles' *The French Lieutenant's Woman*, a best seller last year—and a brilliantly written book—it is really soap opera at one level. That is his basic story. But underneath that are the other levels, which are so fantastic. So if I can find within a piece of work—whether it's an idea, or a published book, or my own thing—something that appeals to me as a six-month's challenge, then I'll go at it. But if it's just an assignment—forget it! That's why I'm doing television now, because in this period where assignments are fewer between than they used to be a year or two ago, and where the projects that I write myself—and I've got four or five of them that I have written and I can't get financed—you've got to have something steady to support your arrogance. And this is why I'm back in television.

FROUG: I was going to ask you why you decided to take on the heavy burden of TV production as executive producer on your own series, "Longstreet"?

SILLIPHANT: Only for that reason. Just to have some kind of

continuity of income. I have a small production company with something like eight people working, and sometimes when I look at the payroll I get nervous, because even when I don't pay anything to myself, just to open the doors costs a lot of money. And I think, "My god, I'm an entrepreneur. I've got an office, a big office, telephone bills, cables, we don't have a foreign cable address." That kind of status is just too much for me.

FROUG: Then "Longstreet," in effect, is what is supporting your moviewriting?

SILLIPHANT: That's about it. I'll give you a good example. I mentioned *The Silent Flute* earlier. I wrote it last September but I worked on it for two years with the actor Jimmy Coburn. He and I and a young Chinese cat named Bruce Lee did it together. It's an original. We need about $1 million, somewhere between $1 million and $1.5 million to make it, and that's not paying ourselves anything. It's an expensive picture to make, because we have to shoot it in Japan and in Thailand and in Morocco. I can't even describe it to you except to say it's very weird. It's a metaphysical statement and deals with martial arts and is to me my favorite thing. But I can't get anybody to give us the negative money. We're dealing at the moment with private sources, and trying to tell them, look, don't ask us what it is. We're going to give you in color a film with a lot of action and Jimmy Coburn. And Bill Fraker's going to direct it. And we have a great cat in the East, Eliot Elisofon who is going to be our color consultant, and do things with infrared and all kinds of wild things. Polarity printing and fourteenth-generation prints. You see a bird leave a branch and it goes off in a series of fluttering held-frames, and all kinds of crazy things. And all these guys dig the script, just the way it is, and want to make that movie. Now the fact that it comments on our existence and the personal metaphysics of both Mr. Coburn and myself which is a mixture of Zen and a faith called Sufi shouldn't enter into the financing of *The Silent Flute*. This is a very religious film to us. This is the way we think about our existence. I worked on that two years. Well, someone's going to have to support me and my staff while I'm indulging in that sort of thing. That's why we're back in television.

FROUG: So even with names as substantial as your own and James Coburn and William Fraker and Elisofon, the raising of $1 million is not easy?

SILLIPHANT: Not with this kind of material, it isn't. Because they think we're crazy. I mean, we don't explain who this cat is, we don't explain where you are, or what time of the century it is, and there are weird mixtures of things. Like in the middle of a scene you're in a bamboo forest and some Japanese cavalry comes charging out of the twelfth century at you. And maybe three scenes before you've been in Bangkok, with automobiles. It's kind of screwed up. And they don't quite understand what we're after. And we say don't worry about it. Just let us make the movie. Have faith.

FROUG: In your choice of material you have reached out into all different areas and I'm thinking now of *A Walk in the Spring Rain.* That was an unusual story. What intrigued you about that project?

SILLIPHANT: I picked *Brief Encounter* as a prototype. There had not been a *Brief Encounter* for two decades. It seemed shameful to me that the people of my age, that is, people past forty-five, were not represented sexually on the screen. What are we supposed to be, robots, nonsexual vegetables? I feel, if I may say so, as or more virile than I did when I was a pimply kid. I experience things more deeply, and this is true of most people who are lucky enough to enjoy good health and a fairly active head. So I said, "Well, what about *us*? Why do we all have to be twenty-two?" I've seen so many films where eighteen-year-olds or twenty-two-year-olds were stumbling into their first love affair and wandering around France in beautiful color with foreground filter and I just got a little weary of the whole goddamned thing and I said, "I'm gonna make one for us." Well, I did. Unfortunately, it was a bomb. It just didn't work.

FROUG: Why was it a bomb?

SILLIPHANT: I don't think I ever licked the script. The kind of script I tried to write, when we came to shoot it, didn't work. And I don't know whether that was because the director didn't achieve what the script set out to do or whether no one could have shot the script because it didn't work, and I'll be specific in a moment. We had to go back to a straight-line story, and the story is much too dull and too pedestrian and too quiet to mean anything, so that it was essentially very boring and nobody really cared about Ingrid Bergman and Tony Quinn in the springtime in the Tennessee mountains. I mean, it was just like you'd say, "Yeah, well, what else have you got? Bring on the second movie." But the whole idea was that a very urbane lady in the city takes a walk from point A to point B in present time in the spring rain, and in the course of that walk remembers an experience which happened last year, in the Tennessee mountains, and different people that she meets on her walk kick her back into the past so that we don't know by the end of the walk whether she is going back to this bittersweet love affair, or back to her husband. And it all takes place in a walk which lasts ten minutes, but her memory covers a six-month period of last year. We ended up only showing the flashbacks. Cut from A to B. We took the walk out, except for the very beginning and the very end, because somehow it just didn't work. Don't ask me why. It worked magnificently in the script. Or so I deluded myself. But for some reason it didn't work visually, and I don't know why. The result was we had neither fish nor fowl. We had to cut the thing together and it starts with her going back and meeting him and all this stuff, and leaving him at the end. And you don't really care that much. There were two or three very effective scenes in there. That's what I mean by two or three terribly powerful scenes, but the total failing, versus the total working.

FROUG: Can you give us examples of the scenes that worked?

SILLIPHANT: One between the mother and the daughter, which truly had a dialogue of great honesty between two generations. If I say so myself, it's a very memorable scene. I'm quite proud of it, but it made many audiences very uncomfortable. It was much too honest. It was really a scathing scene between the two people, in which the mother dares to say, "Look, I have my own life to lead, and it's more important to me than your life." And you're just not supposed to say that if you're a mommy. Mommies are supposed to sacrifice. It's ironic that Ingrid spoke out of her own life experience where she personally once made that very choice. It is quite a scene, and it rips you apart. And many young people cried after that scene and came out and then were very antagonistic and said, "That's very unfair, it makes us seem like selfish people." And I said, "But you are, baby. Don't apologize. This is your nature. Don't be ashamed of it. You're young. You can afford to be selfish. But those of us who are older and have learned to be unselfish also deserve the luxury of being selfish on occasion. Give us the same right we give you." I think it's a terribly important scene, but the picture was immensely unsuccessful. The reviews were, at the best, unkind. Some of them nasty. That is, in Hollywood. Out around the country, in newspapers, they were somewhat kinder. By and large the national media really ripped into the film. Just attacked it. I was aware that we had a serious problem, particularly when the *Variety* review indicated that if this film had been released in 1940 it would have been old-fashioned. Things like that rankle, and I must say I try not to be disturbed by reviews only because I think the one thing I have learned is not really to listen to other people. I don't mean in my work. I mean in terms of what *I* am. To me one of the great plays of all time is Sartre's *No Exit*, which, simply said, bottom line, that hell is other people. Other people's opinion. If you really have searched your soul and have lived with yourself for many years and undergone all kinds of grinding and exhilarating experiences, you reach a certain kind of conclusion about yourself. You make a kind of a deal with yourself, right or wrong, and other people do nothing but bounce back things that are their problems, not yours. So, as a whole, I try to live my life in total separation from the reactions of other people. In short, I don't really care, honestly, what anyone thinks about me. I really don't. If someone thinks that I'm this or I'm that, I don't even want to know what they think, because it's of no interest. And if they came and said, "I want to tell you about yourself," I'm not a guy that says, "Sit down and tell me, I want to know." I don't want to know. Because I know what I think of myself, and I've got enough problems with that. So, relating this to the critics, I wasn't disturbed by—I won't even call them reviews—I'll call them indictments that were served on that unfortunate film. But since I owned an immense chunk of it, 50 percent, as a matter of fact, was the deal I had at Columbia, I decided I would get out and do something positive about it. I made a tour of twelve major cities and set down with the critics in each of those cities, individually, and at lunch, and said, "Look, you haven't seen the film yet. It will be screened for you shortly. You may hate it and I'm not asking you not to hate it, but I am coming and talking to you up front, because so far the reviews in the trade papers have been brutal, and it may be that I have produced an immense bomb here, and if so, great, and you will exercise your opinion stating that. But I do want to tell you what I had in mind, what my intention was, so that when you do savage me you will do it with love and understanding." And I must say that I do think that trip had a great bearing on the reviews we got around the country, which by and large were not only not bad, some of them were quite laudatory. Because I think they were reaching out, these critics, to try to say, "The man has attempted to make the film ipso facto very boring and dull because that age group tends to be a little more placid than the kids who are on the motorcycles or doing their thing in the VW and the whole bag." My lovely older people are not beautiful people in those terms. We can't show them with their clothes off in the candlelight because their bodies are a little lumpy and maybe they have varicose veins and maybe Tony's chin is sagging slightly, so we can't appeal to the esthetics of clean, youthful, lean, lovely bodies. We have to appeal to something else. Well, unfortunately, that just doesn't seem to be box office. And that's where we were with the picture. I'm not ashamed of it because it failed commercially. I am ashamed of my inability as the producer to have succeeded in photographing my script. And that bugs me. Because there's nobody to blame but me for that. And that's kind of an unforgivable thing. That's where the failure is.

FROUG: You once said that being a producer is a demotion.

SILLIPHANT: Well, it is a demotion, it really is. For instance, on this television thing we're doing, I've got a great, great guy as producer, Joel Rogosin. Very lucky to steal him away from Universal. Well, poor Joel is in here at the studio at eight o'clock every morning until nine o'clock at night, worrying about should the harness on the white guide dog be brown or black or white, and he called me up to say what do you think, and I said, "Joel, I'm going to leave these decisions totally to you. I want you to run a unilateral ship. I don't give a damn if the dog doesn't have a harness on. I don't want to know about that." He is going through hell with these stupid things. All kinds of questions about things that you would never dream of. Now that's a demotion.

FROUG: What makes a great screenplay?

SILLIPHANT: Maybe a year or two ago I would have said truth, but I think that that isn't correct, totally, because I think you have to create your truth and if you do that then the screenplay is powerful. For instance, *Rosemary's Baby* is an example of a created truth. Any fine play creates its own reality. That's really what I mean by truth. It's a reality within the rules which the playwright or the screenwriter sets down which causes the viewer to become totally involved in terms of creditability, in terms of believability, in terms of fascination. That would be my first requisite. That a film must have total reality. Then, obviously, what I will call the singularity of the film, it's own being, its own separate existence. The concept of the film has got to be a singular thing and has got to move in one direction. And make a total impression.

FROUG: Who is your favorite screenwriter?

SILLIPHANT: My favorite screenwriter is Robert Bolt. For all kinds of reasons. In the first place, Bob—I call him Bob, I don't know him, I wish I did—is an author and a playwright without recourse to source material. He is a creative writer. He creates his own material. *Lawrence of Arabia* was not all that derivative, even though there was great source material. The scenes had to be created. The same thing is true with *Doctor Zhivago*. *Ryan's Daughter* is an original and an unfortunate film which I think fails in its direction more than anything else.

FROUG: The direction perhaps overpowers the screenplay?

SILLIPHANT: Essentially, it's a very simple story and should have been done simply. But back to Robert Bolt—taking things like *A Man for All Seasons*, which was a brilliant play. Now you see, it's a simple thematic story about a man and his principle against an established authority. That's what I mean by a singular thing. Its concept was to tell that story through the eyes of this man and his family, and I will go on record as saying that one of the great, great, great scenes ever written for the stage or for films is in the scene in which his family comes to visit him in prison before he is going off to be sentenced. I just recommend that as a scene, every writer, every student writer should read and reread dozens of times for its evaluation of human feeling against a heroic background. Because there were no heroic speeches in it. It was all very simple and very honest, where a wife says to her husband, "Why are you doing this? Tell them you're sorry." And his reasons for not doing it were totally convincing. And not on the basis of a false reality, of saying this is a story about a man who's a hero, but on the basis of any one of us in that situation might say, "I'm going to take this position. I'm not going to say I'm sorry. I'm going to stick to my guns." Well, that's pretty grown-up writing. Bob has another great talent, and that is the ability to get in and out of a scene economically and cinematically and effectively by only going to the core of it, which is something I have tried to do in *The New Centurions.* For example, *Doctor Zhivago,* there's a scene early on, in which Rod Steiger, having made love to the mother of Julie Christie, comes out, more or less like a cock of the walk, adjusting his clothes. You haven't seen a sex affair, but you know what has gone on. He comes out, still sated from having made love to the mother, that good feeling that a man has at that moment, and, through the door, fresh, wind in her hair, snow in her face, looking absolutely ravishing with fur around her face, comes little Julie Christie. And the two confront each other. And in the expressions on their faces, and the non-writing, it's all there. And then Steiger asks her, "How old are you?" and she answers, "Seventeen." And he shakes his head and goes out. That's all. ". . . how . . . old . . . are . . . you . . . Seventeen." Five words. Brilliant scene. You couldn't have said any more with a thousand words, you know? Later on, at the end of the picture, when Alec Guinness is narrating and saying the government said no one was to come to the funeral, but thousands came, you see people walking around the coffin. He's in the center. Julie Christie comes running across through the crowd and up to him and she says nothing sentimental, after all they've been through in this movie together. Russia has fallen. Millions have been massacred. These people have been through hell. Her man is dead. They've been lovers. And she says to the brother, "I *knew* him," and the brother says, "I know." And she says, "Can you help me?" That's all there is to the scene. All of human love, and despair, is within that scene. Tears you apart. Now that is writing. It's writing because it's what I call un-writing. It strips down to its very essence the emotion of the scene. Those human cries people utter at those moments. And that's all he shows you. He doesn't do a big introduction, and people and all that, he just goes *wham*!

FROUG: That's subscribing, I presume, to the theory that less is more?

SILLIPHANT: Exactly. That's why I do all this research, so I can forget it all. And only then take the very, very peak. That's Hemingway's one-eighth theory, with seven-eighths below the surface. But to build the top of the iceberg, you've got to have it afloat. And it's in knowing what you can leave out, because you *know* it, that you have confidence. But you have to know *how* to write it, before you don't *have* to write it.

FROUG: When you're working on a screenplay, Stirling, how many hours a day do you devote to your actual writing?

SILLIPHANT: I get up at six in the morning, have coffee, and do a few exercises, and start writing about seven. Then I'll work until noon, usually twelve o'clock, and then I will go to lunch—usually a business luncheon—then come back at two, do mail, return calls, and try to get back to the typewriter by four o'clock and then work till around seven. So, all in all, that's five days a week. That's roughly six or seven hours a day of writing. On the weekends I write probably ten hours a day. In other words, I work my ass off on Saturdays and Sundays. That's when I get most of it done. Saturdays and Sundays. I'll put in twenty hours between the days. Sometimes more. All the phones in the world have stopped ringing.

FROUG: So that you always work, when writing, on a seven-day-a-week schedule?

SILLIPHANT: As a matter of fact, when it really gets going well, then I just don't stop. I mean, I'll just keep writing until my eyes start to close, until I really feel physically exhausted. Then I will lie down and sleep and when I wake up I'll start writing again.

FROUG: How many drafts do you write for yourself before you turn in to the studio or to the director a so-called "first draft"?

SILLIPHANT: Well, quite a few, Bill. I write on the typewriter. And what I will do is, I will write a scene which, let's say for the sake of argument, is three pages long. I just knock it out on yellow paper. Better on the eyes, incidentally, than white paper. Then I will edit that. And then I will retype the edited copy. Then I will edit that, and then I will retype that. Then the process is repeated on the next scene. Now, every morning when I get up and start writing at seven, before I begin to write, I read from page one up to wherever I have ended. And I re-edit that once—or many times—more. Or, if as happened this morning, in working on a television script, something had troubled me all night. I got up earlier this morning—I got up at five because I couldn't sleep. This scene was really troubling me. I discovered the scene invalid and incorrect. I jut threw the whole thing out. That meant rewriting the prior and the following scenes to bring it all together again. This time it seemed to work. It snapped right into place. So, actually, the first hour or two of every day's writing is a backup on the previous day where I rewrite and rewrite and rewrite. I would say that there is no way to calculate. By the time I have finished what I turn in, my first draft, it has probably been rewritten fifteen or twenty times. And represents to me the very best approach I have to the film. As a matter of fact, I will sound very arrogant and say that I feel that my best work has never really been on the screen.

FROUG: Why is that?

SILLIPHANT: Well, only because it's maybe daring and outrageous and reaches for impulsive things, and you tend in these committee meetings with director or producer, or actor, or whatever, to grade things down to a more acceptable level which is based on other people's experiences and attitudes in life.

FROUG: You cut off the highs and cut out the lows and remain safely in the middle?

SILLIPHANT: Right. And I would be willing to state categorically that the things of which I am the proudest will never be made. The scenes which really have something unique about them. There's a scene, for instance, in *The New Centurions* in which, after a separation of one year, the wife of one of our main characters comes back to have him sign adoption papers. She's getting remarried. And I play the scene in which he was at first very hostile when she came in because he really didn't know what she wanted and she goes to bed with him, makes love to him. And after she makes love to him, she tells him. Well, I couldn't get my producer and my director to permit me to do that. They said, "No, that makes her a real bitch." And I said, "But she is. And anyway she isn't. She was married to this guy, they had a baby together. She comes back. He's a good-looking guy, so he's drinking a little, and he's kind of horny, and she's a good-looking chick, and she says, 'I still find you attractive, Roy.' And he says, 'Oh, come on, you know, what are you going to do? Ball me?' And she says, 'Well, would you find that so objectionable?' He says, 'Yeah, I think it stinks. Why, I don't want to ball you! What are you talking about?' And they end up in the sack." Now to me, that's the way life is lived. But I can't get that through. Instead, we have a nice, safe scene where she comes back and they play she wants her new husband to adopt the baby. This has happened all my writing life. The things I feel are the way life is, kind of outrageous and funny and sad, you can't usually get anyone else to agree to.

FROUG: They're playing safe.

SILLIPHANT: They're not willing to fail.

FROUG: So even in the beginning the screenwriter never has control over his screenplay?

SILLIPHANT: Absolutely not. I have never, never, never, with the exception of "Naked City" and "Route 66." Those were the four happiest years of my life, because Bert Leonard, my partner, and I had creative control in our contracts. We had right of approval. The networks didn't. This was the last time that ever happened. This went out, as you know, Bill, around '64. We were able to force networks to put our work on the air. Now that gave us a sense of exhilaration and freedom, and responsibility. In those four years I think I really learned my craft, because there were no rules. There was nothing I couldn't do. Nothing I couldn't experiment with, and it was such a heady thing, and such an inspirational thing, that I look at some of those scripts today with wonder. I ran one last week as a reminder because now I'm dealing with my new TV show, "Longstreet," which is essentially case-oriented and all the bullshit and guns and guys in jeopardy and all that crap, you know? I keep trying to simplify this show down to human terms, but it's very hard to get a network to listen. And so, as an example of total simplicity, where nothing happens in the story, and yet somehow it works, I got a couple of "Route 66"s and ran them for some people and they were crying in the projection room and carrying on. No one could work for an hour afterwards. They said, "What happened to those days?" I said, "What happened is very simple. You can't do that sort of thing anymore."

FROUG: Why not? "Route 66" and "Naked City" were considered and still are considered two of the best series that were ever on television. Why the change?

SILLIPHANT: It's changed because when Senator Dodd

brought those ridiculous accusations against the networks back in the sixties that we were corrupting the youth of America and we were doing all kinds of naughty things and making people violent and inspiring crime by our comic strip stuff. The networks, instead of fighting that, kissed ass. They let it happen for a very good reason. They wanted control of programming. At that time, control of programming was vested in the studios and in the many creative advertising agencies. Now, when you've got fifty people all fighting and competing for the free market, doing creative things, you've got a chance; but when you've got only three . . .

FROUG: The networks . . .

SILLIPHANT: The three networks, you're dead! In those days it was a free ball. Some guy could come along from nowhere with a great show and suddenly he'd be doing his thing. No way now. Now it's all by committee. You have to check every story outline with New York before it gets approved—first with the studio, then with the local network contacts, then with New York. So a writer comes in and says, "Hey, I want to write for your show," and you say, "You're a good writer, you're hired. What do you want to do?" "Well, I have an idea where so and so . . . " You say, "Okay, hold it up." Now you make a phone call and you say, "We got so and so here, Bill Froug wants to write a story about so and so." And they say, "Well, Bill's a good writer, sounds good. Have him put a couple of paragraphs down." So now I say, "Bill, put a couple of paragraphs down." So you put a couple of paragraphs down. Now we send that into the studio. Three or four days go by while they look at the paragraphs. They then send it to the local network guys here. They meditate on it. Then it goes back to the network guys in New York. Finally a week later someone says, "Could be an interesting concept, have him write an outline." Now by this time the writer has forgotten what the hell the meeting was about. So you call him back in and say, "Remember that thing last week where you wanted to do the story, Bill, about the so and so?" And he says, "Yeah." "Well, we got a tentative okay to go to outline." So now you go to outline and it sounds like you're going into delivery. Everything is a step hedged all the way, so that there is no spontaneity, no chance for error, no chance for anything good. Now the writer writes his outline. And this could run anywhere from five to thirty pages. He brings it in. Everyone reads it. Now look at the irony. It's too fat for them to read, it's too tiresome. So the network guys now ask you to synopsize the outline that this poor guy has written. So now you give them a page and a half synopsis of the outline he's written, which is hardly more than the original paragraphs he first brought in. You're into the second or third week by now. So maybe you get that approved after another week while your writer waits. He can't afford to wait because he's got to eat and you're only paying him somewhere around $800 for his story. In all this time he can't eat on that, so meanwhile he's out taking other assignments. So when you finally call him and say, "Hey, we're ready to go," he says, "Well, I can't get at it for two weeks because I'm doing a 'Mannix' or doing an 'F.B.I.'" So *why* do writers have to take multiple assignments? So they can eat! Anyway, finally he goes to script. And you wait anywhere from two weeks to a month, and the first draft comes in. Now everybody reads the first draft. And everyone comments on it. The network comments on it. The studio comments on it. And you get all those reactions before you can tell him to come in and have him make his changes. So the process runs from two to three months to write one lousy fifty-five to sixty-five page episode. That's the system today. Now let me show you the difference. Bear in mind that in each of these steps there are these committees with different attitudes, different reasons for liking or disliking the material, all essentially negative forces. They are not there for a creative or affirmative purpose. That's not what their function is. If that *were* their function, great. I'm not saying great, but at least it would be better. They are not there for that. They are there to pass judgment and how are they going to pass judgment? If you look at the record of what they have achieved in their passing judgment—what have the networks contributed, in terms of dramatic television, which is so startling in the last five years? The good shows get cancelled right off the bat. "The Senator" right off the air. No way. Okay, here we go. Now look at the difference. When we were doing "Naked City" and "Route 66," Bert Leonard and I were accountable to no one except ourselves. What we would do is we would go out to lunch and we would say, "We need a story for next week. What are we going to do?" "Well, let's see. What *haven't* we done?" "We haven't done anything about jury fixing. Why don't we do something about jury fixing?" "Okay. That's not a bad idea. Now let's see. We haven't done a story for two weeks about a very interesting girl. Suppose there's a girl who is a very sexy girl. And we'll get so and so to play the part. Just a minute. I'll call her and see." Now you pick up the phone and call X and say Stirling wants to write a "Naked City" or a "Route 66" for you. She says, "Groovy. What's the story?" "We don't know, we're just sitting here kicking it around. But are you going to be free on such and such a date?" So we'd book the shows this way. We've had the best actors and actresses in the business. We got them without scripts. We'd call them and say, "Do you want to be on the show?" and they'd say, "What's the story?" and we'd say, "Well, we'll work it out; don't worry. We'll be in touch." Now we know who the actor or the actress is and we'd write for them. That was what made it so great, because I was able to write for specific people.

FROUG: I heard in those days you were sitting with one hand on the telephone, one hand on the typewriter; your phone was ringing continually, and you were turning out an hour script almost every week.

SILLIPHANT: Yeah. Yeah. Well, that's because of this freedom. And see, that's what I mean, Bill. We were totally inspired by it. We'd talk at lunch and I'd make a few notes, and that would be it. Now, we didn't check with anybody. I'd go home and I'd start writing. I'd come in in a week with a first draft. We'd look it over and we'd say great; we'd shoot it. The only thing we would ever have to do is we would have to submit our shooting script to the network continuity acceptance department, which is the censor, to be sure we hadn't said fuck or something like that. But we knew what the "no-nos" were and we really never had much trouble with the continuity acceptance people. Either at CBS or ABC. Now that freedom is lacking today. Totally lacking.

FROUG: ABC told me that part of the reason they bought "Longstreet" is that you agreed to write the first thirteen episodes.

SILLIPHANT: I agreed originally to do it, but that was amended to six when I discovered how stupid I'd been to promise thirteen.

FROUG: Did you have any idea that the television situation had changed so drastically?

SILLIPHANT: No. I had heard ugly rumors, but I must tell you I'm getting quite an education. To the point where I can honestly tell you I am only on my third script now, after three months. And I find it very, very difficult. The situation in six years has changed critically for the worse. Now my heart goes out to these television writers. I don't know how the hell they put up with it. It is demoralizing and debilitating, and I am beginning to understand why they are called hacks, because that's all the people want. They want it safe. They want so many standard stories. They want case stories, where the plot is more important than the people. Now they want people to be interesting, they say, but what that means is they want them to be catchy. You know, you have to be able to look at a character and right away dig that's some freaky, special cat. Well, that's the worst kind of superficial writing. You can't just take ordinary people and do them in depth. Because they say they aren't interesting. You can't do anyone in depth, because the moment you get to literature in the sense that very, very fine short stories are written, Irwin Shaw, Malamud, and Salinger, you're dead. You wouldn't dare to do "It's a Perfect Day for Banana Fish," Salinger's great, great story. Wouldn't dare do it because some idiot would say how come that guy kills himself in the end? He was just out on the surf making this wonderful conversation with this little kid. He goes up to his room, his wife is in the other bed sleeping, he opens his suitcase, takes out a 7.65, checks the clip, puts it back in, blows his head off. End of story. Who is this freak? They miss the whole point of the story. They don't understand things like that. If you had a guy who did that, you'd have to freak him out from the first frame so you'd marked him as a real strange weirdo.

FROUG: Is this because the networks are running scared?

SILLIPHANT: I don't know what they're running scared of. They got the only game in town. It's *their* network. What are they scared of? The FCC?

FROUG: Yes.

SILLIPHANT: If I had all the money that CBS had or NBC had—I mean, NBC is RCA, that's a pretty big corporation—I wouldn't let four or five guys sitting in Washington scare me that much. With that kind of power, man, you can go after those boys. So I don't understand why they're scared. *I'm* not scared and I got nothing. Imagine if *I* owned RCA. Why, hell man, we'd take over the country.

FROUG: Maybe they're afraid of loss of revenue?

SILLIPHANT: Well, that's another problem, but that's not going to be enhanced by their lousy programming, it seems to me. I have never felt that bad programming is the way to commercial success. If it is, and I can be wrong, maybe it is, then they're doing the right thing. Wouldn't that be dreary?

FROUG: Will you continue on beyond your six script commitment on this series?

SILLIPHANT: Not if I can help it. Not if I can help it.

FROUG: Do you think that the Writers Guild is ever going to be able to establish through bargaining, with strikes or whatever economic weapons are available, a stronger role for the writer in the finished product of his film?

SILLIPHANT: I don't think so, Bill, ever. I'm just not at all optimistic about that, until the writer is willing to work for nothing. That's the only way.

FROUG: As the Dramatists Guild has negotiated it, the writer has control because he owns the material?

SILLIPHANT: And I must agree with that.

FROUG: Now, *The Silent Flute* being a case in point, you've written that screenplay entirely on your own and you intend to insist that it be done your way, or not at all?

SILLIPHANT: You better believe it. Absolutely. All we're looking for is the bread.

FROUG: One million or 1.5 million dollars?

SILLIPHANT: Right. And someone just to give us a check and get lost.

Fay Kanin

1942 SUNDAY PUNCH *(Joint Screenplay)*

1954 MY PAL GUS *(Joint Story and Screenplay)*

1954 RHAPSODY *(Joint Screenplay)*

1956 THE OPPOSITE SEX *(Joint Screenplay)*

1957 THIEVES MARKET *(Joint Screenplay)*

1958 TEACHER'S PET *(Joint Story and Screenplay)*

1961 THE RIGHT APPROACH *(Joint Screenplay)*

1962 SWORDSMAN OF SIENA *(Joint Screenplay)*

1965 MEETING AT A FAR MERIDIAN *(Screenplay)*

1969 THIS MUST BE THE PLACE *(Original Story and Screenplay)*

1972 HEAT OF ANGER *(Original Story and Screenplay)*

PLAYS

1950 GOODBYE MY FANCY

1954 HIS AND HERS

1961 THE GAY LIFE

1964 RASHOMON

Film critic Arthur Knight calls screenwriter Fay Kanin "the Jewish Ava Gardner." As president of the Screen Branch of the Writers Guild of America, west, she is also the Guild's Golda Meir. Her diplomacy is the equal of her beauty.

Whatever catchphrase one uses to describe the elegant and poised Mrs. Kanin, the fact remains that she is an extraordinary as well as talented woman. (I once confessed to her husband, screenwriter and artist Michael Kanin—brother of Garson—that I was in love with his wife. "Oh," he replied, rather wearily, "another one of them.")

Not even Madison Avenue has surpassed Hollywood in the exploitation of the female. The movies either extol her bust measurements while denigrating her intellect or present her as Superwoman valiantly supporting weak-kneed men. The woman writer in Hollywood, if she is ambitious, is said to be aggressive. If she is feminine, she is said to be using her sex. In either case, she is called castrating.

It is not surprising that there are only a handful of successful screenwriting women and that many of them shy away from the public view. Harriet Ravetch of the highly successful husband-and-wife team, Irving Ravetch and Harriet Frank, Jr. (*Hud*, *The Reivers*, *Hombre*, *The Cowboys*), flatly refused to be interviewed: "I think writers sound pompous no matter what they say," she told me. Carole Eastman (*Five Easy Pieces*, under the name of Adrien Joyce) is a well-known recluse. Her agent devotes much of his time to protecting her fierce need for privacy. "She does not want to be interviewed under any circumstances," he told me.

Working in a male-dominated world as a member of a mini-minority, Fay Kanin has managed, nonetheless, to transcend all of the stereotypical nonsense that surrounds her sex.

Against all odds, she maintains both femininity and an elan that is uniquely hers. She describes herself as garrulous, which may be true; but she is also unflappable.

Mrs. Kanin was born Fay Mitchell in New York City in a year she takes great pains not to disclose. ("No dates, Bill, please!") She was raised and educated in Elmira, New York.

When she was in the eighth grade she won the New York State Spelling Contest and was presented to then Governor and Mrs. Franklin D. Roosevelt. The Roosevelts took a liking to the young girl and sent her birthday cards every year and flowers when she graduated from high school. Later, when she was editor of the Elmira College yearbook, she visited the Roosevelts at the White House.

In 1936 the Mitchell family moved to Los Angeles, where Fay completed her fourth year of college at the University of Southern California, majoring in English and drama.

A studio biography, in classic Hollywoodese, says, "At the tender age of nineteen she stormed the citadels of the motion picture studios. She carried with her a portfolio bursting with her best English themes and her college newspaper and magazine stories."

It's easy to picture the bright and beautiful brunette, just off the campus, winning interviews with important studio story editors. Women's lib notwithstanding, the female of the species, in any industry, is not always at a disadvantage.

Three months out of college, Fay Mitchell went to work as a writer at RKO. "The triumph was short-lived," she says. "A week later the head of the studio left and there was a clean sweep of all his appointees. I was swept out with him."

She landed a job in the story department as a reader and spent the next two years reading screenplays, prowling the sound stages and the editing rooms, and learning her craft.

At RKO she met a young screenwriter just arrived from New York with a seven-year contract; a year later she and Michael Kanin were married.

For fifteen years Fay and Mike Kanin were a successful screenwriting team, interrupted briefly while Mike and Ring Lardner, Jr., collaborated on an original story and screenplay, *Woman of the Year*, which won them an Oscar.

During World War II Fay conceived a radio program designed to explain women's role in the national defense scheme. She convinced the government it ought to be aired and she convinced NBC they ought to donate the time as a public service. Fay became both writer and commentator of "The Woman's Angle."

Concurrently she wrote a short novel with Elick Moll, *Beauty and the Beast*, and studied acting at the Actor's Lab. And in her spare time she wrote a play on her own about a summer visit she had made to her old alma mater, Elmira College. It was called *Goodbye, My Fancy* and ran for a year and a half on Broadway. Michael produced it. ("We mortgaged our house to help raise the money," says Fay, "but it paid off.")

Fay and Mike wrote another Broadway play, *Rashomon*, based on the Japanese film, which has become a part of many college repertoires. They spent a year writing and living in Europe.

But the Kanins decided to break up the team and write separately. "It was important to our marriage," says Fay candidly.

The Kanins are very much a part of the Hollywood Establishment, supporters of liberal causes and charities, dedicated to their community as well as to their craft.

Fay's work in the Writers Guild is prodigious. "I just love writers. They're the most wonderful group of people in the whole world." The screenwriters obviously reciprocate. They elected her their president this year.

Our interview took place in the Kanins' home on the beach, just below the city of Santa Monica. What was once a major Hollywood playground is now a receding cluster of frame houses, vintage twenties and thirties, repainted and remodeled, an island of past splendor in a sea of encroaching commercialism. Hot dog stands and parking lots inch closer every year and Marion Davies' massive and palatial home became first a hotel and now a beach club as landowners and lawyers wage a last-ditch and admittedly futile battle against the advancing bulldozers.

"We're thinking of moving to the desert," says Fay, "or even France. There's a friend over there who tells us they have whole villages for sale. What if a group of writers got together? . . ."

As we talked, a massive yellow-brown haze hung ominously over the ocean, stretching as far as the eye could see. We could taste the foul air and our eyes smarted from the fume-laden smog. Fay sucked cough drops and Michael wiped his eyes and left for his studio above the garage.

"Poor darling," said Fay, "he can hardly see to paint these days. What are we all to do?"

Outside, on the Pacific Coast Highway at the Kanin's front door, diesel trucks, campers, cars, and motorcycles were knotted in a massive traffic jam, belching noise and gas fumes.

Inside, the Kanin home was an oasis of comfortable living, good taste, warmth, hospitality.

"Everything's changed so," said Fay.

It might have been an epitaph for Hollywood.

ON THE UPPER FLOOR (BACK TO PRESENT)

Frank is staring at Jessie - pale, tormented.

FRANK

No, I -

JESSIE

Why not?

(~~relentlessly~~)

Why not, Frank?

FRANK

I -

JESSIE

Say it -

(he can't)

Say it!

FRANK

(it bursts through)

I wanted to quit! I couldn't stomach anymore. I had enough!

(anguished)

Only he wouldn't let go. He was like - high - but not on drugs. On his own juice -

STILL SHOT (REPEAT) - ROY LIFTING FRANK TO HIS FEET

ROY'S VOICE

Get the hell up and fight!

STILL SHOT (REPEAT) - FRANK STANDING UNSTEADILY

ROY'S VOICE

(~~amused~~, shrill)

Stand up on your feet ~~and~~ - show me! Show me how tough you are - !

The STILL COMES TO LIFE as Frank sways dizzily. Roy comes into the SHOT in front of him, jabbing at him, taunting, teasing, then backing away provocatively.

ROY

What's the matter, Big Mouth? You were gonna beat me up? Let's see you do it!

Frank stares at him blearily, blood trickling from the corner of his mouth.

FROUG: Fay, what is the primary function of the Writers Guild?

KANIN: Well, I would say the Writers Guild is first and foremost a labor union, and it does what every labor union does. It negotiates and enforces collective bargaining agreements. In that sense we deal with wages, hours, and working conditions and all of the concerns that are common to labor unions. But I think we have two rather unique functions that very few other unions do. Even in our industry. One is the responsibility of determining the appropriate screen credits for our members and setting up the procedures for that. The other is defining and reserving rights in material for our authors, which is very special to us.

FROUG: How does a writer go about joining the Writers Guild? If he writes a screenplay, must he join? And at what point is he eligible to become a member?

KANIN: Let's take, first, who has to join the Guild. Any writer who is employed by a company that's a signatory to our minimum basic agreement has to join the Guild. The basic agreement provides that any writer employed by a producer shall be or become a member of the union in good standing no later than the thirty-first day following the beginning of such employment. So a writer gets a job and thirty-one days later he must become a member of the Guild.

FROUG: Are most producing companies signatories to this contract?

KANIN: Oh, yes. I would say the great majority. Certainly all of what we used to call "the majors" and pretty much all of the independents. For instance, my husband and I have a production company through which we have done some of our own work. And we are signatories to the Guild M.B.A. I use that as an example, because that happens in a great many cases. Now let me tell you what the procedures are for becoming a member. The minimum requirement is that an individual has had employment as a writer for screen or for television or for radio within the past two years, or that he sold original material to one of those media within the same period. If a writer meets these requirements, then he must complete an application, support the application with a copy of his contract for his writing services or some other evidence of sale or employment, and pay the initiation fee of $200. His application is then reviewed and presented to the Guild's membership committee, and if it is in good order, he's automatically a member. There is no apprenticeship period or membership roster or waiting list. He is a member.

FROUG: After he becomes a member, what are his dues?

KANIN: The dues are ten dollars a quarter plus one percent of gross income from writing. The ten dollars is credited against the first $1,000 of earnings.

FROUG: Fay, in the course of the interviews for this book we've had references to the arbitration system, whereby the Writers Guild determines the credits for the writers on screenplays. Could you explain the system for us?

KANIN: To preface it, Bill, I want to say I am very proud of the fact that it is *writers* who decide writers' credits. No producer or director or studio can dictate the writer's credit that appears on the screen. A writer knows that his final credit will be determined by those who are, after all, best qualified to judge his participation and his contribution—his peers. Now, for the way the arbitration procedure works. When a producer has completed production he's obliged by the terms of our contract to inform the Guild and *any* writer who's been associated with the film of the writing credits that he, the producer, is recommending to be on the screen. Any one or more of the writers on the film can request a credit arbitration. If any of the writers on the film has a supervisory function on it, there's automatically a credit arbitration, because then certain definitions have to be made. Then the Guild requires that the employer immediately submit three copies of every item that was connected with the writing. Every single piece of paper, starting with the basic concept. We then inform all of the writers who are named on this project that they may submit their views in a letter to us, their arguments, in a sense, and any other material they want to give us. Because we have found occasionally that the producer has lost, either through negligence or design, certain of the materials the writer feels are very substantive. At that point, any writer has the option to come in and look at this whole mass of material. No one in a credit arbitration can say, "I don't know what is going on" at any point. It's all open to him. We have a panel of arbitrators, renewed every couple of years. It's a hard job because it often means reading mountains of material and making very responsible and careful decisions about a fellow writer. You want to do it well, because you want it done well when it's your turn. If in any arbitration a writer feels very strongly that the arbitration was unfair to him in some way—for instance, if he feels that certain materials were omitted that would change the arbitration or if certain of the procedures were not followed—he can request a review.

FROUG: Then the writer has an appeal?

KANIN: Right. If he appeals with new evidence or some proof that correct procedures were not followed, he certainly would get a review. There would be three new readers of the material, and, in a sense, a new arbitration.

FROUG: Fay, how will the amalgamation of the screen and TV branches affect the screenwriter?

KANIN: I don't think, Bill, that it's going to affect them unduly. Most writers are operating now in both media, as I am. For instance, I am now doing a ninety-minute movie for television. My first. Someday it might show up on the big screen, who knows? I expect to move back and forth; I know television writers who are moving into screen. So rigid divisions really don't exist anymore, and what we are trying to do in the Guild, with amalgamation, is to reflect a condition that is already here.

FROUG: Some screenwriters have said that they felt that because of the numerical strength of the television writers, as opposed to the screenwriters, that the television writers tended to control the Guild. What do you feel about that?

KANIN: I have here the number of active current members in each branch: screen, 640; TV, 977. I've been on the Guild Council for quite a few years. The council has an even division of screen and television representation. I can tell you, Bill, that in all those years I can't remember one issue in which the TV members of the council voted as a TV block, or the screen members voted as a screen block. We differ greatly on the council, but it's never in terms of "I'm a TV writer," or "I'm a screenwriter." So I don't think that that is an issue. I don't think TV is going to say, "We'll throw our weight around and do things that will be bad for the screenwriter." I just don't think that's going to happen.

FROUG: Partially because most TV writers want to be screenwriters too?

KANIN: I do think everyone aspires to that big screen. Maybe just because it's bigger. Maybe because it has a longer history—I don't know what its glamor is. But, beyond that I think, at least in the Guild, we are trying to erase that kind of polarization of our membership. More and more, we're becoming a homogeneous group and I think it's very healthy.

FROUG: When you speak of polarization, then you also bring in the hyphenate issue, automatically. The group which you once said to me should be called "writer-executives." Some writers claim that the hyphenates have too much control in the Guild.

KANIN: Again, I really don't know what you mean by "control." You mean that they will influence—what? What would their "control" represent?

FROUG: The inference from the TV writers is either that the screenwriter represents an elitist group, or the hyphenates are an elitist group, neither of which are really concerned with that workaday television man who is making a living from TV series.

KANIN: You know, in the old days when it was the Screen Writers Guild, before we had the Writers Guild of America, there used to be a feeling that the highly paid screenwriters were the elitist group and that the writers of the "B" picture at that time were, we could say, in the position the television writer is in now. And there used to be some talk like, "Well, those fellas up there couldn't care less about the little guys." It just wasn't so. The writers who had the most clout used to sit at the bargaining table and work the hardest to raise minimums. All the things that didn't actually concern their own livelihood, that didn't change their economic lives one whit. But everyone I know who really had that kind of power and prestige used it for the whole Guild. I never heard a writer saying, "Oh, I made $100,000. What do I care about the writer who's going to make $5,000?" It just never happened. I just don't see it in my fellow Guild members. I find them as a group very generous. And I don't see people grabbing power or furthering their own ends. Not in the Guild. In the individual employment situation, there may be another story. But in the Guild, I don't see it. I also want to say something about writer-executives. As we said, at some point maybe every television writer aspires to write for the big screen. It's my feeling that the highest aspiration of the writer is to be a writer-executive in the sense that he goes on to control his material in one further aspect by producing or directing it. I believe every writer who can should try to accomplish that. Because it's the best way he can get his work done well.

FROUG: How can the screenwriter gain more control over his work short of becoming an executive or producing or directing his screenplay?

KANIN: From my point of view, the best way to do that is to write original works. The writer who starts a piece of work from a blank sheet of paper is generally in a better position to control it, to get better terms, certainly to have separation of rights. He or she has all kinds of advantages that the writer who sells his services—the adapter—doesn't have. Happily, I see a return to writing originals; I notice it more and more from the Guild registration service. While other crafts have to sit around chewing their fingernails waiting for a movie to be put together, writers have one great strength. They can sit down and generate their own employment and determine their own fate to a great extent by the degree of their discipline, their guts, and their talents. As the bottom has dropped out of the employment picture in Hollywood, suddenly we've noticed at the Guild office we're doing a land-office business in registrations, because writers are writing original screenplays. I think that's enormously healthy, both for the writers and for films. As far as I'm concerned, it's as honorable to write a good original screenplay as to write an original play for the theater. And as more writers do it, and more good films derive from originals, its honor will increase.

FROUG: Can a nonmember register his material with the Writers Guild? And what protection does that offer the screenwriter?

KANIN: First of all, this registration service is open to both members and nonmembers. It's open to any writer. It establishes the identity of the project and the date on which it was finished. It protects the writer in terms of any litigation, because he can establish that he registered this property as of this date and to prove it, here is the property in a sealed envelope. That's really all the protection even the Library of Congress copyright in Washington gives you. The registration fee is two dollars to members of the Guild and five dollars to nonmembers.

FROUG: How long is that material kept?

KANIN: For ten years. After that time, if writers wish to renew the registration, they can renew for another ten years for an additional fee.

FROUG: Fay, what steps, if any, has the Writers Guild taken to combat the auteur theory?

KANIN: Whenever the Guild has recognized an outrageous or arrogant assumption or omission of the writer's contribution in the news media, it has tried to bring it to the attention of the critic or columnist or article-writer who's been a party to it. On some occasions it has even sent a copy of the screenplay in question to a particular critic or columnist with generally excellent results. As a Guild, that's really all we can do. For myself, I think the word auteur has been used, misused, paraded, fought over, intellectualized, and interpreted to the point of boredom. As I understand from my French, auteur means author. And I cannot see how someone is an author who, having a concept for a film, does not at some point sit down and write it—words on paper, an outline of its action and/or dialogue—I don't care what form it takes, how formal or informal it is. Originally, I gather, the designation came from Europe where auteurs were directors who wrote, or writers who directed. Bergman. Fellini. Now suddenly scores of directors who accept a complete and finished screenplay from a writer talk endlessly to the press about "what I really am saying in this film is so and so." And I ask myself, "If that's what he wanted to say, why didn't he just tell his actors what he wanted to say and bypass that unimportant and anonymous screenwriter?" By the way, I've seen a few of the films in which the director has done just that. And we'll be kind and not talk about those. The director who does not write has a considerable contribution to make to a film. That is, to interpret the writer's statement in valid and exciting cinematic terms, according to the degree of his own talent. It can be and has been a distinguished contribution. Only an insatiable ego or an intolerable sense of inferiority could lead a director to ignore the basic creativity of the men or woman who thought it up, sweated it out, and delivered those precious pages into his hands.

FROUG: Recently a meeting was held at the Guild offices by women writers to discuss problems that particularly concerned them. Can you tell us something about the role of women in film writing today? Are they discriminated against?

KANIN: There's no doubt they're discriminated against in the sense that there are fewer of them employed than men writers. I think we've all heard the kind of statement which goes, "Oh, this is a picture I really should have a woman writer for," or "I wouldn't want to have a woman writer on this picture." As movies moved into the super-male cycle which we seem to have been in for a long time, with male movie stars dominating films, the numbers of women employed in screenwriting did shrink. I know that when I came into this industry the great stars were women. Shearer and Harlow and Crawford, Roz Russell and Hepburn and Stanwyck, Bette Davis, Garbo, Jean Arthur—I can't even start to name them all. In that day, you were doing pictures for women, and women were supposed to know women. Obviously, women are not supposed to know men. Then it got to be John Wayne and Glenn Ford and Steve McQueen and Paul Newman and Lee Marvin, etc. Suddenly I think the reasoning was, "There aren't many 'women's pictures' anymore, so let's not have women writers." Well, of course, that's nonsense. Writers know people, though I do concede that some writers might know how to write for John Wayne better than others. I don't think it has anything to do with sex. If you were to ask me, "Have you, yourself, been discriminated against?" I would say I've never felt that I was. I've worked very happily in this industry, worked extremely well with male producers and directors. In some cases, I thought being a woman was a decided asset. But I am sure there were movies that I was not considered for because I was a woman, that a man was preferred for some assignments, even though it was not said openly to me. It was either said to my agent who didn't tell me, or wasn't even said to my agent. It was just thought. "Fay Kanin? Oh yes, very good, but I just don't particularly see her on this picture." I don't think a producer said aloud, "I don't see her on this picture because she's a woman," but I think that's what he thought.

FROUG: How do the women writers feel they can combat this sort of thing?

KANIN: Well, I suppose first of all by doing their research thoroughly. And organizing their statistics. They don't want to go off half-cocked.

FROUG: You should forgive the expression . . .

KANIN: Or embrace it. I don't know which.

FROUG: Assuming women writers—and I don't doubt for a minute they can—accumulate such evidence of sex prejudice, what can they then do about it?

KANIN: They can do what all minorities do. They can first publicize the facts, make a little stink about it. You have to alert people to the facts, what's wrong, before you can start to change it. I think some of the men will be shocked and say, "Who, me?" I think some of the men will really be surprised that in many cases it's an absolutely unconscious process on their parts. So—the first thing is to bring it into people's consciousness. Men and, oddly enough, women too. I don't think women writers are going to go out in hot pants and picket producers' offices, although they may, who knows? But I imagine they'll take every step that's available to them to try to broaden the employment picture for women. In extreme cases the ultimate might even be some recourse to the courts.

FROUG: Fay, can you tell us as the president of the Screen Branch what you think are the primary problems facing the screenwriter today?

KANIN: Well, I think the primary problem is shared by the screenwriter with everybody else in the motion picture industry. And that is adjusting to the shrinking feature film market, accepting the realities of the employment picture. I don't think it is something one can explain just by saying we are in an economic depression. I think rather it's a reflection of a historic change in the world and in our social mores. There were fewer people in 1971 going to the movies than in any year since talkies arrived. Part of this is attributable to the fact that other countries, who have subsidized film industries, have been making more films and taking a good deal of the market that the American film industry once claimed. Part is the rise in TV viewing; part is a shift in audience makeup. But the overwhelming fact is that we are now living in an increasingly hostile society. More and more, people are afraid to go out of their houses. I'm not so sure that's going to get better. It may get worse. Not only in terms of what goes on in the streets, but in the air or lack of it. It's getting difficult to breathe. Pretty soon it's going to be not quite such a good idea to take your car out when it isn't absolutely necessary. You're going to stay more and more in and around your home. And I think, as that necessity grows, people will want to see films in their own homes through some form of cable or pay television. I expect that there will be an enormous explosion and a demand for films beyond anything any of us has ever envisioned.

FROUG: How far ahead do you imagine that will be?

KANIN: Lord, I don't know. The way things move these days I have a feeling it's going to come fast. This past year, for instance, CBS showed on prime time, quite surprisingly, a series of films, "The Six Wives of Henry VIII." They wouldn't have dreamed of doing that two years ago. I think they're beginning to admit that there is a growing selectivity in the audience—which is what cable TV reflects, although free TV as we know it can't really completely cater to that. I think they're signalling us that it's coming.

FROUG: The screenwriter appears to have more freedom than the television writer, in subject matter, in style, and content. Do you think he'll have that freedom in cable TV?

KANIN: Oh, I do. Because in cable TV you'll buy what you want. If you want to see an X-rated movie, and let's just use those designations because we have them now, you will buy that X-rated movie on cable. You won't buy it if it offends you. You'll buy something which suits your taste. There will be an audience for everything. None of the strictures that operate on network TV, as we know it, will operate on cable at all, because there will be no advertiser who is fearful of public prejudice or reaction in relation to the purchase of his product.

FROUG: Fay, for some time now, the Writers Guild has maintained what it has called an open door policy which has been to encourage members of minority groups who want to become screenwriters. Could you tell us how that program is progressing?

KANIN: Actually, open door policy is not quite the correct name. The open door committee of the Guild has been appointed by the council and funded by the Guild to operate a kind of mini-school, in which a certain amount of minority students are being taught something about the craft of writing for screen and television by professional screen and TV writers. In addition to the training, there has been effort on the part of the teaching staff and the committee to assist talented students in the selling of their work. And we've had a good deal of success. Writing is a difficult thing to teach at best, as you know, Bill. But I've always thought that the best way one taught writing was to give students a set of disciplines. To give them a place to bring their work, to give them a deadline, to give them someone who ways, "This is good or bad," or "Start again," or "Think that part over," or "I expect that on Friday." I think that's the way you start, by making someone know that you're waiting for those pages. We have been able to do that for a group of people who might otherwise have never had access to that kind of stimulation.

FROUG: Has the new freedom available to the screenwriter in film today affected your thinking about your own work?

KANIN: Yes. Definitely. It's like getting yourself out of handcuffs that you've worn for years. In the first screenplays I wrote, the double bed didn't exist. If you had married people in a film, you had to put them into twin beds. As for unmarried people, I guess they just sat up all night. The most arduous kind of verbal censorship existed, for example, in a film we once wrote called *Teacher's Pet.* It was centered in the city room of a metropolitan newspaper, full of tough, hard-talking newspapermen. We were forced to use all our ingenuity to invent phrases and expletives that sounded strong but were, according to the code, inoffensive. In contrast, a couple of years ago, I did a script at Universal which dealt with a crummy burlesque show in the Chicago of the forties. I found it absolutely exhilarating to be able to write those people as they were, to have them talk as they would. It was like coming alive as a writer. Right now, I'm doing an hour-and-a-half film for TV, my first, which is possibly going to be a series. And, having felt the taste of freedom, I can hardly bear the thought that I may have to be saying, "gosh damn" again for the TV censorship.

FROUG: After fifteen years of marriage and collaboration with your husband, Michael, you wrote, on your own, *Goodbye, My Fancy,* which became a hit on Broadway. What motivated you from film to the play form?

KANIN: As always, an idea. I went back to visit my first college, a women's college in the East. I got some very strong feelings about the whole nostalgia of going back, of looking back at yourself. And somewhere along the line, I decided to put those strong feelings down in the form of a play.

FROUG: Having written that hit play, were you tempted to remain in the theater or did you still want to return to the screen?

KANIN: At that time the theater was the most exciting thing for a writer, because theater did belong to the writer. There was no doubt about who was the auteur. It was the writer's play. And not a word of it could be changed unless he agreed to it. I have never been able to sign my name to the contract that one signs in Hollywood, which says that the studio is the author of your screenplay, without feeling angry and humiliated. I've had it explained to me very diligently by my agent, by producers across the bargaining table, that it is a matter of copyright. That the studio is purchasing the copyright and that the law dictates that they be named the legal author. But giving that away to a corporation has always seemed to me the ultimate indignity, and maybe the only thing I've ever really disliked about being a screenwriter. Because I always really loved screenwriting. And I loved Hollywood. When I came into it, it was like all your childhood fantasies come true. It was full of beautiful people, having a simply marvelous time. I think the distinguishing thing I remember about it all was that everyone enjoyed what they were doing so much. Picturemaking was a ball, and from Louis Mayer down to the kid on the bike who delivered the mail, it was great, great fun. It was glamorous in the truest sense. You walked out on the studio lot at lunchtime and even that was exciting. I'm not trying to say that people didn't have frustrations. And that I wasn't occasionally angry and disappointed. But you were among people who loved making films, and today I don't get that feeling. I feel it in some of the young filmmakers who seem to be enjoying doing their thing. But in terms of the studio system, as I see it today, and as I knew it, it's as different as day and night. I see frightened people, unwilling to make a decision. Certainly not enjoying the making of the film because the end result is so perilous, so in question. The economics have become so all-important and terrifying. Sometimes I go to a screening at my alma mater, RKO, or walk down the empty streets at 20th Century-Fox or MGM, where I had very happy times, and I find it very sad.

FROUG: Fay, you are one of the few screenwriters ever to work in the Soviet Union. Could you tell us something about that experience?

KANIN: It happened quite accidentally. A friend of mine, Lester Cowan, owned a novel called *Meeting at a Far Meridian.* He had several screenplays on it, none of which had been satisfactory. I was on a visit in the east and he asked me if I would read the material as a friend and give him some opinions on it. I did it as a friend, upon which he then pressed me into service. He said, "I'd like you to go to the Soviet Union. I'd like you to work with a team, a Russian team, and then to work on a screenplay." This appealed to me enormously. Also the material which was, I thought, volatile and interesting. It was to be, at that time—which was around 1965—the first Soviet-American co-production—Lester's company and MGM, and Mosfilm. All film studios are state owned in the Soviet Union, but Mosfilm is the giant parent in Moscow. I was the sole screenwriter and the only American besides Lester involved in the preproduction phase. The co-producer, the director and all the technicians were Russian. It was to be shot in San Francisco. And the actors were going to be mixed, Russian and American. Two male stars, one an American and one a Russian, were to be the principals. I went to Moscow as a guest of Mosfilm which, believe me, is the way to go. I arrived there with an outline of what I wanted to do with the script. The idea was that I was to work with my director and producer for four or five weeks, we were to agree on the major progressions of the story, and then I was to come back here and write my screenplay.

FROUG: Were you working through an interpreter?

KANIN: Yes. I thought it was going to be very difficult. But it was fascinating that after the first two minutes one completely forgot that there was an interpreter. My interpreter was a woman, an Intourist guide who was extremely proficient, spoke beautiful English. She was so adept that as I spoke, we'll say, to our director, she would be translating simultaneously. We seemed to be talking to each other and there was never any sense that we were waiting for someone to grind out the words. I had a feeling that she was getting every nuance, all my shades of meaning because I could tell from the reactions to what I had to say. I'm no expert on the Soviet Union after having been there six weeks, nor am I an expert on the Russian people, nor am I even an expert on the Russian film industry. But I have observations that are extremely personal to me of the film people that I worked with. In the first place, I found them extremely hospitable. They meet you at the station, en masse, with fruit and flowers and gifts until you begin to feel like a visiting potentate. You have to remind yourself you're a writer. And you ask yourself who in Hollywood has ever been met at the station with flowers, except the reigning star. At any rate, they had designed an elaborate schedule to show me all of the things that it was important for me to see in Moscow. The film was a contemporary film. It was to be the first film to show modern Moscow, and to show world-wide audiences, particularly Americans, what daily life in a Soviet city was like. The film was about a relationship between two astrophysicists, an American and a Russian. The body of the film was concerned with the visit of the American to Russia, and then there was a small return visit by the Russian, to America. I was apprehensive at first about the story conferences. But I found that very soon it shook down to exactly the same things that would be happening if I were talking to Larry

Weingarten or Charles Vidor or to any of the people I had worked with here. I had one little bump to get over. That was to build their confidence in me, which, I guess, is the same bump you have to get over in any working relationship. And the additional one—that I was an American. I think there was an initial feeling, though they never expressed it, that I might slant the characters in some way that would be biased.

FROUG: Was there any political content in the story?

KANIN: Not really, except in the sense that everything is political. It was about the field of science where there is, I must say, the greatest kind of exchange and communication. But there were some extremely sensitive scenes. In one of our initial conferences, we were discussing a scene in which the American physicist arrives in the Soviet Union to meet his Soviet colleague. They are two men who have built a relationship through correspondence and have an enormous respect for each other, though they have never met. In an early outline I had been given, which we were talking about, the American arrived in Moscow expecting to be greeted by his Russian counterpart, only to find that he was busy and kept him waiting almost a week before they met. I said to them, "I don't like that. I think your man is a boor." They said to me, "What do you mean?" And I said, "I don't want Americans to see, as the introduction to our Russian character, a man who is too damn busy for a week to see a man who has come all the way across the world to see him. I just don't like that. I think that's playing right into a kind of prejudice or a kind of stereotype about boorish Russians that I don't want this character to be saddled with. Not if I'm going to write him." Well, they were a little taken aback and a bit defensive, and they said, "Well, you know, when we came to the United States, we knew Stanley Kramer. We called Stanley up and we told him we were there and he was busy and couldn't see us for three or four days. So you see, it does happen." I said, "Not the same at all. You came to the United States primarily to have conferences with me and the studio. In the course of that, you casually called Stanley Kramer, and he was working on a film. He said to you, 'I can't see you immediately, but I'll see you in a few days.' And he did see you in a few days. Fine. But if I came all the way across the ocean, as I have done now, to your country in order to work with you, and you said to me, 'Sorry, we can't see you for a week,' I would say to you, 'Fellas, I don't want to work with you.' And I would go home.'" There was a long pause, and they had a little conference in Russian. After a moment they came back and said, "Well, maybe there is a point there. Why don't you just write that sequence as you see it." I just use that as an illustration. Because they realized that I was saying to them, "If you had any idea that it's my intention to make Russians look lousy and Americans look great, you're wrong. I want to write about people—good, lousy—but as they are. And for no other reasons." We never had any serious story problems after that. At that first story conference, there was a gentleman whom I had never seen before. They introduced him to me by name. He sat there while we were conferring, saying nothing. Finally, I asked Lester who that was and he said, "Well, that's a man from the Party." It made me quite uncomfortable and finally I guess somebody noticed it and that man didn't appear at our conferences anymore.

FROUG: How did Mosfilm Studios compare physically with our own here in Hollywood?

KANIN: Well, when they first took me to visit the studio, I thought I was back at MGM. Here was this big, beautiful lot, wide streets, large roomy stages. An enormous amount of production seemed to be going on. On one set they were shooting a biographical film of Lenin; on another set they were doing what seemed to me a sort of thirties melodrama with an Americanized-looking nightclub set. Then on one stage, there was what looked like a sentimental, young-love story with two young principals.

The director was wearing a beret, puttees, and carrying a small riding crop. When we spoke through my interpreter, he said to me, "Oh, you know, I visited in the United States. I was on a lot of sets." And I figured there was no doubt he'd been on a Cecil DeMille set. I also noticed that a great many of the technicians were women. Camera operators, even grips. Women grips wore the traditional overalls with tools hanging around their waists and were busily climbing around all the catwalks, hanging lights very expertly.

FROUG: Do the Soviet screenwriters have a union?

KANIN: There is one vertical union of the entire film industry. It's called the Creative Union of Cinematographers and it embraces everyone who works in the film industry—directors, writers, actors, cameramen, technicians, everybody. They took me to dinner one night at Domkino, the building which is the home of this union. It's a large, impressive building—three to four floors—which has a theater, a restaurant, galleries on the upper floors where they have displays related to films. When I was there they had a show consisting of stills of the early work of Eisenstein. In the little vestibule gallery outside the restaurant, they had paintings by the art directors in the industry. Our art director had been the one on *War and Peace*, an extremely gifted man. And a lot of his work was on display there. Our entire team—cinematographer, art director, producers, director, production men and women—all dined together that night at Domkino, a very gay dinner with much champagne and wine and many toasts. The Russians are very big with toasts. And then we went into a showing of a Russian film. When it was over, all of the people connected with the film (the major functions) walked up on the stage from the audience for a discussion period. My interpreter identified them for me. I'm glad she did, because, interestingly enough, the stars of the film were no more prominently aligned on that stage, or the director, than, let's say, the art director or the cinematographer or the writer. They stood in a rather straggly little line, no one more important than anyone else.

FROUG: Since the various crafts form one union, which includes all phases of filmmaking, with whom do they negotiate?

KANIN: I don't think they negotiate in that sense, nor do I think they strike. However, if they ever wanted to strike, and I can't imagine it, they'd have one hell of a strong union.

FROUG: Is there, in your opinion, any realistic likelihood that the diverse interests such as the directors and producers and actors might unite with the writers into one union?

KANIN: I really don't know. In my work with the Guild, I see many instances in which we all work together very well and I see many issues in which we are in agreement. Whether that could ever broaden to encompass such a union I don't know. But I would hope that it would.

FROUG: During the six weeks you were working in the Soviet Union, did you find that the enthusiasm among the filmmakers in Moscow more or less matched your experience of the days you spoke of in Hollywood when people were excited about their work?

KANIN: Yes, I found great pleasure in filmmaking there. First of all, they have unlimited schedules and almost no economic pressures, as we know them. When I was going around the sets at Mosfilm I would ask, "How long have you been shooting?" There was one film, hardly an epic, which had been shooting something like eight months. The actors were appearing in the same play in the evenings in a Moscow theater and so the shooting day was a short one. And, occasionally, there were days they didn't shoot at all. You know that *War and Peace* took three or four years to complete. When its director got seriously ill, it closed down at one point for a year until he recovered. There was no problem of sets having to be taken down; there was no problem of economics. Under those circumstances you can see that there's a relaxation about filmmaking. Whether that makes films come out better or worse—well, that's another story. Whether some of the exigencies of our business make our films better, I can't say. But you asked me about enthusiasm, and there's a lot of it. Also, there's enormous interest in our films in Russia. Under the Cultural Exchange Agreement between the U.S. and the Soviet Union, there have been exchanges of films. In the first group of films given to the Russians under that agreement was a film that Mike and I had written, *Rhapsody*, starring Liz Taylor, one we had done at MGM. It was an enormous smash in the Soviet Union. Michael has some relatives in Odessa who kept writing him letters saying, "We've now seen *Rhapsody* six times and we're going to see it again." It kept playing round and round endlessly. When my team found out that I was the writer of *Rhapsody*, well, the red carpet went out double. And my interpreter said to me, "Mrs. Kanin, I'll bet you I know the words of *Rhapsody* better than you do." I guess I must have looked confused, so she explained. When foreign films are shown in the Soviet Union they're neither dubbed nor titled. They're run in their original version and an interpreter stands at the side of the screen with a microphone and translates simultaneously for the audience. She said, "I've translated *Rhapsody* about fifty times. I know every word, every inflection in it. I even know the place where the symphony plays for five minutes and I go out and get a smoke."

FROUG: What became of your Russian-American film? Was it ever made?

KANIN: It had an unfortunate demise due to that little altercation called the Vietnam War. It got to be a little chancy to get involved in a six-month project which, because of the volatile times, might blow up somewhere in the middle. However, I finished a shooting script MGM was most excited about. And, though I sometimes rage at the frustration of writing for the shelf, I felt the whole experience had been a signal one and very valuable for me. Perhaps, one day, the film will still be made.

FROUG: Have you had any contact with the Russian filmmakers since the demise of the project?

KANIN: Whenever they come to the United States every now and then, I get a phone call and an interpreter gets on the phone and says, "Mrs. Kanin, Sergei Gerasimov wishes to speak to you." And then Sergei comes on and he's got about three beautiful words in English, and then we lapse into French. But, as I say, whenever he comes to Hollywood he always calls and we try to see each other. As for the others, they haven't been here since. I wrote to them, naturally, expressing my appreciation and feelings of friendship. I got some cards, but no letters in return. Very few Russians correspond with Americans.

FROUG: Why do you think that is?

KANIN: I think it might be, and it's only speculation on my part, that it's frowned upon. I just think there might be certain risks involved. Whatever it is, in no way does it alter my knowledge that these people were enormously fond of me, just as I was of them. But there are other considerations. I think probably the most difficult thing for creative people in the Soviet Union is a lack of personal freedom and personal expression. I think they enjoy a spirit of community; I think they have great opportunities for following their craft without economic worries. All of that. Nobody gets tremendously rich but there is a sort of hierarchy which comes with talent and the recognition of that. But, in the end, I believe that to be a creative person and not to be able to express it in your own terms is difficult, and eventually intolerable, for any human being anywhere.